The ART and HISTORY of
THE DANDY

75 YEARS of BIFFS, BANGS and BANANA SKINS

WAVERLEY
BOOKS

The Art & History Of The Dandy
– 75 YEARS of BIFFS, BANGS and BANANA SKINS

First published 2012 by Waverley Books,
an imprint of DC Thomson Books Ltd
144 Port Dundas Road, Glasgow, Scotland, G4 0HZ.

Text is by Morris Heggie, *The Dandy* Editor 1986–2006; Craig Graham, *The Dandy* Editor (current),
Michelle O'Donnell, Deputy Editor, *The Dandy* (current), Christopher Riches and Waverley Books.
Editor-in-chief Christopher Riches

The publishers gratefully acknowledge the assistance of Dave Torrie, *The Dandy* Editor 1982–1986;
Dave Robertson and Dave Marr, *The Dandy* sub-editors under Albert Barnes;
Jim Barnes, Lorna Richards, Amanda Fraser-Mills, Erica Farmer, Bill Holroyd, Steve Bright;
and Ray Moore for permission to include material from *The Dandy Monster Index*.

ISBN: 978-1-84934-241-4

Printed and bound in the EU.

CONTENTS

THE DANDY

FOREWORD

BY MR DESPERATE DAN

Howdy folks! My old buddy Dog-Ears Montana picked up some news off a' the telegraph wire this mornin'. Dog-Ears has such good hearing he just listens to the words coming along the lines, near a wonder he don't get lynched fer phone hackin' nowadays. Anyways, he tells me that 'The Dandy' editor wants me to write a foreword for 'The Art and History of The Dandy', seein' as I been in near every 'Dandy' that there ever has been. I ain't no man fer book larnin' and writin' ain't one of my best skills but I am due that man a mighty big favour seein' as it was him first persuaded my dear Aunt Aggie to bake me up a cowpie back in '39. These ol' pies have been my favourite ever since, I must've eaten a fair size herd of cows by now.

Well folks, when I joined up with 'The Dandy' I was a pretty rough diamond on the wrong side of the law. I guess that's why they named 'The Dandy' after me. DAN-D. They were too frightened to call it anything else. They teamed me up with a real nice feller called Dudley Watkins. Watty and I were pards for more than thirty years. He drawed with his pen all the crazy things I got up to, and there was a lot of laughter as I recall. He designed me a swell Texas town to live in, called it Cactusville, and filled it with buses from London, British post boxes and stone houses like you have back in the UK. We enlisted in the British Army, Navy and Air Force when the Second World War came along. Watty made me a pea-shooter that could knock enemy planes out of the sky. Mighty amazing guy.

I got along with a bunch of other good pencil pushers too. Charlie Grigg, Pete Davidson, Ken Harrison, David Parkins, John Geering, Stevie Bright and Jamie Smart - I knew them all - every stroke of every pencil - some were sharper than others but they all made me look good. I broke a lot of stuff over the years, destroyed poor old Cactusville quite regularly. It wasn't all my fault though, I just didn't know my own strength. My nephew and niece, Danny and Katey, spend a lot of time with me, in fact they helped me launch my own Cowpie Eater's Club in 1978. Had near half a million members by 1980.

I've seen good neighbours come and go from 'The Dandy', I spent long whiles with 'Winker Watson', 'Brassneck' and 'Corporal Clott' but my biggest buddy was 'Korky the Cat'. He's been with me near all my life. We sorta had words and he stuck his claws in my rear in 1985 when I took over from him on 'The Dandy' cover - but he got over it. Next week was another issue of 'The Dandy' and we had fun all over again.

Me and my friends said a lot of funny things and cracked a lot of jokes over the years and it all appeared in fancy little speech bubbles - more bubbles than you could make in a trillion baths. Not that I have too many baths, I still prefer showering under a waterfall every spring whether I need it or not.

So here we are, the story of 'The Dandy'.
75 Years of Biffs, Bangs and Banana Skins.
Where did they get that title from?
Nothin' to do with me.

D. Dan.

THE DANDY

INTRODUCTION

Albert Barnes – A Portrait

Editor 1937–1982

*Desperate Dan:
a character synonymous with the first
Editor, Albert Barnes.*

ALBERT BARNES

THE FIRST DANDY EDITOR

1937–1982

ALBERT BARNES was born in Dundee in 1913 and joined D.C. Thomson direct from school at the age of 15. He was to remain with the company until his retirement in 1982 and was very much a 'company man'. By the mid-1930s he was the senior sub-editor on *The Wizard* and *The Rover*, giving him great experience in the minutiae of running comics that contained both prose stories and a limited number of comic strips. R.D. Low, the managing editor of all the D.C. Thomson comics, felt that there was a great opportunity to create a second series of comics which had a greater emphasis on humour.

The first comic was to be *The Dandy*, and Low chose Albert Barnes, then just 25, to be its editor. Neither of them could have imagined that Albert would remain editor (apart from war service) until 1982. *The Dandy*, therefore, is very much Albert's creation. He described the physical humour of *The Dandy* by saying 'There is never any real violence, only the cartoon kind to be found in "Tom and Jerry" where the victim always springs back unharmed. It gives children a chance to cock a harmless snook at authority.' He controlled the content and the look, he selected the stories for publication, he approved all the characters to be developed as strips and selected and directly managed all the artists who worked on the comic. He firmly believed that no-one should have dealings with freelance artists unless they had already met them and for many years he ensured that only he met artists.

Albert played a key role in developing the most famous characters in the comic. With the artistic genius of Dudley Watkins, he developed 'Desperate Dan' noting that 'he is to be the roughest, toughest cowboy. He has to be the strongest man in the world: a man who can chew iron and spit dust.' Dan was also a man with a huge chin and Dudley Watkins drew inspiration from Albert's own chin to create the character that personifies the *The Dandy*. Albert wrote most of the scripts for 'Desperate Dan' and for 'Korky', rather than delegating these tasks to staff writers, as most editors would have done.

In 1940, less than three years after the first issue, Albert was called up and spent the remainder of the Second World War

*First **Dandy** Editor, Albert Barnes.*

in the Royal Navy. The editing of *The Dandy* was overseen by R.D. Low and Albert saw very little of Dundee until he returned from the war. Starting as an able seaman, he soon was serving on a minesweeper out of Archangel. His talents were quickly recognised and he became an officer. These navy years had a great influence on him. It reinforced his love of direct, physical humour and of playing practical jokes. He learnt much about man management as an officer – handling temperamental artists was nothing compared with sorting out a group of sailors on shore leave in some exotic port or other.

After the war he returned to his editor's chair and so began the golden age of *The Dandy*, which was soon selling over 2 million copies a week. In these early post-war days he was alert

THAT WAS MIGHTY NICE OF THE BOYS MAKING ME A LITTLE SALAD SANDWICH FOR HELPING THEM OUT!

The illustration above shows Desperate Dan as he appeared in the first edition of **The Dandy**.

Many say that Desperate Dan's chin was based on Albert Barnes.

to changing tastes, which led to the ending of prose stories and an increase in the number of strips.

He was very supportive of the artists he selected; his copious correspondence with them, shows him encouraging and cajoling them and they responded with great loyalty. Some became personal friends of the family, though others were certainly in awe of his opinions (even such artists as Davey Law and Jack Prout). He had particular foibles – he never trusted anyone who wore a bow tie or wore sunglasses in winter (the downfall of at least one potential artist) nor would he read a script if it was stapled at the top right-hand corner instead of the top left, and those who worked for him had to adjust to these whims. He would occasionally even reject a script he was

happy with, just to ensure that the scriptwriter did not become complacent in his ability.

Because of the success of **The Dandy**, he was held in great respect by the company and was able to run the comic with very little intervention, only once being made aware of their criticism (over a particular 'Corporal Clott' strip (in the 1960s). However, Albert was disappointed not to be offered R.D. Low's job when he retired in 1974 (it went instead to George Moonie, the first editor of **The Beano**). Even Moonie, however, trod carefully around Albert, answering any letters of complaint from readers directly without showing them to Albert.

After the death of Dudley Watkins, he began losing

COMIC CAST

Podge.

Mugg Muggins the Crazy Inventor.

The Two Brave Runaways.

Barney Boko.

Smarty Grandpa.

Sammy and his Sister.

Freddie Fearless Fly.

Our Gang.

Desperate Dan.

Korky the Cat.

The Bellhop

the drive that had made **The Dandy** what it was. The decision to reprint old 'Desperate Dan' strips rather than find a new artist was symptomatic of this, as was his response to the greater success of **The Beano**. He felt that **The Dandy** was not giving enough to its readers who, he thought, wanted more to read – so, for example, he decreased the typesize of the words below the pictures in 'Black Bob' to squeeze in more text, even if this made it difficult to read.

Albert retired in 1982 as his health was failing (such was his position that the company never raised the question of retirement with him). His legacy is celebrated in this book and in the pleasure **The Dandy** has brought to millions of readers.

*A selection of characters from the first issue of **The Dandy**.*

Air castaways from 'Lost on the Mountain of Fear'.

Red Hoof.

The Tricks of Tommy.

Invisible Dick.

Keyhole Kate.

Kelman, the fair-haired boy from 'The Magic Sword'.

Magic Mike and his Magic Shop.

Bongo and Pongo from 'Bamboo Town'.

The Daring Deeds of Buck Wilson.

Hungry Horace.

Wig and Wam.

Wee Tusky.

When the West Was Wild.

Jimmy and his Grockle.

11

THE DANDY

The Birth of *The Dandy*

1937–1939

THE BIRTH OF THE DANDY

The cover of the first edition of **The Dandy**.

IN THE early 1920s D.C. Thomson had seen the great potential in adventure stories and began a series of comics aimed at boys. Starting with *Adventure* in 1921, *The Rover* and *The Wizard* followed in 1922, *The Vanguard* in 1923, *The Skipper* in 1930 and last, but not least, *The Hotspur* in 1933. All these magazines had strands of humour in them. While *The Vanguard* ceased in 1926, the other titles were so successful that they were referred to as the Big Five. The Big Five pioneered the comic strip format.

The creative force behind the Big Five and all the juvenile publications was the head of the children's publications department for D.C. Thomson, a shrewd Scot, Robert Low, more usually known as R.D. Low or just R.D. As the 1930s came to a close there was more and more humour in all the comics, and along with the action illustrations, the artists began to turn their hands to humour. In 1937 R.D. set about building a second Big Five, starting with *The Dandy* in 1937, *The Beano* in 1938 and *The Magic Comic* in 1939. Only the start of the Second World War stopped further expansion.

Each of the new titles was built to the same formula. Whereas the Big Five were adventure papers that included

Poor old Pussy on the prowl—Meets the Frog. now hear him howl.

YOU, TOO, CAN HAVE FUN WITH THE JUMPING FROG. THERE WILL BE ONE FREE INSIDE EVERY COPY OF "THE DANDY" NEXT WEEK

Advertising for **The Dandy** *appeared in all the top comics of the day. The first two issues had a bonus in the form of a FREE gift, either the express whistler or the jumping frog pictured here and on the following pages. In the advertisement above, note the rhyming couplet, a regular feature of comics at that time, and the bane of the sub-editor's life.*

PAGE EIGHT

FREE TO EVERY READER WITH THE NEW COMIC. JUMPING FROGS

THE DANDY COMIC OUT ON FRIDAY 10TH DEC.

GET THE DANDY EVERY FRIDAY FOR FUN AND THRILLS PRICE 2D

Printed and published by D. C. Thomson & Co. Ltd., 12 Fetter Lane, London. E.C.4.

some humour strips, the New Three were humour papers that included some adventure strips, a complete change of emphasis. They brought in a type of humour that was powerful in visual slapstick and scorned officials and authority. This had been done before but the new vigorous trio pushed its gags and situations further, which built their appeal to children all the more strongly.

The first issue of *The Dandy*, edited by the youthful Albert Barnes, was published on December 4, 1937, at the price of 2d for 28 pages. It was D.C. Thomson's first weekly comic but its the line-up of artists and scriptwriters were far from newcomers to the field of comic art, much of it for already established Thomson publications.

'Chic' Gordon had drawn 'Cheery Chinks' for *The Rover* as early as 1922, while Allan Morley had drawn innumerable strips for the boys' papers ('Nosey Parker', 'Silias Snatcher', etc.) since 1924. Dudley Watkins, starting as a boys' paper illustrator in 1925, had progressed to

drawing 'The Broons' and 'Oor Wullie' in **The Sunday Post** 'Fun Section' in 1936, and, though they had not done any strip work as such before **The Dandy** No. 1, both Jack Glass and Fred Sturrock had been 'heading block' artists for the Thomson boys' papers since the 1920s.

Also, directly linked with the Thomson publications, James Crichton and James Clark had drawn nursery strips for Thomson's co-publisher (John Leng) in *Fairyland Tales* since the mid-twenties, James Crichton drawing 'Billy and

Bunny' and James Clark drawing 'Willie Waddle'.

The sales ledger figures show how close and how large the immediate sales were of both **The Dandy** and **The Beano**. The first **Dandy** amassed sales of 481,895 copies and the first **Beano**, published six months later, 442,963 copies. The circulation of **The Wizard**, the most popular of the Big Five, was around 350,000 per week at this time so it is no exaggeration to say the comics were an immediate success.

Not content to let their free gifts attract readers, this eight-page mini comic was inserted into **Adventure** *ahead of the publication of the first* **Dandy**. *It gave readers samples of what they could expect to find in the new comic.*

STORIES to READ and PICTURES to SEE
In No. 1 of "The Dandy," Out on Friday, December 3

THE MAGIC SWORD

The shining sword of the shining sun
In the hands of a boy—the Fair-Haired One—
Shall bring death to the tyrant, so, Tyrant, beware
Of the sword of the sun and the son who is fair!

This story tells about the strange up-bringing of the fair-haired boy who was destined to save his country from a tyrant.

WHEN THE WEST WAS WILD
—The thrilling adventures of a family bound for the Golden West in their prairie waggons.

THE TWO BRAVE RUNAWAYS
—Tells how an orphan girl and her cripple brother ran away from their cruel home and started a life of adventurous wanderings.

THE TRICKS OF TOMMY
—Fun with a youngster who can imitate other people's voices.

RED HOOF
—The young Highland stag that was saved from death and kept as a pet by a deer-stalker's son.

LOST ON THE MOUNTAIN OF FEAR
—The picture story of three castaways stranded on top of a mountain.

FREDDY THE FEARLESS FLY : HUNGRY HORACE
SMARTY GRANDPA : BOASTER BILLY & *many others*

WEE TUSKY

The thrilling jungle life of a young elephant, specially written for "The Dandy."

JIMMY AND HIS GROCKLE

Told in words and in pictures. The funny adventures of a boy and his pet—and that pet is the queerest animal you ever saw!

THE DANDY

ISSUE

No.1

*So what was the first **Dandy** actually like? Over the next twenty-eight pages the complete first edition is reproduced, showing the balance between strips and prose stories, the latter a feature of greater significance than we might now expect. To find out more about the strips and who illustrated them (where known), consult the index at the back of this book.*

'Korky the Cat', drawn by James Crichton for twenty-five years, may have been based on Otto Messmer's successful 'Felix the Cat'.

22   *The start of some things big: 'Keyhole Kate' (by Allan Morley) ran for nearly twenty years while 'Desperate Dan' (here by Dudley Watkins) still remains larger than life today.*

Queerest Beast to Walk on Land—Jimmy's Grockle Beats the Band!

JIMMY AND HIS GROCKLE

1—Jimmy Johnson got a present in a parcel from his uncle in South America. It was a great big egg—so big that Jimmy thought it was an ostrich egg.

2—There wasn't a hen in the hen-house big enough to sit on it and hatch it out. But Jimmy thought of putting it in the warm oven.

3—He listened at the oven door for a long time. Presently he heard queer sounds like these—"Grockle, grockle, grockle!" The egg was hatching.

4—But it wasn't an ostrich that walked out when he opened the oven. It was the queerest animal you ever saw, right from its funny grin to its funny, spiky tail.

5—Jimmy thought it might be hungry. It was!—for when he put down a basin of potatoes, it gobbled up the potatoes and tried to gobble up the basin as well!

6—What an appetite that animal had! It ate anything, from Pa Johnson's Sunday boots to the cabbages in the garden. And it grew and grew and grew.

7—One day Jimmy tied a string round the queer animal's neck and took it out for a walk. He wanted to show it off to his chums in the street.

8—But round the corner of the wall at the end of the street he met Big Bill Brown, the town bully. Brown was in an ugly mood and started getting tough.

9—Then he spotted the string in Jimmy's hand, and thought Jimmy had a dog with him. So he flattened Jimmy's nose and grabbed the string.

10—Meanwhile Jimmy's queer animal had lingered round the corner to chew up an old tin can. But when Brown heaved on the string, round it came.

11—Wonder of wonders! — Flames streamed from its mouth and set Brown's pants on fire! And Brown ran so hard, his boots must nearly have gone on fire, too!

12—When the strange animal came back Jimmy looked at it. It looked like nothing else on earth, so he called it by the name which it called itself—Grockle.

The funny grin on his funny clock'll—Be here next week; watch for Jimmy's Grockle.

Dreams of the 'ultimate pet' became a staple of comics. This strip (by James Clark) shows the favourite style of Albert Barnes with both speech balloons in the drawings and text beneath each picture.

Fun With a Joker Who Can Imitate Other People's Voices.

"I ALWAYS MIX SOME WHITE SAND INTO MY SUGAR"

"I DON'T GIVE MY CUSTOMERS VALUE FOR THEIR MONEY"

"I BELIEVE IN SWINDLING MY CUSTOMERS"

PEARS

NEW LAID EGGS

THE TRICKS OF TOMMY

The Boy With 100 Voices

"TOMMY," said Mrs Payne, as she bustled round the breakfast table, "I want you to call in on Mr Crosspatch, the grocer, on your way to school, and ask him to send these groceries. I won't have time to go for them myself, and I must have them for the dinner."

She gave Tommy a list of the groceries she wanted.

"Must I go, Mother?" Tommy grumbled. "You know Mr Crosspatch always growls at me, and I'm late for school as it is."

"Yes, Tommy, you must go," said Mrs Payne. "I must have those things this morning. Run along, now. The clock is ten minutes fast, so you'll be in plenty of time."

"O K, Mums," grinned Tommy. "Cheerio! And cheerio, Christina!" he added to his little sister, who was not yet old enough to go to school.

He went out whistling. But when he reached the street his whistle quickly died away. He never whistled when he was going to the grocer's, and the reason was that he didn't like going to the grocer's.

Old Crosspatch was a mean and nasty customer. Some people even said he was a cheat and a swindler. And he was thoroughly hated by nearly everybody in the town of Crockford. He had got Tommy into trouble more than once, and nowadays Tommy kept away from him as much as he could.

Now Tommy had a strange gift. He could imitate other people's voices. He had been able to do this ever since he was a little toddler. When a person frightened him at that early age, he would answer back in that person's voice.

Gradually he had got over this, and as he got older he had learned to control the trick, until now he could speak with anybody's voice at any time, after hearing it only once. All he had to do was to think hard of the person he wanted to imitate.

Another strange thing about Tommy's imitation of anybody's voice was that it didn't seem to come from Tommy, but just seemed to float out of nowhere.

Tommy looked around to see that there was no one about in the street. Then he thought hard of old Crosspatch.

"Ah, you young varmint!" he growled in Crosspatch's voice. "I'll set the police on your track!"

Tommy rubbed his hands. That was exactly how the grocer spoke, and he knew old Crosspatch would say something like that.

"Old sour face!" thought Tommy as he came in sight of the grocer's shop.

The shop was big and dark, and there were stacks of biscuit tins and sacks of potatoes piled up just inside the door, so that you walked along a sort of alley to get inside the shop.

Tommy had turned into this alley and he was about to step into the shop when he came to a sudden halt. A small boy's cry of pain had rung through the shop, and it was followed by old Crosspatch's angry voice.

"Shut up, you young rascal!" Tommy heard the grocer say. "I don't want any of your snivelling tricks in here. Now what are you going to tell your mother?"

There was no reply—only a sound of sobbing. Tommy peered round a pile of biscuit tins to see what was happening. There was Crosspatch, leaning right over the counter and gripping a little chap a bit younger than Tommy by the collar.

"Well, what are you going to tell your mother?" repeated the grocer, shaking the little chap until his teeth rattled.

"I—I don't know!"

"You do know! You're going to tell her that you and some of your young scoundrels of companions ate those apples which she says were missing from the basket of groceries you took home to her. Now, that's what you're going to tell her, isn't it?"

"N—no!" stammered the boy. "I—I didn't eat them."

"You're going to say you did!"

"But I didn't. You couldn't have put them into my basket."

Tommy's fists clenched as old Crosspatch shook the boy again.

"Listen!" snarled the grocer. "You'll tell your mother you ate those apples, or I'll tell the police you were playing football in the street last night and nearly broke my window!"

A scared look came into the little chap's eyes, and he was silent for a moment. Then he seemed to decide that a whacking from his mother wouldn't be quite as bad as being reported to the police.

"All—all right, Mr Crosspatch," he faltered at last, and when the grocer let him go he scurried away into the street, not even noticing Tommy as he flashed past.

Tommy peered into the shop again. There was the grocer, smiling broadly.

"That was easy money!" Tommy heard him say.

"The dirty twister!" growled Tommy, and he drew back, boiling with rage.

It was quite clear now that Crosspatch was really a cheat, just as some people said. He had taken the money for the apples from the little fellow, but hadn't given him any apples. His mother had received all the other groceries she had ordered, but had sent her son back for the apples. And now Crosspatch had bullied the boy into promising to tell his mother that he had eaten them.

It was a mean, foul trick, such as only the greediest miser would think of playing. Tommy wondered what he should do. If he told the police, the grocer would only laugh at his story.

So he racked his brains desperately. The only thing would be to show up the grocer in his true colours, but how could that be done?

Then Tommy hit on a great idea. He decided he could fix old Crosspatch if he could make him wild enough to come along and complain to Tommy's Headmaster, as Crosspatch usually did when he was wild at boys. The Headmaster was quite a big man in Crockford, and when he saw Crosspatch shown up he would know how to deal with him.

The problem of how the showing up was to be done didn't worry Tommy just then. He just shoved his hands into his pockets and strode into the shop with the idea of making Crosspatch wild!

He advanced to the counter and handed over Mrs Payne's list of groceries.

"My mother wants you to send these things along this morning," he said.

"Ah, you young varmint!" growled Crosspatch, using the exact words Tommy had known he would use. "We've had peace since you started going to school. I suppose you're pestering the teachers like you used to pester me. Go on," he grunted. "Be off with you. I'll send these things along."

Tommy turned away, and at once saw a means of making the grocer jumping mad. On a box near the door Crosspatch had laid a tray of sugar lumps. Tommy coolly stuck his hand out, grabbed a handful, and put them into his pocket.

Sure enough, Crosspatch saw him. The grocer let out a yell.

"I'll teach you, you young rip, you highway robber! I'll have you flogged up at that school of yours, you wretched thief!"

Tommy dived for the door. But he tripped and fell forward, and his outstretched hands went slap into a crate of eggs. He broke about a dozen, and covered his hands and arms with yellow yolk. But he picked himself up quickly, and ran as fast as he could.

Doubling around a few corners, he was soon able to slow down. Crosspatch had given up the chase, and Tommy just had time to get to the school and clean up before the bell rang.

"Well, Crosspatch ought to be wild enough now!" he chuckled.

Shocks for the Teacher

TOMMY was worried. Mr Paxton, his teacher, was giving a history lesson that morning. He was telling the class briefly about the Kings of England, and had got as far as Henry the Eighth. But Tommy was paying no attention to him. His mind was on old Crosspatch, and he was wondering how he was going to show the grocer up in front of the Headmaster.

Just then Mr Paxton, who saw that Tommy was dreaming, fired a question at him.

Tommy's ability as a ventriloquist allows him to have fun at the expense of adults.

"Payne!" he rapped. "Describe in a few words the kind of man Henry the Eighth was."

Tommy started from his day-dreaming and blinked. Mr Paxton repeated the question.

Tommy didn't know what to do, but Blossom, who was the biggest fellow in the class and a proper bully, slipped Tommy a note. Tommy opened the note under his desk and began to read its contents aloud.

"Henry the Eighth was called Bluff King Hal because he was good at bluffing his way out of tight corners. He was married six times and he became a great film actor. He was a star in a film that was shown at The Kinema along the road three weeks ago."

The class was doubled up with laughter, and Blossom laughed loudest of all. Mr Paxton was furious. He took his cane and gave the bewildered Tommy four stingers.

"And now, my pretty Blossom that bloometh in the spring," purred Mr Paxton. "You are enjoying yourself. So perhaps you'll tell us the names of Henry's six wives?"

Blossom stood up and cleared his throat. This was Tommy's chance to get revenge on Blossom for the nonsense he had written on that note. He thought hard, very hard of Blossom, and then spoke out with Blossom's voice.

"Sure, I'll tell you. The six dames that Henry fell in love with were Greta Garbo, Myrna Loy, Ginger Rogers, Joan Crawford, Gracie Fields, and—and Nellie Wallace!"

The class was dumb with awe. This was going too far. Blossom would get it in the neck this time. And Blossom did!

Mr Paxton was speechless with rage at first. He choked and spluttered, and just then the bell rang for the morning break. As the other boys trooped out the teacher took the frightened Blossom by the collar.

"Come, Blossom, we'll see what the Headmaster has to say about this outrage!"

"But, sir, it wasn't me. I didn't say anything!" cried Blossom.

"Don't make it worse by lying," said Mr Paxton between his teeth.

It was a very sore Blossom who came back to the class a quarter of an hour later. Tommy grinned. That would teach Blossom not to get other people into trouble!

Mr Crosspatch on the War-Path

BUT Tommy was still puzzling over his problem. How could he show up old Crosspatch?

And his chance arrived before he was ready for it. A boy came in with a message that Dr Blott, the Headmaster, wished to see Thomas Payne in his study immediately.

Tommy left the room nervously. Now for it! He tapped gently on the Headmaster's study door.

"Come in," called the Head.

"That's the villain! That's the blackguard!" shouted Crosspatch, waving his umbrella as Tommy entered the room.

"Really, sir!" interrupted Dr Blott. "Please allow me to handle this affair!"

Crosspatch only scowled.

"Payne," said Dr Blott, turning to Tommy, "I have received a very serious complaint about you. Mr Crosspatch has stated that you stole his goods and destroyed a crate of his eggs. Now, what have you to say for yourself?"

"The breaking of the eggs was an accident, sir. I slipped," began Tommy.

"Take no notice of the little scoundrel!" growled Crosspatch. "He did it on purpose."

The Head looked at Crosspatch very coldly. It was clear to Tommy that he didn't like the old grumbler, and that he hated all these interruptions. Tommy saw a slender chance. If he could cause these two to quarrel, he might manage to make Crosspatch show himself up. So he thought very hard about the Head. Then very clearly he imitated the Head's voice.

"Shut up, you old twister!" he said. Crosspatch snorted furiously.

THIS GREAT **JUMPING FROG** **FREE** TO EVERY READER NEXT FRIDAY

"Old twister! What do you mean, sir? How dare you call me an old twister?" The Headmaster looked puzzled.

"I assure you, sir——" he began.

"—that you are a dirty swindler!" continued Tommy in the Head's voice.

"And you, sir, are a pompous old madman. I'll have the law on you for this!" shouted Crosspatch. "I'll report you to the education authorities. I'll have you sacked. No wonder the boys are thieves and wreckers. Their masters are no better!"

Things had gone a bit further than Tommy had meant them to go just yet. Dr Blott lost his temper thoroughly, and he told Crosspatch in very strong language what he thought of him and his continual complaints.

It was all very funny, but it was not what Tommy had meant to happen. He had hoped to imitate Crosspatch's voice and say things about the grocer that would show him up properly. But now they were both shouting so loud that Tommy didn't have the lung power to make his imitation of the grocer's voice heard.

They hurled threats at each other until they were both breathless, and then Crosspatch grabbed his hat and strode out, nearly pulling the door off its hinges. Tommy looked uneasily at the panting Head.

Dr Blott was wild with anger, and he had to have something to vent his anger upon.

"So you are the boy who caused all the trouble!" he roared. "Good! We'll see what we can do to curb your frisky goings-on."

It was a painful ten minutes for Tommy. His plans had gone all wrong, but as he limped away he vowed between clenched teeth that he would have Crosspatch run out of the town yet. This flogging only made him more determined than ever!

Tommy's Revenge

TOMMY got the idea for his plan of revenge from Christina, his little sister. His father had brought home some sand, very fine, white sand, to do a job in the garden. Christina was playing with it.

"Look, Tommy!" she shouted. "Sugar!"

That gave Tommy the idea. After his tea on Saturday evening, he went along to Crosspatch's shop. The shop was full of people doing their week-end shopping, and Tommy had no trouble in mixing among

them without being seen by Crosspatch.

He mingled with the customers at the counter, and found that Mrs Breen, the wife of an important man in Crockford, was being served by Crosspatch. She was giving her order.

"A pot of marmalade, two pounds of butter—Empire butter—a dozen fresh eggs—mind they are fresh, Mr Crosspatch. And let me see, yes, three pounds of sugar."

This was Tommy's chance. Mr Crosspatch was an old-fashioned grocer, who didn't bother with the new-fangled methods of selling sugar that was all ready made up in bags. He kept loose sugar in a bin at the back of the shop, and weighed it out as he needed it.

Tommy cleared his throat, and thought hard of Mr Crosspatch.

"Oh, Mrs Breen," Crosspatch's voice went floating over the shop, "I really wouldn't advise you to buy my sugar. I always mix some white sand into my sugar, and it wouldn't suit you, I know. You should go along to Moffat's Stores and buy their wrapped sugar. It's so much better value!"

"Really, Mr Crosspatch!" gasped Mrs Breen.

Tommy spoke out again in Crosspatch's voice.

"Oh, shut up, you old hen! You think because your husband is on the Town Council that you are the Queen of Crockford!"

The other women in the shop tittered. Mrs Breen wasn't very well liked. She had become very proud since her husband had been elected to the Town Council.

"I've never been so insulted in all my life. Sand in the sugar, indeed! Old hen, am I? I'll fetch my husband around to you. I'll fetch my husband!" shouted Mrs Breen, and stormed out of the shop.

"What does she mean? Did she say there was sand in the sugar? What is she talking about?" said Mr Crosspatch in amazement.

"You said yourself that you put sand in the sugar," snorted a woman. "It's terrible the way we housewives are treated. I for one am not going to be insulted by a grocer. Good-day, Mr Crosspatch!"

There were mutterings among the other women, and they all trooped out of the shop into the street. The news spread quickly over the town, and soon a crowd of women gathered around the shop, all of them shouting and shaking their fists.

"He puts sand in the sugar! He said so himself!"

The police had to come and clear them away.

There was an awful row in the town over Mr Crosspatch. Mr Breen, the councillor, wrote a very learned letter to the local newspaper. The town chemist sampled Mr Crosspatch's sugar and reported that there was no sand in it. It was good, pure sugar. But the townspeople were very upset over Mr Crosspatch. There were quite a few who had heard him say that there was sand in it.

So Mr Crosspatch decided to sell his shop to Moffat's, who had wanted it for a long time.

On the day when he was leaving Crockford he wrote a letter to the newspaper. He said he was glad to get out of the town, that the children were wild, that the parents couldn't control them, and that the teachers were not fit to teach them.

But nobody worried about that. And Tommy worried least of all. All he felt was gladness, for he knew he had done the people of Crockford a good service by getting rid of the surliest, best-hated man in the town.

Next Friday in " The Dandy "—There will be another great complete story about some more of "The Tricks of Tommy."

Funny Fellows, Every One—Join Our Gang and Have Some Fun.

OUR GANG

All these boys and girls play in the famous Hal Roach films of "Our Gang," and appear here by courtesy of M-G-M.

| Spot The Pup | Alfalfa Switzer | Scotty Beckett | Darla Hood | Billy Thomas | Porky Lee | Patsy May | Spanky McFarland | Buckwheat Thomas |

1—There was a big meeting in the Gang Clubhouse the other day, with Buckwheat Thomas, Scotty Beckett, Alfalfa Switzer, Billy Thomas, Darla Hood, Spanky McFarland, and Porky Lee all present. Even Spot the Pup was there, and everybody except Alfalfa was trying to think of something the Gang could do. Alfalfa folded his arms and thought of nothing. You see, he sprained his brain when he was learning the A B C, and he hasn't done any thinking since!

2—Then in came Baby Patsy May with a proper brainwave. "Let's make a fire engine," she said. Billy Thomas got so excited at the notion that she hit Alfalfa on the head with the mallet. But nobody noticed this, because it made the same sound as if the mallet had hit the wooden box. Porky was dreaming of food as usual, and his dreams came true, for his hair was ironed out by Scotty's meaty feet.

3—And here's how the Gang got busy with the job of building their fire engine. Just look at Scotty with the old back axle, and Buckwheat Thomas with the garden seat. Buckwheat was mighty worried about that seat. He couldn't help thinking, "Wonder if Pa will get a drop when he sits down in the place where it was and finds it isn't there?" Darla Hood vowed she would take a lesson in snake-charming before handling a fire hose again.

4—But there was no slacking. In two wags of Spot's tail that fire engine began to look real, with wheels, seats, a bell, and even a ladder. Then along came Buckwheat and Spanky McFarland with an old barrel to serve as a water tank. Billy Thomas cheered them on, but they wouldn't have thought so much of her cheers if they had known she was inside the barrel.

5—"What will we do for a motor?" asked Spanky. "Motor nix!" said Buckwheat. "We gotta dog." And Spot was trying to tell everybody that he was only a 1 Dog Power dog when Alfalfa came along with a 10 Horse Power horse. It was a real fireman's horse, too, for it wore a helmet—though it was only a straw helmet. However, they yoked him up and got ready.

6—"I'm firemaster on this job," chortled Spanky. As he was the best fighter in the Gang, no one argued. So off went the latest 1937 fire brigade, and the four-legged engine, galloping along with a horse-laugh on its face, was a great success. It had lost a shoe, and had a bit of a limp until Scotty found that one of his father's boots fitted its hoof!

Hal Roach's 'Our Gang', as drawn by Dudley Watkins, would have been familiar to readers from the cinema.

Our young scamps on the ramp—Make the tramps rather damp **7**

7—Round the town they dashed, but never a fire did they see. However, they upset Fruity Funnyface's apple cart and Alfalfa did himself a bit of good by catching the fruit as it fell. Buckwheat was greedier. He tried to catch a lot in his hat, but forgot that the hat had no crown! Ninety-year-old Gaffer Smith had to hop out of the way like a nine-year-old, and the engine was two miles away before he got his breath back.

8—Then all of a sudden, as they thundered up towards Buttercup Farm, where they thought they might start a fire of their own, a couple of nasty tramps sprang out and stopped the engine. "Scram outa this!" said one. "We don't want you guys snooping around!" snarled the other, and he presented Alfalfa with a copy of his fingerprints, and Spot the Pup with a sample of his footprints.

9—So the Gang had to turn and go back, and they went with their hearts in their boots. Even the horse's heart must have been down in Scotty's father's boot. "It's funny these brutes turned us out," said Scotty. "They've got no right to the farm. It don't belong to them!" Alfalfa gave a shout. "Gee! You're right. Guess they're up to no good. Maybe they're the two toughs the cops are looking for."

10—Meanwhile the fire engine had drifted back to town, and Scotty and Alfalfa had just wandered off to see if they could smell out a fire when Fatty came tearing up. "Hi, kids!" he yelled. "I got the good news." Yes, sure enough there was a fire up the road. The engine was turned round faster than a merry-go-round. "All aboard," roared Spanky, and off dashed the brigade.

11—Up the road they went like a streak of greasy lightning. And they took the first bend so fast that there was a biff! and a smack! That fire engine had given the two town cops a tip,—yes, a tip into the ditch! But the Gang didn't mind. They were getting the hose ready. Alfalfa was jumping up and down as if his pants were full of nettles. He could see smoke ahead.

12—Near Buttercup Farm they found the fire all right. Clouds of smoke came pouring over the hedge. So Firemaster Spanky grabbed the hose while Scotty worked the pump. Porky got the bellows, Billy Thomas used her water pistol, Darla Hood filled her mother's jug, and Baby Patsy May got so tied up in the hose that she splashed enough tears to put a damper on any fire.

13—The water went whoosh! over the hedge. And what do you think the fire was? The two tramps had stolen a chicken and were roasting it for dinner over a fire they had built in the field. The water flattened them out, and they hadn't had a bath for so long that they nearly passed out with the shock. So the Gang jumped on them.

14—Then up came the cops. The Gang thought they were in for trouble, but when the two boys in blue saw the tramps they gave a cheer. "Great work, kids!" they sang out. "Them's the two we want, and there's a fat reward for capturing them." And so the Gang had puffs and pies and pastries galore that night. And who ate most? Why, Porky Lee!

Our Gang has lots of laughs for you—In next week's "Dandy," No. 2.

Even in its first issue, the big screen was having an impact on **The Dandy**'s *small page.*

The Great Story of a Boy and a Young Stag.

RED HOOF

Son of a Deer-Stalker

THE wind blew keenly down Glen Gorm as a boy toiled up the slope on the western side.

Sturdy, red-cheeked, sure-footed, Ian Duncan was quite a little fellow, yet already he was perfectly at home in the hills. Whenever he got back from school it was his daily task to take his father's lunch to him, wherever he might be in the vast Gairnshee deer forest.

To-day he knew he would find his father somewhere at the head of the glen, where in a certain hollow a good many deer had come down to feed on the tender new heather shoots.

In his hand he carried a large basket containing sandwiches and a flask of hot tea. Big John Duncan would be glad of the tea, for he was the head deer-stalker on this estate, and had been out since early morn watching the herd.

The basket was heavy, and more than once the boy set it down to rest his arm. Several times he turned to glance back down the glen, where in the distance he could see the roof and the smoking chimney of the croft where he lived. There, he knew, his mother would be preparing the mid-day meal, and his small sister, Bessie, would be playing on the hearthrug. He would be glad when little Bessie grew big enough to come out with him on the hills.

Ian loved the hills, and the heather-scented wind on his face. Already he knew every burn and every crag within three miles of his home in the Highlands. Already he knew the haunts of the deer and their movements throughout the four seasons.

Now he was at the top of the slope on the west side of the glen, walking more easily along the ridge, and straining his eyes for a glimpse of his father. If he had been bigger and stronger he might have shouted, but the wind was so powerful that he knew it would drown his voice. So he had to rely on his eyes to find his father.

Suddenly he quickened his step, turning slightly towards the east. He had seen the deer, more than two hundred of them, sheltering in the far end of the hollow which he had been heading for. There were many young calves feeding with them.

On the hill ridge above the deer he saw his father, big, boldly outlined against the grey sky. John Duncan had already seen his son, and was waving his stick.

Ian smiled gladly. There would be no fear of his father having a late lunch this day. It was not yet twelve o'clock.

He started to run, and before long came up with the broad-shouldered man, who leaned on his stick watching the movements of the herd below. John Duncan was a slow-moving man, with clear, all-seeing eyes, slow to anger and slow to rouse, but a man who could hold his own out there on the hills with either man or beast.

Others said he was the finest stalker in all Ross-shire. Ian quite believed this. To him his father was the finest and cleverest man in the world. There was not a thing he did not know about the wild birds, the deer, the foxes, the mountain cats, and the eagles.

"Hullo, son, you found me quickly to-day!"

"That's because there's no mist," said the boy. "I was thinking, Father, it would be a good idea if you made me a big whistle. Then when it's misty I could blow that, and when you heard it you could shout, and so guide me to wherever you were."

John Duncan smiled broadly. He knew his son badly wanted him to make a whistle, and knew that when Ian had it he would wish for mist every day so that he might go out on the hills and blow it.

"I'll make you one for your next birthday, Ian," he promised. "See that tiny calf down there? I think that's the smallest one I've ever shown you. It's the youngest deer in the herd."

Ian watched the mother deer busily licking her tiny calf. He would have been happy to stop there all the afternoon, watching the deer, and listening to his father, but after half an hour or so John Duncan sent him back home. By that time the basket and the flask were empty, and the stalker was looking pleased with himself and with the world.

"Away with you now, Ian, and don't loiter on the way home. Your mother will have the dinner ready, and she'll worry if you're late. Be a good lad and hurry."

Ian promised, and went off along the hillside as fast as his legs would carry him. He could have gone down into the glen almost at once, but he chose to keep on the ridge, where he could see much further. He even had hopes of glimpsing some of the big stags which he knew would be away on their own, ranging the hills.

The wind was now behind him, but the air was still keen, and he felt hungry enough to eat everything which his mother was sure to have waiting for him. He was eager for his dinner.

Then all at once the boy stopped, and shaded his eyes. He had seen a soaring bird in the sky, a huge bird, which swooped down on outspread wings.

Ian Duncan crouched and became as still as the rocks around him.

"An eagle!" he muttered to himself.

He was very excited. It was not often he saw an eagle flying so low, and this one seemed to be coming lower. It was almost level with the hilltop where he stood, and was diving nearer, coming in towards the steep hillside below the spot where Ian stood.

The great bird passed below the boy's level, and vanished from sight. Ian waited a few moments, then crawled forward to the edge of the steep hill, and peered over.

There was the eagle hovering close to a ledge about twenty feet below, and on that ledge lay something which at first the boy did not recognise.

Then it dawned on him that a deer lay there, still and motionless, quite dead. Whether it had climbed up from below, to stick on the ledge and perish, or whether it had fallen from above, he could not tell, but there it was, attracting the hungry eagle.

Ian watched silently. He had never before seen an eagle feed. He saw it go closer and closer, until at last it alighted on the edge of the narrow ledge.

What was that? Ian forgot all about the eagle, and sat up and stared in amazement. Something had moved behind the dead deer, something which lay close beside it.

It did not take the stalker's son a couple of seconds to realise that there was a calf with that dead mother deer, and that the calf still lived.

Saved From The Eagles

IT was quite a sturdy little deer calf, with a dull red coat, and it stood between its dead mother and the rocks behind, staring wide-eyed at the eagle. The great bird fluttered its wings and drew a little closer.

Ian no longer wanted to see the eagle feed. He felt sure it was going to attack the young deer, and kill it.

So he shouted and clapped his hands. The eagle looked up at him, stiffening in alarm. The deer calf made a whimpering sound, and the boy seized a large stone.

"Get away!" he called, and hurled the stone at the eagle.

The stone bounced on the hillside, but that was enough to frighten the bird. Flapping its powerful wings, it rose skywards. But it did not fly away. Another eagle appeared, and both of them hovered high above the hill.

Ian Duncan bent again to look at the young deer. One day it would be a glorious stag with noble antlers, fleet-footed on the hillside, but that would only be if it lived.

There did not seem to be very much chance of this, unless someone helped the little creature. It had no mother to protect it. Down there it would either die of hunger, or fall from the ledge, or be killed by the eagles.

Ian looked about him doubtfully. He could not go back and ask his father for help. It was too far to go, and the deer calf might fall to its death before he got back.

He peered over the edge of the rock wall,

Once again, the bond between boy and animal comes to the fore.

When are peas like soldiers?—When they are shelled!

and carefully lowered his legs. He was going to try and climb down to the ledge.

It was a dangerous climb. More than once he slipped, and only the tough roots of the heather growing out of cracks in the rock prevented him falling. His mother would have been very angry if she had seen him doing that climb, but Ian did not think of her then. He was thinking only of the young stag, whch was still making those whimpering noises.

No ordinary boy of Ian's age could have got down that rock wall, but he had been scrambling about on the hills almost as soon as he could walk. Not many minutes later he arrived on the ledge, breathless, and with his fingers sore, and one of them bleeding.

He did not mind that. The deer calf had drawn away to the end of the ledge to stare at him. He could see its soft eyes on him as it wondered whether he was friend or foe.

"It's all right," he said softly. "I've come to help you. Keep still."

But at that moment a great shadow fell across the ledge. It was the shadow of one of the eagles, which had grown bold enough to swoop lower. Ian snatched up a stout stick and waved it to scare the great bird away.

Ian was afraid the deer calf would jump away from the swooping eagle and go over the edge, but it seemed to have the sense to know that the boy was not going to harm it. It remained quite still until he actually touched it.

He was surprised to find how big it was. From above it had looked quite small, but now that he stood beside it he marvelled at the boldness it showed, and the sturdy way it planted its feet.

He caught hold of it and fondled it. Maybe the deer calf liked the warmth of his hands, for it nuzzled against him. Ian frowned when he got his arms about it and felt how heavy it was.

"How can I get it up the hillside?" he asked himself.

He had to do something. The mother deer was quite dead, and time was getting on. If he did not want to worry his own mother, he must go straight back home at once.

In his pocket he had some stout cord, and when he got this out he made the deer calf lie on its side while he tied its legs together, the two front hoofs to the two hind hoofs. The animal struggled, but once Ian had it down he was strong enough to hold it there. And as he tied the hoofs he noticed that, although three of them were black, there was one that was not quite red.

"Don't get frightened, Red Hoof," he whispered. "I'm only doing this so that I can carry you."

It took all his strength to lift the kicking calf, and to get its body across his shoulders, with its bound legs across his chest. But once it was in place he had his hands free, and he knew he could manage the climb.

Ian was hot and weary by the time he got back to the hilltop, but he was very proud of himself. He had rescued the baby stag from certain death. The next thing was to know what to do with it!

He could not turn it loose, for it would only die. He could not give it to another mother deer, for she would know it was not her own calf, and might kill it.

"I'll take it home and look after it," decided the boy, and, after untying the tight cords, he carried the calf in his arms down the hill.

It was very heavy. More than once he stumbled because of the weight of it, but Ian had all the grimness of his father. Once he made up his mind to do a thing, he kept on trying.

He reached the foot of the hill, and the little stag struggled, nearly knocking him over.

"Quietly!" he panted. "I'm going to take you home, where it's dry and warm. Maybe we can get something for you to eat. Be patient!"

Long before he reached the lonely croft in its neat garden at the foot of the glen he was running, and as he ran he was shouting—

"Mother! Bessie! Look what I've found! Come and see what I've found."

Mrs Duncan heard the noise, and came to the gate. She stared in amazement when she saw her son, hot and weary, staggering along and carrying something half as big as himself.

"What in the world have you got there, Ian?" she cried.

He reached the gate, and held his burden out to her.

"Look, Mother, it's a baby deer, a young stag. Its mother is dead, and it had fallen over a cliff. An eagle was going to kill it. I saved its life, Mother. Can't we do something for it? I'm sure it's cold and hungry."

The Story of the King Stag

MRS DUNCAN carried the young deer into the house, and very strange it looked in their neat kitchen, shivering and trembling on the hearthrug in front of the fire, staring about it with wide, frightened eyes, wondering whether to run or stop where it was.

Bessie was just as frightened as the calf. She hid in the corner behind the rocking-chair, and refused to come out and be introduced.

Ian forgot his own hunger and tiredness. He wanted to see the calf eat. He rushed into the garden and pulled handfuls of grass, but it turned its nose away from this.

"It's too young to eat grass, or anything else but milk," declared Mrs Duncan. "We'll heat up some milk and see if it'll take that."

They put some warm milk in a saucer, but it was no use. The animal sniffed, but did not seem to know how to drink.

Then Ian had a brainwave. He went to the cupboard and fetched the old feeding-bottle that Bessie had used when she was a tiny baby.

"It's only a baby stag, Mother, so perhaps it'll use this!" he suggested.

Mrs Duncan did not think so, but she filled the bottle, held the rubber end to the little animal's mouth, and, sure enough, it sucked greedily.

Ian danced with glee. Even Bessie came out from her hiding-place to watch. The baby stag emptied one bottle, and wanted another. It followed Mrs Duncan all round the kitchen as she prepared more milk. She said she had never before seen such a friendly little animal.

"And it's got no mother and no father," said Ian. "Can't we keep it here until it gets big, Mother?"

Mrs Duncan felt the creature's soft nose against her fingers as she held the bottle, and she smiled rather wistfully.

"Who ever heard of keeping a wild stag, even a young one?" she said. "You'll have to ask your father about it."

After this Ian could scarcely wait for his father to come home in the middle of the afternoon.

As soon as it had fed the deer calf wanted to sleep, and they made a comfortable place for it with some rugs and old blankets in front of the fire.

There it slept as though it had no care in all the world, and Ian and young Bessie sat down beside it, as still as could be, to watch its heaving sides.

Almost before they expected him, John Duncan arrived home, weary but full of good humour. He knew there would be a good, hot meal awaiting him, and his day's work on the hills was over. With him he brought Rob, the big deer-hound, which went everywhere with him, and it was the savage growl of Rob that told him there was a stranger in the house.

Then Ian rushed at him, grabbed his hand, and dragged him to the kitchen.

"Look, Father, a real young stag. I saved its life. Its mother is dead. Please, can we keep it and look after it?"

"Yes, please let us keep it!" piped up Bessie, who was no longer afraid of the stranger from the hills.

The stalker looked down at the red-coated creature, and as he did so it opened its eyes and looked at him. Its eyes were clear and unafraid. John Duncan stooped and lifted it in his arms, while his son poured out the story of how he had saved it.

"A baby stag, it's true, but what a size!" marvelled the stalker. "It can't be many days old, yet look how big it is! It's going to be a monster when it's full grown."

The boy's eyes shone.

"But that won't be for a long time, Father! It won't grow up for ever so long. I want to keep it. I'll look after it, I promise I will."

"Well, maybe you can keep it just now, but not here in the kitchen. We'll empty out the stuff from the old barn, and put some hay in there. But look at the breadth of it, and the set of that head! It's no ordinary young stag this, Ian."

"What do you mean by telling the boy it is no ordinary stag?" asked Mrs Duncan. "Why is it different?"

"Because I know the signs, my dear. I know what I'm talking about. If this ever grows up it will be a monster stag, one of the Monarchs of the Hills, maybe even a giant like the one that killed my grandfather, fifty years ago."

"You mean the King Stag they still talk about in the hills, Father?" cried the excited boy.

"Yes, I never saw it myself, but my father told me it stood nearly ten feet high. For years it lorded over all the other stags, and ru'ed the hills in these parts. Once every fifty years or so such a one appears, but never in my time has there been a King Stag—unless this is going to be one."

Ian looked at the big calf with pride, not unmixed with fear.

"What happened to the last one, Father?"

"It was my grandfather who shot it when it was old and lame," said the stalker. "He brought it down, and thinking it was dead he turned it over to skin it. Suddenly it leapt up, and with one tearing blow from its hoof it killed him. Then it died. Since then there's never been a stag like it in these parts. You can see its antlers up at Gairnshee House."

Ian swallowed hard, then threw his arms about the deer calf and hugged it.

"Red Hoof won't do anything like that. He's a good stag, and he's going to be friends with everyone. Can I really keep him, Father?"

The stalker glanced at his wife, then looked thoughtfully out of the window at the rocky glen and the purple hills, with their tops hiding in drifting clouds of mist.

"Well, you can keep him just as long as he chooses to stay, or just as long as he doesn't make himself a nuisance. But don't set your heart on keeping him too long, Ian. Nobody can keep a stag and make it a pet like a dog. They belong to the hills, and to the hills they always go."

Next Friday in " The Dandy "—The story of how Red Hoof fought his first battle.

---

*Unsurprisingly, the romantic scenery of Highland Scotland is a recurrent presence in **The Dandy**'s stories. Note also the unconnected joke at the top of the page, a feature repeated on many story pages.*

The Thrilling Picture Story of Three Air Castaways.

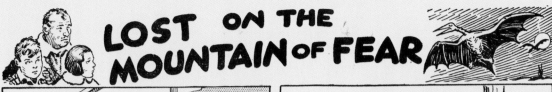

LOST ON THE MOUNTAIN OF FEAR

1—Major Bryant turned from the wreck of his round-the-world 'plane and looked at his two children, Peter and Patricia. "It's a serious business!" he said. "The old 'plane's wrecked completely, and we're stranded up here." Along with the Major's man-servant, Handy Clark, the Bryants had been going round the world by aeroplane, but they had crashed on a level stretch of a broad mountain top in the Andes Mountains of South America.

2—The mountain was the queerest one they had ever seen. Its top was like a big island raised several thousand feet above the surrounding country on a great pillar of smooth rock. It was impossible for anyone to climb down. But suddenly Peter had an idea. "What about the parachutes?" he suggested. "Couldn't we jump over this overhanging edge and float to the ground?"

3—It was a great idea. But when the Major examined the parachutes, his face fell. All but one of them had been damaged in the crash. "Well," he decided, "I'll have to parachute down myself and bring back help. I'm leaving the children in your charge, Handy. There are enough stores in the 'plane to last you a few weeks—so, be brave, kids!" And after kissing little Pat and shaking hands with Peter and Handy, the Major dived into space.

4—Down, down he went, dropping like a stone. Then his parachute billowed out, stopping his fall, and he began to float earthwards. Peter and Pat watched until Handy's voice broke in on their thoughts. Handy had been a sailor and he was a first-class handyman. "Well, shipmates," he said cheerily, "let's see if we can rig up a tent out of what's left of the parachutes."

5—But Peter was thinking of something else. "It may be months till Dad reaches a town and gets help," he said. "If he's away all that time we'll soon forget what day it is!" "That's right," chimed in Pat. "Why, we might even forget our own birthdays!" "Well, I know what I'll do," said Peter. "I'll cut a notch in this tree for every day we're stranded here. Then we'll always know the right date."

6—By this time, Handy, in his clever sailor's way, had rigged up a trim-looking tent. And while Peter went to help him, Pat said she would go and draw water from the little stream that ran down from the peak in the centre of their mountain top. Suddenly Peter and Handy heard the girl's frightened voice. "Come here! Come here quick!" she cried.

Before television and the internet, reading was the only way to find out about faraway places.

7—Handy grabbed a thick spar of wood to use as a club, and he and Peter raced to the girl's side, thinking she was in danger. But when they arrived they found Pat examining some queer footprints on the ground. "What made them?" she gasped. Handy examined the footprints. "Why, it must have been a Three-Toed Sloth," he said at last. "Look—there are only three toe-marks."

8—Handy followed the footprints for a short distance, then pointed to the branches of a tall tree. "There he is!" he cried. "Watch him!" Up there, hanging by its toes from a branch, was the Three-Toed Sloth. "That's how he spends most of his life—hanging upside-down!" Handy said. "He's slow on the ground, because his feet weren't made for walking. But he's a fast mover when he's up a tree."

9—"This is better than being at the zoo!" cried Pat. But as they made their way back to the camp, Handy was looking worried. "Sloths are harmless," he said, "but where there's one animal there are bound to be others—and some of them might be dangerous." His eyes lit on a lot of spiny cactus plants growing nearby. "There's an idea!" he cried. "We'll build a fence of thorns right round our camp. That'll keep any prowlers out!"

10—With Peter and Pat to help him, Handy carefully built a thorny fence right round the camp. Then, as darkness fell, they made a blazing camp fire and cooked a meal, using the first of their stores from the 'plane. Afterwards, Handy rose to his feet. "Now then, youngsters," he smiled, "off to bed with you! I'll take the first spell on guard duty." And Peter and Pat, tired out after their thrilling day, were soon fast asleep.

11—But there was no sleep for Handy Clark that night. All night long he sat on guard at the tent door gazing into the darkness, and even to a hardened, experienced wanderer like him it was an anxious night. Beyond the thorn fence he could make out shadowy forms prowling round the camp. Their glaring eyes reflected the firelight, and occasionally their howls rang through the night. "Panthers!" Handy thought, but he couldn't be sure that he was right. He had no gun, but he gripped a stout club and waited for the dawn.

12—At long last the sun rose and chased away the mysterious shadows. "Wake up, there!" Handy roared, and Peter and Pat poked out their sleepy heads and blinked to find that it was a new day. They went at once to their look-out spot on the cliff top. Where was their father by now? Peter saw the look of fear that came into Pat's eyes, and swallowing the lump he had in his throat, he raised a cheer. "Hurrah!" he cried, turning to cut another notch in the lone tree. "This is our second day here. I wonder what will happen?"

What does the future hold in store for the three castaways? See their next amazing adventure in "The Dandy" next week.

This story combines a fascination for the exotic with a thrilling storyline to great effect, and was drawn by Fred Sturrock.

31

The Story of a Boy Sent to Fight a Tyrant King.

OMAR, The Wise Man.

The shining sword of the shining sun
In the hands of a boy—the Fair-Haired One—
Shall bring death to the tyrant, so, Tyrant, beware
Of the sword of the sun and the son who is fair!

THE MAGIC SWORD

KELMAN, The Fair-Haired Boy.

JASK, The Tyrant King.

The Song of the Sword

JASK, King of Shirak, was in a very happy mood. He had spent most of the day watching his treasurers counting the money which his tax-collectors had gathered in from the long-suffering people of Shirak.

It had given the King hours of joy watching his treasurers at work. And now he had arranged a feast in the palace to celebrate the filling of his coffers.

The scene within the great hall was one of splendour. Jask himself, in wonderful robes, sparkling with jewels, sat at the head of the table. On either side of him were ranged more than a hundred lords and nobles.

They did not all like Jask. Many of them hated him for his cruelty. They thought him the worst tyrant who had ever ruled over Shirak. But they did not dare refuse his invitation to the feast.

There was a great deal of noise and merriment in the vast hall. But suddenly, at the top of the table, there was a crash. The King had dropped the goblet of wine which he had been about to raise to his lips. His face turned pale, and his eyes widened with fear and anger.

"What does that mean?" he roared, and all eyes followed the direction of his shaking finger.

He was pointing at the farthest wall, which, like the other walls, was covered with rich cloth hangings. All the lords and nobles turned their heads and gazed with open mouths.

The biggest of the hangings no longer bore the usual royal designs. There were words on it done in needlework with blood-red threads. The words formed a rhyming verse, and it was quite easy to read that verse:—

" *The shining sword of the shining sun*
In the hands of a boy—the Fair-Haired One—
Shall bring death to the tyrant, so, Tyrant,
beware
Of the sword of the sun and the son who is
fair!"

Voices murmured the verse aloud, until Jask, shaking with fury, leapt to his feet and swept everything from the table in front of him. Everyone cowered back in terror as the tyrant bellowed:

"The Chamberlain! Where is the Chamberlain?"

Shasta, the Chamberlain, came forward and threw himself on his knees before the King.

"What traitor dared to hang up that verse?" demanded Jask, in a terrible voice.

"I know not, Highness. It was not there when the feast started. It must be magic."

"Magic? Bah! It is some trick. I'll strike off the head of the villain who did that. What does it mean?"

The King glared around, and every man there lowered his eyes, for they all knew this verse by heart. The words were the words of a mysterious song which everyone in the Kingdom of Shirak was now singing.

Nobody knew who had written the song, nor who had first sung it, but it was on the lips of all those suffering people who were ground down by the cruel Jask.

Children sang it on the mountainside as they looked after their fathers' goats, men muttered it over their work, women sang it softly to themselves in their homes. The words had become deeply stamped in the minds of all the King's subjects.

Yet this was the first time Jask had seen it. He nearly choked with rage as he demanded:

"Where is this sword, and where is this fair-haired boy? Bring them to me!"

The Chamberlain spread out his hands helplessly.

"Highness, that cannot be. In all your kingdom there is no fair-haired boy. We people of Shirak are dark-haired. Therefore the rhyme is meaningless."

A look of relief came over Jask's face, and he sat down and stared at the mess before him.

"Let this rubbish be cleared away!" he commanded. "Bring a clean cloth for the table!"

Dozens of slaves dashed forward to do his bidding. The traitor's rhyme was torn down from the wall and thrown into the fire. Then six men brought forward a huge silk cloth, which they unfolded on the table before the King.

Suddenly everyone gasped. The King stared as though he could not believe his eyes. There, once again, worked into the design on the new cloth, was that haunting verse:

" *The shining sword of the shining sun*
In the hands of a boy—the Fair-Haired One—
Shall bring death to the tyrant, so, Tyrant,
beware
Of the sword of the sun and the son who is
fair!"

King Jask bounded upright, snatched out his sword, and struck down the nearest of the servants. The rest fled, screaming, and the nobles hurriedly scattered before their wrathful ruler.

"Send me my soldiers! Send me Khast, the Captain of the Guard!" raged Jask. "I will get to the bottom of this. I will find this fair-haired boy and kill him!"

Khast, the Captain of the Guard, arrived in great haste. The King gave him orders to summon the soldiers. They were to make a house-to-house search through the whole city, and the King was going to march with them and see that they searched properly.

"He shall be found, even if we have to enter every house in my Kingdom of Shirak!" vowed Jask, in a towering rage.

But he was really tortured with fear.

The Hunt for the Traitor Boy

THE news of what had happened at the King's feast spread rapidly through the city, and everyone trembled. Long files of soldiers, with drawn swords, marched through the streets, calling at house after house.

"Open your doors, or we will smash them down!" they shouted. "Bring out your children!"

The shivering children were brought before the King, who looked only at the boys. Some of them he took by the hair, and he tugged at it until they cried. One or two, whose hair looked a shade lighter than that of the other boys, were seized by his order and scrubbed until their heads were sore. King Jask wanted to make sure they were not fair-haired boys who had had their hair dyed.

From house to house, from street to street, went the armed men, and they searched every cellar and every attic. But they found no trace of a fair-haired boy. Everyone in the King's capital was dark-haired.

Still the search went on, and as they came near the outskirts of the town a tattered and dirty beggar came and threw himself on the ground before the King.

"O Highness, I think I know where there is a fair-haired boy!"

Jask's face twisted into a cruel grin.

"Speak, and I will reward you with many pieces of gold!"

The beggar looked round fearfully.

"I may be wrong, Highness, but I have heard that Kashan the Swordsmith has a son whose hair is the colour of ripe straw."

"Kashan the Swordsmith—a maker of swords, eh?" snarled the King, and he looked meaningly at the Captain of the Guard. "Who is this Kashan? Where does he live?"

"We all know Kashan," replied the officer. "Many times have I been to his forge, but never have I seen or heard that he had a son."

"Let us go there now!" commanded the tyrant. "If he has a fair-haired son—he and his son shall die."

Once again, the theme is how the underdog can prevail.

The soldiers marched through the outskirts of the town to a clump of trees beside the main highway. There stood a forge, with a cottage beside it, and a sign saying that Kashan made swords of all kinds.

But no smoke came from the forge as the King's men surrounded it. They could not hear the bellows working, nor the clang of the hammer. All was silence.

"He has run away!" said someone.

"Burst open the door and search!" ordered Jask.

So the door was burst open, and the soldiers poured into both the forge and the cottage. They found nobody. Kashan, the maker of swords, was not at home. There were the remains of a meal on the table, and one of the soldiers pointed out that it had been a meal for only one.

"Huh!" scowled the King. "That beggar must have told us a false tale. Let him be flogged instead of rewarded, but when this maker of swords is found he must be brought to me and questioned."

He peered at all the swords hanging around the walls, and carried one or two of them to the doorway to examine them more closely. But in no case did he find a sword that looked in any way unusual. In no case did he find one that might have been called the "Sword of the Sun."

He led the way back to the dusty highroad, and was about to mount his horse when suddenly the horse reared back from something on the ground.

The King and his guards glared. There, written in the thick dust as though by a mighty finger, were the words of the verse:

"*The shining sword of the shining sun*
In the hands of a boy—the Fair-Haired One—
Shall bring death to the tyrant, so, Tyrant,
*   beware*
Of the sword of the sun and the son who is
*   fair!*"

One bellow of fear the King gave, and he leapt upon his trembling steed, drove in his spurs, and fled from the spot—fled back to his palace, where he locked himself in his highest turret-room.

King Jask's eyes were the eyes of a haunted man!

Kashan's Fair-Haired Son

AND about that same time, some miles back in the hills from the spot where the swordsmith's forge stood, a tall and strong-looking man wearing a leather apron was entering a dark cave hidden behind trees and bushes. It was Kashan, the maker of swords, and as soon as he entered, a boy jumped up joyfully from a rough couch at the back of the cave.

Much more powerfully built than any other boy of his age, dressed in a garment of goat-skin, with bright fair hair the colour of ripe straw, he bounded forward.

"Father!" he cried. "It is good of you to come and see me again to-day. I was very lonely."

The swordsmith placed a huge hand on the boy's shoulder and felt the firm muscles under his fingers. Straight in the eyes he looked his son, and studied him keenly. What he saw was good to look upon. In all Shirak there was not a boy so straight, so strong, and so quick on his feet.

"Kelman, my son, you will not have to remain here much longer. You have been a good boy. All your life you have lived in this cave, away from other boys, and away from the city."

"But why—why, Father?" asked Kelman, the Fair-Haired Boy.

"Because it was the order of Omar, the Wise Man, who was your godfather. It was

he who gave me the oils, the herbs and the ointments which have made you grow so strong and so healthy. It was Omar who ordered that you should hunt down your own food, chasing the deer on the mountainside, and the goats among the crags, until you were as fleet and as sure-footed as they are. It was Omar who told me to train you like this, and now I think he will be pleased with you. I am very proud of you."

The Fair-Haired Boy frowned.

"But why am I different from other boys? Why has Omar wanted me to be so strong?"

"That you will learn soon, and meantime remember that you are happier here than you would be in the great city. All these years I have hidden you here, away from the eyes of men, and perhaps you have believed you have missed many things. That is not so, my son. All you have missed is unhappiness. The people of Shirak are very unhappy under their tyrant King. Here in your cave you are perhaps the happiest in the land. Tell me, lad, have you been wrestling with those trees as I taught you?"

"Yes, Father, and now I can uproot a tree a foot thick," said the boy, proudly.

"That is good." The swordsmith stripped off his apron and his tunic, baring himself to the waist. "We will have a match, lad. It will be my strength against your cunning and speed. Come and see if you can throw me yet."

They faced each other in the cave, circling round with hands held ready. And then, with the speed of light itself, the boy darted in and grasped his father's powerful leg. He gripped with both hands, but the swordsmith promptly fell forward on top of his son, caught him by the waist, lifted him high in the air, and dashed him down with great force.

"You were not quick enough, son," he

panted. But then he broke off with a gasp of sheer amazement.

He had thrown the boy with such force that Kelman should have fallen heavily on his back. But the fall had not come about! The fair-haired youngster had landed on his feet, as lightly as a feather, and darted in a second later.

This time he caught his father by both legs, and heaved. The swordsmith was a mighty man. He stood like an oak tree in the wind, scarcely swaying. But suddenly the boy straightened his supple back, and Kashan the Swordsmith found himself flat on the ground, with his son kneeling on top of him, pinning his brawny shoulders down.

The swordsmith gave a roar.

"Loose me, son, for you have won! You have thrown me! For the first time in thirty years someone has thrown me, and it is my own son who has done it! I am prouder of you than ever."

The boy helped him to his feet, and stood there panting with his efforts, his face flushed with triumph.

"I really won, Father?" he asked. "It was a fair throw? You were trying your hardest?"

"I tried harder than ever before, but there is no wrestler living who could have stood against that second attack of yours, my boy. I am very, very pleased with you."

He slipped his arm about the boy's shoulders, and as they stood like that for a moment, something whistled between their heads, and stuck quivering and humming in a crack in the wall beyond.

Father and son sprang apart, and stared at the weapon which had come hurtling through the cave entrance.

"It's a javelin, Father, and there's a piece of paper tied round the shaft," cried the Fair-Haired Boy.

A strange look came into the swordsmith's face as he reached for the javelin and examined the paper. In bold, plain letters on it was a message:

"Kashan, the time has come. Your son is ready for the tests. You have reared him and trained him as I ordered. Now I must see the result. Bid him come to my secret cave. Let him take the path beside the brook as far as the dark wood, then follow the hooting of the owl until he comes to the big rocks. There I shall await him.—Omar."

The swordsmith had read the strange note aloud, and the boy's eyes widened.

"What does it mean?" he whispered.

"It means, my son, that the time has come when you will learn what the future holds for you. You must go to Omar the Wise Man, following the directions he has given, and you must not be afraid. He will tell you the great task in store for you, and what you are going to do for your country."

The Fair-Haired Boy gazed out through the cave mouth, looked at the clear sky, and the waving trees. So far he had seen very little of the world beyond the woods where he had lived hidden all these years. Now he was anxious to see more of it, and to learn why he had been brought up in this strange way.

"I will go, Father," he said softly. "I will go at once."

Next Friday in "The Dandy"—The Fair-Haired Boy faces the first of his terrible tests.

Courage, resilience and a handy magical weapon are all it takes, apparently!

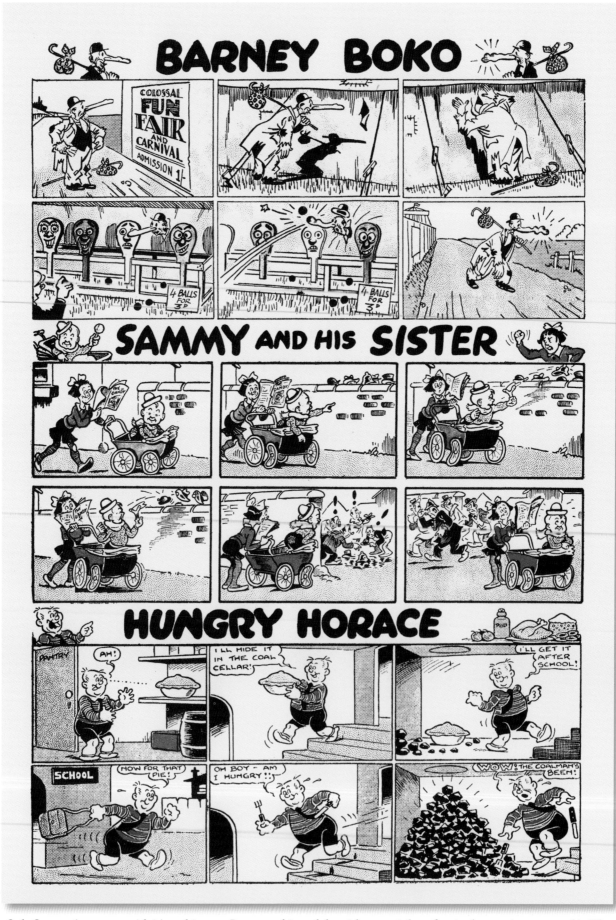

Only Sammy 'gets away with it' on this page. It seems pelting adults with stones is less of a sin than nosiness or greed in **The Dandy** *universe! Strips by John Mason, Frank Minnitt and Allan Morley.*

Smarty Grandpa himself bears more than a passing resemblance to Granpaw from 'The Broons', also by Dudley Watkins. The other strips are by Allan Morley and Sam Fair.

35

The Wanderings of a Girl and Her Cripple Brother on the Open Road.

THE TWO BRAVE RUNAWAYS

Hard-Hearted Aunt Mary

BETTY BROOK came in at the back door of her aunt's house and crept up the stairs very quietly. She kept one eye on the kitchen door, for she did not want her Aunt Mary to see her.

She was a little late in getting home from school, and if she was caught it would mean trouble. She wanted to change her shoes and hang up her coat, so that she could pretend she had been in for some time.

But at the top of the stairs she stopped. The sound of low sobbing came from the little room on the right. It was her little brother, Jack, who was crying, and the girl's face grew grim as she softly opened the door.

Jack had not been at school that day. He was a cripple. His leg had given him trouble ever since he was a year old, and he couldn't walk without the aid of a crutch. Some days the pain in his leg was very bad, and he was unable to go to school.

Betty tip-toed to the bed, where he lay face down. She was only a year older than her brother, but she had always been like a mother to him ever since their own father and mother had been killed in a railway train accident.

That was why they were living with Aunt Mary, who was not very kind to them.

Jack lifted a tear-stained face when he heard his sister beside the bed. He wiped his eyes in his handkerchief, and Betty sat down beside him.

"What is it, Jack? Does the leg hurt very badly?"

"No, it's not my leg, it—it's Aunt Mary!"

"What's she been doing now?" asked the girl fiercely. "Has she been beating you?"

"No, but she won't give me any tea. I accidentally touched her sore toe with my crutch, and she got into an awful temper. She said I was a useless mouth to feed, and —and that I always would be useless!" sobbed the boy.

Betty looked furious. Nobody had the right to speak to her brother like that. It was not his fault that he was a cripple, and it was cruel to taunt him about his lameness.

Aunt Mary should have been the last person to do it, for she was well enough paid for keeping the two children. Their father had left a little money, which provided fifteen shillings a week for their keep.

"You stop crying, Jack," Betty whispered. "I'll bring something up to you after tea. I'll hide it and slip upstairs with it."

Jack cheered up a little after this. He

was a good-looking boy in a dark, frail way, and he worshipped his sister.

"Don't you let her catch you, or she'll whip you," he warned.

Betty said she would be careful, then changed her shoes and went down to the kitchen. Aunt Mary, a big, stern woman with glasses, was already sitting at the tea-table, and she glared fiercely at the girl.

"Huh, I didn't know you were in! I've a good mind to give you no tea for coming late. Sit down! Don't stand there fidgeting like a little idiot! Your brother won't be here. I've sent him to bed."

Betty did not dare tell her aunt that she was very cruel to do this. She sat at the table and tried to munch her buttered bread. But Jack's unhappiness had upset her, and the bread felt dry and stuck in her throat. Her aunt was reading a paper, and did not even look at her.

On the rug lay Rufus, the big mongrel dog which her aunt loved more than the children. She was always buying good meat for it, and often made the children go without some of their food so that there should be more for Rufus.

Now he watched Betty steadily, and raised his head with a low growl when she doubled up a couple of pieces of buttered bread and hid them under her pinafore. Her aunt did not take any notice.

Betty grew bolder. There was only one piece of cake, and she took it and slipped it away with the bread. Jack would not go hungry after all.

A few minutes later she asked to be excused, and got down from her chair.

Betty started for the door, but before she got there Rufus bounded up to her, pushed his nose against her hand, and knocked the food out of her grasp.

"Oh!" gasped Betty in dismay, and just then her aunt looked up.

"You greedy little wretch!" screamed Aunt Mary. "You're more like a pig than a child. What you can't stuff down your throat you try to take away with you. I've a good mind to whip you. Don't touch it! Leave it there! Here Rufus, you can eat it."

She made Betty stand there while the big dog gobbled up the food meant for Jack. Then she ordered the girl up to bed.

There were tears in Betty's eyes when she joined Jack a few minutes later. He looked up eagerly to see what she had brought, but she could only shake her head and say she had nothing.

She told him what had happened, and her blue eyes sparkled as she went on to say—

"It's horrible, Jack. We aren't wanted here. I believe Aunt Mary only wants the fifteen shillings a week. The best thing we can do is to run-away."

Jack was on his feet in a moment, reaching for his crutch.

"Yes, let's run away, Sis. Where can we go? What can we do?"

"Oh, we can go somewhere where they treat us better than Aunt Mary does. I've got that sixpence the teacher gave me at school for being the best in the class at singing. We can get two tickets on the bus and go ever such a long way for sixpence. Let's pack our things and go while she's out doing her shopping before supper."

Jack Brook nodded. He was willing. And so they moved softly about, collecting their few belongings in two small bundles.

The Man From Filmland

WHEN Aunt Mary took her shopping basket and went out, Betty and Jack were crouching at the top of the stairs ready to run away.

Rufus was always left to guard the house, and when Betty saw him sitting at the back door she felt very nervous.

"He'll never let us pass," she said. "And we can't go out by the front door. The neighbours might see us."

Jack said nothing. He limped down the stairs and made straight for the dog. The huge brute rose to its feet and turned to face the boy, baring its teeth and growling as if knowing he meant to go out.

But Jack never wavered. Without showing any fear, he went slowly forward, stretching out his hand and speaking softly all the while.

"Good old Rufus!" he said soothingly. "Good boy! Go and lie down, Rufus!"

There was a strange glitter in Jack's eyes, and a soft, thrilling note in his voice. Betty had seen him act like this before, and knew that this brother of hers, so frail and delicate, had a strange power over animals.

She watched breathlessly as Jack's out-stretched hand drew nearer and nearer to the dog's head, and she almost gasped aloud with relief when the great head drooped under the advancing hand. Jack fondled the animal's ears.

"Good dog, Rufus!" he said, and then added in the same tone, "Hurry up, Sis. Open the door quietly and get out. You're a good boy, Rufus. Lie down, now."

Betty tip-toed round behind her brother's back, and, while Jack kept the mongrel quiet, she drew back the bolts on the door and slipped out. Out of the corner of his eye Jack saw that Betty was safely outside, and he backed away from the dog, keeping talking to it until he was also out of the house.

He closed the door quickly, and together he and his sister made for the alley behind the house, and hurried along there to the main road. They boarded the first bus that

Two underdogs must fight for survival in this melodramatic tale.

came along, and although the conductor looked at them rather strangely as they sat down with their bundles, he didn't say anything.

"Two threepenny tickets, please," said Betty, and gave him her sixpence.

Of course, they travelled with children's half-price tickets, so it was quite a long ride they got for their sixpence. It was more than half an hour later when they finally reached the town of Redford. It was now quite dark, but there were plenty of lights in the streets, and they were not at all frightened as they went along looking at the shops.

It was a cold, dry night, and they were glad they had brought their thick coats.

"Where are we going to sleep to-night?" Jack asked, shivering a little.

Betty clung firmly to her bundle. It seemed to be getting heavier every minute.

"Oh, it won't cost much to get us a bed," she said.

"But we haven't any money, not even a penny," pointed out her brother. "We spent it all on the bus."

That was true, but Betty's lips tightened firmly.

They crossed a square, turned into a street that was slightly less crowded, and looked rather enviously in at the lighted windows of several houses, where people were gathering round cosy fires. It began to dawn on Betty that it was not very nice to be without a home on a winter's evening.

Ahead of them they saw a rough-looking man standing on the edge of the pavement, and singing in a harsh, unmusical voice. As he sang he held out his cap to the people who passed.

"What's he doing that for?" asked Jack Brook.

"To get money for food and a bed," cried Betty excitedly. "That's an idea! We can do that! The teacher says I've a good voice, and even Aunt Mary used to say it wasn't bad. I'll sing, and you hold out your cap."

Jack was doubtful about whether they ought to do such a thing or not. But before he had a chance to object Betty had climbed up on the steps in front of a church, and began to sing in her small, clear voice.

It was only a simple little song she sang, but her voice rose clearly like a silver bell in the din of the street. People stopped to stare at the golden-haired girl who sang so well. Jack was so frightened that he forgot to take off his cap.

He felt a touch on his shoulder. The ragged-looking man who had been singing farther along the street now loomed over him.

"Are you with that girl?" he asked gruffly.

"Yes, that's my sister," replied Jack proudly. "Doesn't she sing nicely? You should hear the one about the candy ship——"

"Huh!" grunted the man, and he stepped forward among the crowd with his hat held out.

Of course, the people thought Betty was his little girl, and nearly everyone put some coppers in the greasy hat. Several of them told him what a fine voice Betty had for such a small girl.

Round the growing circle went the stranger, and his cap grew quite heavy with pennies.

Betty stopped, but the man looked up at her and shook the hat so that the contents jingled pleasantly.

"Go on!" he said encouragingly.

"Yes, keep singing, Betty. We're getting a lot of money," called Jack, and Betty flushed with delight as she started another song.

A big car slowed down on the outskirts of the crowd, and the driver honked his horn in an effort to clear a way through the crowded street. But there were so many people eager to hear Betty singing that they paid no attention.

The car was forced to stop, and the door opened and a lady and gentleman got out. Both were beautifully dressed, and anyone who had looked closely at them would have known that the man was the famous Carl Matson. The lady was his wife. Matson was a very well-known film director. He made

films in London, and his name was also famous in the London theatres.

Just now his eyes had opened wide with excitement. He squeezed his wife's arm.

"Do you hear that little girl, my dear? She's marvellous. She's got a better voice than any other girl of her age I've ever heard. And she's actually singing in the street! I must get hold of her and test her. She could make a fortune with that voice of hers."

"Are you sure she's good enough?" asked his wife excitedly, wrapping her fur coat more closely around her.

"Certain!" replied the famous film director. "With me in charge of her, her name could be made world-famous. She's wonderful, and pretty, too! I could put her into my new film, and she'd be the talk of London at once."

He pushed into the crowd, but just then there was uproar. Jack had seen the man with the money in his hat in the act of sneaking away. Betty's brother raised his voice angrily.

"Hey, come back! Some of that money is ours. We need it! My sister sang for it."

He ran after the man, who had by then reached the edge of the crowd. Jack gripped his sleeve, but the burly ruffian turned and swung the cripple boy into the gutter, where he fell heavily.

A roar of anger went up from the crowd.

"That brute's stealing the children's money!" cried someone. "Stop him!"

There was a rush to go after the man, and in their excitement the people did not notice that they pushed Betty along with them. She just had time to help Jack to his feet, when they were shoved into a narrow side road, while all around them people were shouting and threatening what they would do to the thief.

The man had disappeared in the darkness down a narrow alley, and more than half the crowd streamed after him. Betty was frightened. She knew she had caused all this bother, and when she saw a big policeman pushing his way towards them, she plucked Jack by the arm.

"We've got to get out of this, Jack. The policeman may lock us up for being the cause of this row. Let's run!"

So, hand in hand, they ran right up to the end of the street, away from all the uproar. Jack used his crutch with surprising speed, and in next to no time they were out of sight of the church steps from which Betty had sung.

Little did Betty know she had just missed the chance of a lifetime. The gentleman who had got out of the car was looking for her everywhere in the crowd, and even asking the policeman if he knew who the little girl with the wonderful voice was. But no one could tell him.

A Friend in Need

BETTY and Jack wandered along breathlessly, sick at heart, feeling really frightened now that it was getting darker and darker. They were very hungry.

The run had tired them. When they saw some wooden steps inside a porch, they went in there and sat down side by side, as close as they could be, to try and keep warm.

"Do you think we'll have to stay out here all night, Sis?" questioned Jack.

Before Betty had time to reply, a voice spoke above them—

"Who's this talking about stopping all night on my steps?"

They jumped up in a fright, ready to run. But when they saw that the person who had spoken was a stout, pleasant woman, with a smile on her face, they stood and stared at her. Behind her was an open door leading into a cosy kitchen, and they could smell something good cooking on the stove.

"Why, you're only children!" exclaimed the woman. "Haven't you got any home?"

"No, ma'am," spoke up Betty, and Jack clutched her hand tightly.

"Well, well, that's terrible, and on a cold December evening like this, too!" said the lady of the house. "Come inside, my dears,

and we'll see what we can do for you. Molly Walters isn't the kind to leave two youngsters like you on the doorstep. Come inside. It's almost time for my husband to come home to his supper."

Before they knew what was happening, they were in the warm room beside the fire, with their coats hanging behind the door, and a big basin of rich soup beside each of them.

After that Mrs Walters gave them some delicious home-made bread, with plenty of butter, and a banana each.

The good lady watched them all the time, but did not ask any questions. Her husband came in. He wore blue overall trousers, and carried a tea-basket. He was an engine-driver, and he was a big, cheery man.

His wife spoke to him quietly in the corner, and then he sat down to his own supper, joking with the children and telling them funny stories, until Mrs Walters said—

"I see your eyes beginning to close now. It's time for bed. I've got a nice big, warm bed waiting for you. Come along!"

Tears formed in Betty's eyes.

"Are we—are you really going to let us sleep here?" she asked.

"Certainly you'll sleep here. You don't think you're going out in that nasty, cold street again to-night, do you? Now, off to bed with you."

And sure enough, five minutes later they were in bed, with Mrs Walters tucking them in and wishing them good-night just as though they were her own children.

They closed their eyes contentedly, and then Jack whispered—

"Isn't she nice? We'd never have run away if Aunt Mary had been like that. What do you think Aunt Mary will do when she finds we've gone?"

"Oh, don't worry about her!" said Betty. "She'll say 'There goes bad rubbish!' and she'll be glad we're not there to feed. Don't you worry. Good-night!"

Very little time passed before they were both asleep, for they were very tired indeed. They did not waken all night, and when at last Betty opened her eyes, it was to hear movements in the next room.

Mrs Walters was seeing her husband off to work, and Betty could smell the bacon frying.

"They must have run away from home, the young rascals," Sam Walters was saying. "We'll get into trouble for keeping 'em here, my dear."

"Bless you, what else could we do?" murmured his wife. "We kept the poor things from staying out in the street all night, and saved them from getting their death of cold. Their mother must be terribly worried about them, if they have a mother. On your way down to the railway yard, Sam, you'd better call in at the police station and ask Sergeant Green if he's heard of any small children being missing. Tell him their names are Betty and Jack. Tell him he'll find them here, bless their hearts."

Sam Walters promised to do this, and Betty shivered under the bedclothes when she saw his burly form go past the window.

The police! The thought of being taken by them, perhaps back to Aunt Mary, terrified her. Aunt Mary would give them an awful whipping, and would treat them worse than ever. Mrs Walters did not know about that.

The girl poked her brother in the ribs, and when Jack opened his eyes in surprise she clutched him firmly and hissed in his ear—

"Quickly, Jack! We've got to dress at once and get out of here. Mrs Walters has sent her husband to tell the police about us. We must escape by way of the window!"

Next Friday in " The Dandy "—Read how Betty and Jack are forced to run away again, and how Jack uses his strange power over animals to tame the biggest animal he has ever seen.

Again, strength of character and courage are what really matter in a **Dandy** *adventure story.*

The Story in Pictures of a Singing Cowboy and His Wonder Horse.

THE DARING DEEDS OF BUCK WILSON

1—Buck Wilson, the stalwart young rider from Texas, came down the prairie trail to Five Forks on Snowfire, his great white horse. Buck was a roving rider who carried all his belongings tied to his saddle. And he didn't have a care in the world. He was strumming on his banjo and singing an old Western song. Snowfire seemed to like that song, for he cocked up his ears and whisked his tail and stepped out briskly.

2—But suddenly Buck heard screams coming from outside a shack in a meadow away ahead. All in one movement he hitched the banjo to his saddle, grabbed the reins, and urged Snowfire on with his knees. At full gallop Buck thundered up to the meadow, and there he found a mother and her young daughter shouting for help. Running away towards the mountains beyond was a grizzly bear, with something dangling from its jaws.

3—Buck galloped right up to the mother and brought Snow-fire slithering to a stop. "What is wrong?" he asked. "A grizzly bear attacked us," sobbed the woman, "and it has carried off little Benny. Oh, help us, please!" Buck's mouth tightened grimly. "Look! The bear is running to the mountains," added the girl, pointing to the mountain trail. With a quick word of comfort to the mother, Buck dashed off after the bear.

4—The mountain trail was steep and dangerous, but Snowfire charged up the rocky path at a reckless pace. Swerving round great boulders, he made up on the grizzly until Buck saw the shaggy brute pause on the edge of a cliff not far ahead. "We've cornered him old horse!" he cried—but he spoke too soon. As Snowfire cleared a fallen tree, the bear turned and leaped down to a rocky crag, with the little fellow still dangling from its jaws.

5—Buck peered over the edge of the cliff and saw the grizzly drop on to a wide ledge that ran along the cliff face. There was a big cave on the ledge, and Buck watched with horror as the bear took the helpless boy into that cave. "Must be the bear's den," Buck thought. "Now, if I jump down there the way the bear did, how am I going to get up again?" His heavy riding boots would prevent him climbing. What was he to do?

6—Buck's mind was quickly made up. He led his horse along to a spot right above the bear's cave, uncoiling his strong lariat as he went. Then he tied one end to the saddle and dropped the other end over the cliff. Next he picked up a stout club and took a firm grip on the rope. "Steady, boy!" he said to Snowfire, and the horse braced his forelegs to take the strain as his master lowered himself over the edge of the cliff.

Cinemas were full of Westerns in the 1930s, and Albert Barnes certainly felt they would be popular with readers!

What has three feet but no legs?—A yard ruler.

7—He slid down the rope to the mouth of the cave, and there was the bear crouching over the body of the terrified youngster. It would be madness to shoot it, for the little fellow would certainly be crushed by its vast bulk. The only thing to do was to draw it away from its victim, and Buck hit on a way of doing this. He swung himself into the cave and rapped the bear smartly on the nose with his stick.

8—With a great roar of rage and pain the grizzly rose on its hind legs and rushed out of the cave. The rope had swung Buck outwards, and the bear came after him with gleaming fangs and flashing claws. Quick as lightning Buck dropped his stick, drew his right-hand gun, and fired twice, right between those gaping jaws. Crack! Crack! And the thunder of the shots mingled with the wild roar of the grizzly monster.

9—Those shots had been fired from such close range that the bear stopped dead in its tracks. It swayed on the edge of the ledge, and as Buck swung inwards once more it collapsed and plunged forward into space. Its dying roar rang through the cave and echoed from the cliff face. And before the wisps of smoke had stopped drifting from the barrel of Buck's gun, the grizzly had hit the rocks below.

10—Buck dropped on to the ledge and strode over to where the youngster was crouching in the mouth of the cave. He was a brave little chap, for he hadn't cried at all. But there was blood on his lips, and Buck knew he had been biting them to keep himself from crying. "We'll soon have you home now, sonny!" Buck said. "Come on! Let's see you grin!" And the little chap grinned bravely.

11—With the rope tied round his waist and the youngster in his arms, Buck shouted up to Snowfire—"Back, old horse! Back and pull us up!" The intelligent animal knew exactly what he was expected to do. He strained on the rope and backed slowly away from the edge of the cliff. Buck planted his feet against the cliff face. Then as Snowfire went on heaving, Buck went on walking, and so he brought the youngster to the top.

12—Buck swung into the saddle, and they headed back down the rocky trail to the little shack in the meadow. Never was there such thankfulness as when Benny was placed in his mother's arms. Never was there such a happy scene as when Buck sat down with the family to enjoy a great big meal. And never was there such a contented horse as when Snowfire was put in a stable with a huge pile of sweet hay. When Buck rode out on to the prairie trail to continue his wanderings, he was glad he had been able to give aid to the little family.

There will be another thrilling Buck Wilson adventure in "The Dandy" next week.

This is the second of four Cowboy and Indian-themed stories in the first edition. It was drawn by Jack Glass.

The Thrilling Jungle Life of a Baby Elephant.

WEE TUSKY

Kang, The Tiger

WEE TUSKY, the baby elephant, was very proud of his strength.

And he wasn't the only one to be so proud. There were quite a number of baby elephants in the great elephant herd that roamed the steaming jungle, and these youngsters of the herd were continually holding contests to prove which of them was the strongest.

They would try to pick up big boulders, to push over trees with their heads, to raise logs bigger than themselves, or to uproot trees with their trunks.

To-day Tusky was practising on his own. He was straining and tugging at a tree which simply refused to be uprooted. He had curled his trunk round the bottom of it, and was straining upwards and backwards with all his might. The tree creaked, and some of the roots tore out of the ground, but the rest held firmly.

Tusky paused and stamped angrily round the tree. It was really much too large for his strength, but he would not admit defeat. He felt that unless he got this tree out by the roots he would never beat any of the other baby elephants in the next strength contest. So he was going to try and try until he succeeded.

Again he took firm hold with his trunk, and threw all his weight into one tremendous pull. Straining back with head, body, and legs, he heaved until he felt his muscles cracking. And at last there was a loud, creaking sound from the tree.

He put all he knew into one last mighty tug, and without the slightest warning the tree toppled over on top of him.

So suddenly did it come that Tusky shot backwards. He had not noticed that behind him was a steep slope, hidden by a fringe of bushes.

Crash! Right through those bushes he went, and down the slope. Vainly did he try to stop himself. The slope was almost a cliff. It was bare and smooth. Rolling over and over he went, and then—thud!—he found himself in the bottom of a gorge, shaken, bruised, and very frightened.

But he did not remain long on the ground. Scrambling upright, he stamped around, shook himself, drew in a deep breath, and blew down his trunk with relief.

"Whoooooooo!"

He was not really hurt, and by uprooting that tree he had proved himself to be stronger than even he had thought. He would go at once and fetch the other baby elephants to see what he had done.

Two minutes later he found that that would not be so easy. How could he get back up the slope?

There was no way out of the gorge into which he had tumbled. The slope down which he had rolled was very steep, and he knew he could never climb it. The opposite slope was even steeper. And as for the ends of the gorge, they were closed up with huge rocks that not even a full-grown elephant could drag away. Tusky was trapped.

He became very frightened. What if he could not get out?

The thought made him wild with fear, and he rushed at the slope down which he had fallen. By sheer strength he went up almost halfway, and then he slipped.

Down he tumbled again, and got more bruises.

But Tusky was desperate. He tried again and again. He struggled and scrambled, tried to dig in with his short tusks, but it was no good. Hard, smooth rock beat him every time. He always landed at the bottom again with more bruises.

Panting, the baby elephant gave it up. The only thing he could do was to call for help.

Yet he knew the herd must be quite a distance away now. As usual, Tusky had strayed from the side of Minbu, his mother, and had lingered behind the herd, looking for trees to pull up. And this was the result. Still, he raised his trunk hopefully and bellowed lustily.

"Whoooooooo—whoooooooo—whoooooo!"

The rocks around him echoed his cry strangely, and he was frightened more than ever. It was just as though the rocks were shouting back at him.

Each time he called, Tusky waited a while to listen for an answering call. But there was never any sound except the echoes of his own cry. Again and again he bellowed, but it was useless.

He was a prisoner, lost from the rest of the herd, and if the other elephants moved on to new feeding-grounds, Tusky's plight would become more terrible than ever.

The thought of being shut down there, without food or water, and with night coming on, made Tusky nearly mad with despair.

He filled his lungs with great gulps of fresh air, and then he tried once more, louder than ever before—

"Whoooooo—whoooooooo-oooooooo!"

Surely some of the elephants would hear his call this time! His big ears stood out from the side of his head as he strained to listen, and suddenly his heart gave a great thump. He had heard a movement at last. Was it Minbu, his mother, who was coming?

Joyfully he raised his head, and stared at the edge of the gorge right above him.

The bushes parted, and a head appeared. Tusky took one look at it, and then wished the ground would open and swallow him up.

For the head was that of his worst enemy. It was the head of Kang, the tiger, the most terrible beast in the jungle.

With his huge mouth open and his wicked fangs glistening, his whiskers bristling like wire, and his fierce eyes glittering with cruel delight, Kang peered down at the trapped baby elephant.

"Grr-rr-rrrrrr!" he snarled, and licked his lips in horrible fashion.

Wee Tusky's Hour of Terror

WEE TUSKY knew what Kang was thinking. Kang was telling himself that young elephant was very tender, and that it made a splendid dinner!

Many a time Minbu, the mother of Tusky, had warned him never to go near Kang. Twice Minbu had fought with the striped giant, and twice she had beaten him after a dreadful struggle. But Kang was so strong and so fierce that even Minbu had failed to slay him.

Only old Mawk, the leader of the elephant herd, could have killed the tiger, and Kang was clever enough to keep away from old Mawk. He took care to attack only deer, zebras, baby elephants, and smaller animals—in fact, just the ones he knew he could overpower.

Tusky nearly collapsed with fear when he saw the brute crouching to spring down on him. He knew the force in those mighty paws. He knew the strength of those cruel fangs. Down in the bottom of the narrow gorge there would be no room for him to dodge. He would just have to stand there and be mauled.

He raised his eyes to see what the tiger was doing.

Once, twice, three times Kang leaned over as though to spring, but each time he hung back. And it dawned on Tusky that the tiger was wondering how he would get back out of the gorge again after he had made his kill.

For the first time Tusky was pleased that the sides of the gorge were so steep and so smooth. Kang could spring down on him, but he wouldn't do it unless he was sure he could get back up again.

"Grr-rrrrr-rrrrr!" snarled the tiger, and this time he sounded angry.

He straightened up and looked about him. He was still licking his lips, but for the moment he was baffled.

Tusky breathed again. In the meantime he was safe. But he felt sure that Kang would be clever enough to find some way of getting at him before long.

The baby elephant decided that his one chance was to bring help, so he bellowed again and again.

Crash! A big rock came hurtling down from above and narrowly missed him. The

This story combines two previously-seen themes: the lure of the exotic and the struggle of the underdog.

head of Kang appeared over the edge of the gorge once more. It was the tiger who had pushed the rock over, and Tusky wondered why.

Crash! Crash! More boulders came bouncing down, and Tusky had to move fast to dodge them. He wondered if Kang was trying to bury him alive.

Then all was silent for a time, until he heard something heavy being dragged towards the edge of the gorge. Kang was tugging and straining and grunting as he gripped it with his teeth and heaved it along.

The end of a tree trunk came over the edge. It was slowly moving outwards as the tiger tugged it along by the stump of a broken-off branch.

The baby elephant understood Kang's plot in a flash. Kang had thrown down boulders to form a pile at the foot of the steep slope. Now he was going to topple this long tree trunk over the edge so that it would stand on end on the pile of boulders and reach to the top of the gorge.

Once this was done he would be able to run down it, kill and eat Tusky, and climb up again. His long, sharp claws would easily find a hold in the thick bark.

More and more of the tree trunk came into view. It was beginning to topple over. Tusky watched it with wide eyes, and trembled once more. What could he do now?

Down came the big log, with Kang still clinging to the top end. And then Tusky acted quickly, reaching up with his trunk and gripping the lower end.

The log was very heavy, but Tusky had made his trunk strong by trying to pull trees out of the ground. He staggered under the weight, but managed to push the log upwards.

The tiger could use only his teeth. He growled as he thrust forward.

It was a strange form of tug-o'-war, with the baby elephant trying to push the tree out and the tiger trying to push it into the gorge. It went on for some time, and Tusky began to get tired. He could not keep this up much longer.

Snarling and growling, Kang was using all his great strength, almost falling over the edge of the gorge in his excitement. Tusky panted and swayed from side to side, and then he had a brilliant idea.

When he had been heaving the tree out of the ground at the top of the slope, and it had suddenly given way, he had over-balanced. What would happen if Kang lost his balance in the same way?

It would be a very risky thing to try, but it seemed the only thing Tusky could do.

He timed things nicely. Just as Kang gave an extra hard push, the baby elephant let go and jumped to one side.

Crash! Down came the heavy tree, and down came Kang with it. He turned head over heels as he fell through the air, and then—thud!

He landed on his back with enough force to have killed anything else, but it didn't kill Kang. It only shook him up and drove the breath out of him.

Tusky was shivering with fright, but he knew he had to act again. In another few moments the tiger would be up and at him. The baby elephant rushed in, grabbed one end of the tree trunk, lifted it, and tossed it on top of Kang.

The tiger let out a roar. Tusky had not been able to lift the whole tree, but only one end. Yet even one end of it was heavy enough to pin the tiger to the ground.

But Tusky was not satisfied with that. He did not feel safe until he had stepped up and stood on the tree, adding his ton weight to the weight of the tree.

Roars and screeches of anger and pain came from the maddened tiger. He tore at the tree with teeth and claws, making the splinters fly. But that did not ease the weight on his chest. He was held as though in a vice.

Tusky gradually got back his courage. He even picked up some stones and hurled them at Kang. And that made Kang madder than ever.

Louder and louder rang his cries. The sides of the gorge took up the echoes, and those echoes carried further than the cries of Tusky ever could.

The baby elephant balanced himself firmly. He was going to stand there as long as he could. He knew his doom would be sealed the moment he stepped off.

Minbu to the Rescue

MANY beasts heard the dreadful bellowing of Kang, and wondered what was happening.

Monkeys in the tree-tops and zebras in the grassy clearings, buffalo down by the water and crocodiles in the mud, all heard the uproar. They looked at each other, as if asking what the cries meant. What was happening to Kang? Had the striped terror of the jungle got caught in a trap at last?

Every single animal hoped he had.

The noise was heard at last by the elephants. Old Mawk raised his head and listened. He could tell that there was pain as well as fury behind that outcry, and he grunted with satisfaction. He hated Kang.

The other elephants fidgeted uneasily. The baby elephants were curious, and wanted to go and see what was happening. But their mothers herded them into the centre of the clearing, where all the elephants were feeding.

Minbu, the mother of Tusky, suddenly missed her son, and called for him anxiously.

There was no reply, and she remembered that she had not seen Tusky for a long time. There could be only one reason, she thought. He must have gone to see why Kang was making all that noise.

So Minbu started off at once in the direction of the uproar. Her ears were flapping, and her trunk was curled upwards above her head as she charged through the jungle.

Other beasts who saw her knew that Minbu was very angry, and that there would be trouble for Tusky when his mother found him.

It was easy enough to follow the noise. Minbu came within sight of the gorge, and began to call her missing son—

" Whoooo-whoooo-whoooo !"

But Tusky, down there at the bottom of the gorge, with the tiger making all that uproar close to him, did not hear his mother.

More angry than ever, Minbu went forward. She knew about the gorge, and guessed that Kang had fallen into it. She did not mind about that. In fact, she was rather glad about it. But where was Tusky?

Gradually she worked nearer the edge of the gorge, and it was only by chance that she looked over.

Minbu drew back with a horrified squeal. She had found her son. There was Tusky at the bottom of the gorge, twenty feet below the level of the ground, standing on a tree trunk that rested on the roaring tiger!

Minbu was horrified.

" Whooooooooooooo !" she roared, and Tusky gave a glad squeal when he heard her.

He thought he was safe. Surely his mother could help him now! Looking up, he saw her staring down at him, with her trunk dangling over the edge of the gorge.

She wanted him to try and grasp it and be pulled up, but it was far beyond his reach. Minbu knelt down. She leaned over as far as possible without losing her balance, and that made matters better.

But still Tusky could not reach the end of her trunk with his own. There was nearly ten feet of space between them, even though he was standing on the tree trunk.

" Grrr-rrrrrrr !" roared Kang, making wilder efforts to get free. He did not like the look of Minbu. He knew she was clever.

Minbu was thinking quickly. Her son's life was at stake. She turned away, and a moment later came back with a big rock gripped in her curled trunk.

Down it came whizzing, and landed on top of Kang's outstretched body with great force, knocking the breath out of him again. He lay still, not even snarling. It was only because he was very tough that he did not die.

Tusky knew now what to do. He climbed down from his perch on the tree trunk and quickly piled up the boulders which lay in the bottom of the gorge. He piled them one upon the other against the sloping side of the gorge.

And all the time while he worked he feared that Kang would recover and get loose. That fear made him work very fast, and at last he had made the pile of rocks as high as he possibly could.

Again his mother called to him, and he climbed up to the top of this pile, balanced himself carefully, and reached up with his trunk. Minbu knelt down, and this time she was able to grip the end of her son's trunk.

Tusky hung on for dear life. He weighed a ton, but his mother was tremendously strong. Backing away from the edge of the gorge, she pulled him straight to the top, so that he collapsed on the grass and was safe.

For some minutes he was unable to move. He had received a terrible fright. Down in the bottom of the gorge Kang stirred. He was waking up again and starting to struggle.

Minbu did not want to fight him just then. Kang had been taught a lesson. It was time to go. Night was falling fast.

Nearby was a pool. She dipped in her trunk, sucking up a great deal of water, and squirted it over Tusky. He gasped and stood up. That cold bath had brought him to his senses. He hurried after his mother, trembling at the thought of what he had escaped.

Behind them Kang wriggled and twisted until he managed to get out from under the tree trunk. Then he rushed to the top of the piled boulders and leapt out of the gorge. But he did not go after Tusky. He was too frightened of Minbu.

Sore and bleeding from several wounds, he crept off to his lair to sleep off the effects of his rough handling. He had discovered that even a baby elephant could defend itself when cornered.

By the time he got back to the herd Tusky felt very proud of himself for what he had done. He thought he was quite a hero. He was the only baby elephant in the herd who had ever fought with Kang and won.

But his mother did not seem to be proud of him at all!

She remembered only how he had lingered too far behind the herd, and she led him to a bamboo grove where nice long canes grew.

Tusky began to look sorry for himself. He knew what was coming. It was not as bad being thrashed by his mother as by old Mawk, but it was bad enough, and he knew that when he went to sleep that night he would be almost as sore as Kang.

He told himself that he would look well behind him before trying another test of strength on a tree!

Next Friday in " The Dandy "—Wee Tusky's desperate hunt for water in the dried-up jungle, told in another complete story.

Here's the page that always wins—For jolly jokes and cheery grins.

JOKES AND JOKES AND JOKES

Teacher—" Willie, if eggs were six for a shilling, how many would you get for twopence ?"
Willie—" None !"
Teacher—" None ? Why ?"
Willie — " Because I'd get toffee !"

Cheeky Charlie—" A pennyworth of tacks !"
Shopman—" What for ?"
Cheeky Charlie—" A penny, of course. Do you think I'm going to give you twopence ?"

Mother—" No, Wilfy, no more cake to-night. Don't you know you can't sleep on a full stomach?"
Wilfy—" Well, I can sleep on my back."

" I know a bird that can go twenty years without food."
" What kind of a bird ?"
" A scarecrow !"

" Why weren't you at school yesterday ?"
" I was sick, sir."
" Sick of what ?"
" Sick of school !"

Father—" What are you doing up there?"
Freddy—" Teacher told me to write an essay on a horse."

Angry Diner—" You're not fit to serve a pig."
Waiter—" I'm doing my best, sir."

Billy—" Was Robinson Crusoe an acrobat ?"
Dad—" No !"
Billy—" Well, it says here he sat down on his chest."

Mother—" I left two pieces of cake in the pantry, and now there's only one. Can you explain it, Tommy ?"
Tommy—" Well, it was so dark when I went in there that I didn't see the other bit."

Jack—" Why are you running ?"
Mack—" To stop two boys fighting."
Jack—" What two boys ?"
Mack—" Billy Smith and me !"

Tramp—" Do you buy rags and bones ?"
Ragman—" Yes."
Tramp—" Well, how much am I worth ?"

Beggar—" Spare a penny for a blind man, mum."
Old Lady—" You can see with one eye."
Beggar—" Well, spare a halfpenny, then."

Ma—" Why are you rolling the dustbin about ?"
Billy—" To amuse baby."
Ma—" Where's baby ?"
Billy—" In the dustbin !"

Next Week You'll Get

6 STORIES
The Magic Sword.
Red Hoof.
The Tricks of Tommy.
Wee Tusky.
The Two Brave Runaways.
When the West Was Wild.

5 STORIES IN PICTURES
Invisible Dick.
Our Gang.
Jimmy and His Grockle.
Lost on the Mountain of Fear.
The Daring Deeds of Buck Wilson.

14 COMICS
Korky the Cat.
Barney Boko.
Sammy and His Sister.
Hungry Horace.
Mugg Muggins.
Wig and Wam.
Podge.
Keyhole Kate.
Smarty Grandpa.
Magic Mike.
Freddy the Fearless Fly.
Boaster Billy.
Desperate Dan.
Bamboo Town.

AND

A FREE GIFT
OF A
JUMPING FROG
ALL IN
THE DANDY

Diner—" Waiter, bring me some tea without milk."
Waiter—" Sorry, we've no milk, sir. Will it do without cream ?"

" Who gave you that black eye ?"
" No one gave me it. I had to fight hard to get it."

Cheeky Tommy—" The British Navy is surrounded !"
Jack Tar—" What by ?"
Cheeky Tommy—" Water !"

Teacher—" What comes after ' T '?"
Pupil—" Supper, miss."

Smart Sam—" The postman has just got the sack."
Dizzy Dennis—" What for ?"
Smart Sam—" To carry his letters in, of course."

" You used a car for seven years and never had a puncture ! What kind of a car was it ?"
" A tram-car !"

Teacher—" Name a popular general."
Pupil—" General holiday, sir."

Rastus—" You'd better keep your eyes open to-morrow."
Razz—" Why ?"
Rastus—" 'Cos you won't be able to see if you don't."

Teacher—" If four of your fingers were missing, what would you have ?"
Smart Alec — " No music lessons !"

Henry—" There won't be any school to-morrow, will there, sir ?"

Weary Willie—" I know a man who shaves a hundred times a day."
Tired Tim—" Nonsense. Who is he ?"
Weary Willie—" A barber !"

Old Gent—" What are you going to be when you leave school, Johnny ?"
Johnny—" Happy, sir."

Farmer (to boy up apple tree)—" Come down or I'll tell your father."
Boy—" Tell him now. He's up here with me."

" Will this letter get to York to-night ?"
" Yes, sir."
" That's strange. It's addressed to London."

Bobby—" If you give me a penny I'll imitate a bird."
Mother—" What will you do ? Will you sing ?"
Bobby—" No, I'll eat a worm !"

Waiter—" This half-crown is bad !"
Diner—" Well, so was the dinner !"

BOASTER BILLY

The 'Jokes' page was a regular feature in comics. In later years readers were asked to contribute their own jokes, perhaps an improvement on some of those here!

Another Western tale (this time starring two Indians, drawn by Sam Fair), 'Podge', an early contribution from Eric Roberts and 'Mugg Muggins', drawn by 'Chic' Gordon.

Prairie Waggons on the Danger Trail to the Golden West.

WHEN THE WEST WAS WILD

A Letter From Dad

YOUNG Jack Ryan hitched his pony, Star, to the rack outside the store in the little Western village of Three Springs.

He had ridden the fifteen miles from his home at River Bend in an hour, racing to the village the moment he knew the mail had come in.

There must be a letter from Dad with this mail, surely!

"Good-morning, Jack!" said Old Thompson, the storekeeper, scratching his shining bald head with his thumb-nail. "And how's things out at River Bend? Spring's here at last, and they do say——"

"Is there a letter for us, Mr Thompson?" cut in Jack quickly.

"Letter for you? Let's see!" said the old storekeeper, turning towards the rack behind him. He reached for the letters in the slot marked "R," and went slowly through them, reading each name aloud.

"Rawlins, Robins, Renton, Brent! Brent? How did that get among the 'R's'?" he frowned, and stopped to take the Brent letter and place it in its proper slot.

Impatiently Jack tapped the counter as the storekeeper went back to the pile.

"Reckitt, Reynolds, Robson! That's the lot!" he said, looking over the top of his spectacles. "None for you this mail, Jack! Was you expecting something?"

Jack bit his lip and strove to hide his disappointment.

"We ought to have had a letter from Dad!" he said in a low voice. "From Oregon. Surely he's there by now?"

"Oh, ah! I remember!" said old Thompson. "Your Dad left last autumn with the covered waggon pioneers for the new country, didn't he? Well, don't you worry, Jack. I guess you'll hear from him when the next mail gets in from Oregon to Independence, a month from now."

"A month!" echoed Jack. "And the spring waggon-train leaves in ten days' time! We'd planned to leave by then, Mr Thompson, to join Dad. Are you sure there isn't a letter for us!"

"Quite sure, son!" said the old chap. "Maybe your Dad wrote, but the letter didn't get through. Lots don't, you know! But better luck next time, Jack. I—oh, good-morning, Mrs Brent. Yes! There is a letter for you! Let's see! Brent! Where's the 'B' pile?"

Jack turned sadly away. His disappointment was a bitter one, and he knew that when he reached home it would be shared by Mother and Lucy and young Jimmy, all of whom were waiting anxiously for news.

There were no telephones and no railways in those pioneer days. Letters were carried by pony express riders, who had all sorts of dangers to face when braving those thousands of miles of country where the Redskins ruled and no white man was safe. So it was that six months had gone by since Dad had left in search of a new and richer land, and in all that time there had been no news from him.

Jack climbed into the saddle, and Star turned and moved away. Then old Thompson's voice sounded from the door.

"Hey there, son! Your letter! I found it!"

The boy turned to see the storekeeper waving a crumpled, travel-stained envelope. He was off Star's back in a flash, and ran forward to seize the letter eagerly.

"Reckon my eyesight ain't what it used to be, son!" apologised old Thompson. "It was among the 'B' pile! It's a good job Mrs Brent came in before you'd got out of hearing! The letter's from your Dad, ain't it?"

"Yes! Yes, it's from Dad!" laughed the boy, trembling with relief and pleasure now. "It's from Dad! Good-bye, Mr Thompson, and thanks very much!"

He fairly leapt back into the saddle, and his heels drummed into Star's flanks, urging the pony to race on the homeward trail at top speed.

As he rode, Jack clutched the letter which had travelled two thousand miles over the most dangerous trail in the world. From the far-off new land of Oregon, away on the West Coast of America, this envelope with its precious contents had come.

On into the sunrise it had travelled, until now it had reached the eastern part of America, which was the only part which had so far been really settled by white men.

Half a mile from his home Jack Ryan began to yell. Nearer still, and he was waving the precious envelope excitedly.

His mother, his sister, and his younger brother appeared at the door of the homestead, and came running towards him.

And the sounds of excitement even spread to the next homestead, and a boy a little younger than Jack, and a girl a little older came racing excitedly to hear the news.

Mrs Ryan trembled as she took the letter from her stalwart young son. A tear glistened in her eye as she saw the well-remembered hand-writing. For a long moment she hesitated to break the seal. But young Jimmy and Lucy and Jack shouted for news, and they all went into the house.

The news from Dad was great news. The long letter told how he had arrived in Oregon after many wonderful adventures on the two-thousand-mile-long trail. The journey had taken nearly four months, but Dad said it had been worth it, for he had got a splendid piece of land, which he was going to turn into a farm.

When Mrs Ryan got to this part of the letter Jack and the others gave a rousing cheer. But it was nothing to the cheer they gave when Mrs Ryan came to the bit everybody had been waiting for.

"The only thing I want to make my happiness complete," Dad had written, "is you and the youngsters. I have made all the necessary arrangements for you to leave on the spring waggon-train, which will be getting ready at the town of Independence just about the time when you receive this. Our old friend, Pat Daly, will be in charge of the train, and he has promised to give you all the help he can.

"You know exactly what to bring with you, and as for the journey, there is little advice I need give you. You will suffer all sorts of hardships, but put all your trust in Pat Daly. He's the finest trail-boss in the West, and the Indians seldom attack any waggon when he is in charge.

"This is all meantime, my dear. Give the youngsters my love, and may God bless you and bring you all safely to me.—Dad."

A tear splashed from Mrs Ryan's eye on to the letter. But the youngsters didn't see it. Already they had joined hands, and were whooping round in sheer delight.

"We're going to Oregon! We're going to Dad! Whoopee! Yippy! Hurray!"

"Wait! Wait a minute!" said Mrs Ryan suddenly. "There's another bit here on the back! Listen! It says, 'Mr and Mrs Arnold arrived safely, but to save time they have asked me to tell you to tell Tom and Amy to come with you and join the train in their own waggon. Tell Jack to help Tom and Amy all he can, and to remember that he'll be the man of your little party.—Dad.'"

The two youngsters, who had come from the neighbouring shack, now joined in the excited capering and gleeful shouting.

Young Jack grabbed an old banjo, which he twanged happily. Together the youngsters roared the chorus, which the Oregon pioneers had already made famous—

"Oh, Susannah! Don't you cry for me!
For I'm heading off to Oregon
With my banjo on my knee!"

"Wait for me! Wait for me! Wait for me!" screamed Pedro, the parrot, picking up the words and screeching them out from his cage in the window. But Brush, the sleek black family cat, merely blinked and yawned.

The Town of Covered Waggons

THE Ryan family had a hundred and fifty miles to go to the town of Independence, and ten days in which to get there before the great string of covered waggons left from there on its long trip to Oregon.

But there was quite a lot to be done before they could leave River Bend.

Waggons had to be overhauled and strengthened. Supplies had to be brought in from the village. Belongings had to be packed and the homestead sold.

Yet everybody worked with such a will that in three days everything was done, and three covered waggons, loaded up to the canvas, were drawn up outside the empty homestead.

Pedro's cage had been hung at the back of the leading waggon, which Mrs Ryan drove, with young Jimmy beside her.

Brush, the cat, wide-eyed and wondering, travelled in his basket in the second waggon, which pretty Amy Arnold drove, with Lucy Ryan as her companion.

Tom Arnold was in charge of the third waggon, and young Jack was in command of the whole party, and directed the start from the back of his pony.

It was barely dawn when Mrs Ryan gazed at the empty, forlorn-looking homestead for the last time.

She felt a certain sadness in leaving River Bend, for she had had years of happiness there. But her husband awaited her in this new land of promise, where happiness and fortune awaited them all.

So she whipped up the horses cheerfully, and started off for Independence with the laughter of the youngsters ringing in her ears.

They reached Independence a full day before the waggon-train was due to leave, and, coming down into the great valley, Jack Ryan and the others saw the most extraordinary scene they had ever witnessed.

The " town " was just a straggling collection of huts built in the very centre of the valley. But all around, the eye could see nothing but the white canvas tops of hundreds of covered waggons.

At the entrance to the valley a rough barricade had been erected, and here Jack was stopped and not allowed to proceed until he had shown his papers. Those papers showed that the Government had allowed Mr Ryan to settle in Oregon, and permitted his family to proceed to join him.

" Right ! " snapped an army sergeant, when he had checked the papers and handed them back. " The Ryans and the Arnolds, corporal ! Numbers, please ! "

A corporal with a huge book turned pages swiftly and shouted a reply.

" Remember that, young 'un ! " said the sergeant. " Your three waggons are numbered 102, 103, and 104. That's your position in the waggon-train when it starts ! Now, drive across to the camp for inspection by Colonel Holman. After that, report to the trail-boss. Next ! "

Jack got his waggons on the move again, and after struggling through the heart of the camp he paraded before the Colonel.

His waggons were inspected and his three months' supply of stores roughly checked. Then he was passed on with instructions to be ready to move off sharp at five o'clock the next morning.

It was a job to find enough space to camp for the night. Every yard of ground in the valley seemed to be occupied, and still more and more pioneers were rumbling in.

But at last Jack squeezed the three waggons into a spot that had been overlooked, and left his pony to go in search of Pat Daly.

" If you can't find us again, Jack," said Mrs Ryan with a smile, " whistle as loudly as you can, and I'll start Pedro screeching ! "

From a soldier Jack found out where he would find Pat Daly, and made his way to a wooden shack at the end of the main street of Independence.

He knocked and entered, but at first could not see the man who was one of his father's best friends.

" Hullo, there ! " said a voice from a bunk at the far end of the shack. " Who's there ? "

" I'm looking for Pat Daly ! " said the boy. " Can you tell me where he is, please ? "

" Right here, son ! " said the voice from the bunk. " Gee ! You're Red Ryan's son, aren't you ? Gosh ! You're redder-haired than your father, I guess ! How are you, son ? "

" Fine, Pat ! " said the boy. " I've come to report to you about leaving to-morrow. We're all ready, and our waggon numbers are—— "

" Wait a minute, son ! " said Pat. " Who told you to report to me ? "

" Why, I was told to report to the trail-boss as soon as the Colonel had inspected our outfit," replied the boy.

" H'm ! I don't happen to be the trail-boss this trip, Jack," said Pat quietly. " In fact, I'm not making the trip at all. You see, I was a bit unlucky coming back to Independence last time. I thought I was friendly with the Indians, yet I got hit by an Indian arrow. Now I can't travel for a month or so. Still, I'm glad you've looked in to cheer up an old prairie rat like me, son ! Maybe I can give you a few sound tips."

" I'm sorry you're not going with us, Pat," said Jack slowly. " Dad said you were the best trail-boss that ever rode the Oregon trail. He said you'd promised to help us, too."

" So I did, son ! So I did ! " agreed the wounded man. " And it's a pity it's too late for you to cancel your trip now and come with me next time. 'Cos why ? 'Cos this is the one trip I ought to make if I never make another ! Listen, Jack. Be careful of Dutch Joe ! Avoid him as much as you can, and don't ever get him mad at you. Understand ? "

" Yes. But who is Dutch Joe ? " asked the boy. " I don't know him. I've never heard of him."

" But you will ! " said the old tracker. " Dutch Joe Grutz is the trail-boss on this trip. Once you get out of Independence Dutch Joe is in supreme command ! His word is the law. And he won't like you one little bit, Jack ! "

" But—but I don't understand," frowned the boy. " Why shouldn't he like me ? He doesn't even know me ! "

" He knows your father, son ! " said Pat Daly. " And he's got darn good cause to know him ! Dutch Joe was under me in the last trip we made—when your father went. He knows his job all right, but he's a nasty guy. Nobody likes him. And he was so nasty to your father that when we got to Oregon your Dad gave him the hiding of his life—beat him to a frazzle, Jack.

" So the moment he hears your name—look out. He'll know you in a flash, and he'll make things just as bad as he can for you ! Watch out for him, son ! "

" I'll be careful, Pat," promised the boy. " I'll do my best not to give him any cause to make trouble."

" That's fine," beamed Pat. " Now listen while I give you a few tips."

The Brass Tomahawk

THE tracker drew on his trail knowledge, and gave young Jack valuable hints that were to prove more than useful to him in the days ahead. Finally, he warned the boy about Indians.

" If you're on guard at night-time shoot at anything you may see wandering outside the camp lines," he said. " It may only be a coyote, but, on the other hand, it may be a prowling Redskin. If you do get into trouble with the Redskins, try, if you can, to see a young chief named Double Eagle. He can do much to help you if he knows you're a friend of mine."

He paused to rummage in an old haversack, then handed Jack something he had taken from it. The boy looked at the object curiously, and saw that it was an Indian tomahawk, about half the usual size, and seemingly made of solid brass.

" I want you to hang this on your waggon where everyone can see it, son," he went on. " It's a—a kind of good luck mascot. Don't ever part with it, son. I'll ask for it back when I get to Oregon next time."

" I'll look after it, Pat," promised the boy, admiring the polished brass tomahawk. " And I'll hang it where no one can miss seeing it."

" That's right, Jack," agreed the old tracker. " Just one more tip. You'll hear some queer stories about a man named Death Valley Smith. Take no notice of them. Just remember the name, and if you should ever meet him, well, do exactly as he tells you, without argument, without question. I can't tell you any more than that, son ! "

They talked for a little longer, and then shook hands, and said good-bye. Pat Daly was tired, and so was Jack, and he needed all the rest he could get before the great adventure began the next morning.

Very few of the pioneers slept that night. Bursts of song echoed through the camp, and only ceased when the dawn air rang with the call of bugles.

Then there was a rush. Horses had to be harnessed in the flickering light of swinging oil-lamps. Hasty meals had to be snatched, bedding had to be rolled, and pots and pans loaded.

But at last it was done, and the waggons began to roll away according to their numbers.

Young Jack got his three waggons into position. While waiting to move off he hung the shining brass tomahawk over the driving seat of his leading waggon, and stood back to admire it.

Then Dutch Joe came along to make his final inspection.

He was a big, black-browed, heavily-built man, dressed in leather breeches and a Mexican jacket that was ornamented with silver. He wore a broad-brimmed hat, and carried two big revolvers at his hips.

As he rode towards Jack his keen eyes immediately spotted the hanging brass tomahawk. He scowled and demanded the boy's name.

" Ryan, eh ? " he said, after Jack replied. " How old are you ? Not more than sixteen, I guess ! Where's the man in your party ? "

" My father is already in Oregon," Jack told him. " I'm in charge, and—— "

" Fall out ! Draw your waggons out of the train ! " snapped Dutch Joe. " You're not going ! There's enough for us to do without looking after a parcel of kids ! "

Jack went white and started to argue. Dutch Joe roared angrily at him, and raised his whip.

" What's wrong here ? " cut in a sharp voice, and the boy turned to see Colonel Holman reining in his horse.

" Three waggons falling out, sir," growled Dutch Joe. " They're overloaded, and not in good condition. I'm not taking them ! "

" Show me your papers ! " snapped the Colonel, turning to Jack.

The boy obeyed promptly. The Colonel studied them closely and handed them back. Then he turned to Dutch Joe grimly.

" The waggons have been passed by my men, and the papers are all in order," he said. " Let me remind you, Grutz, that you have signed up to take this waggon-train to Oregon as made up by my men. This party goes with the rest. That's all ! "

Dutch Joe scowled, but said nothing. But as he rode on to the next waggon it was plain to see that someone was going to suffer—later on, when the train was well away from the eagle eye of the Colonel.

Jack Ryan's fists clenched. He knew he and his whole family were going to have a tough time on the trail to Oregon.

Next Friday in " The Dandy " — Read how Dutch Joe got his vengeance on the Ryan family, and how the little brass tomahawk came to Jack's rescue in a queer way.

One Sniff Out of the Magic Bottle—and Invisible Dick Disappears!

INVISIBLE DICK

1—Dick Brett was on his way to meet his pals. "Oh boy, what a day for a game of football!" he cried. And then something amazing happened to him.

2—As he bounced his ball along, he ran into something that felt as solid as a brick wall. "Ouch!" gasped Dick, crashing down in the street.

3—Half-dazed he looked up to see what had knocked him over. And he could see nothing! Then suddenly he spotted a queer-shaped bottle floating in the air!

4—Dick stared hard and his hair stood on end as he made out a dim figure holding that bottle. He turned to run but a deep voice said, "Hold on there, Dick!"

5—Right before Dick's eyes the dim figure slowly turned solid. "Gosh, it's Peg-Leg Pete! Where did you come from?" "Out of the air," said Pete mysteriously.

6—"And here's my secret," he whispered. "One sniff at the queer liquid in this bottle turns anyone invisible! Now I'm going to give you the bottle!"

7—Peg-Leg Pete told how he had got the bronze bottle from an Egyptian who had found it in an ancient tomb. And now Pete was too old to play pranks with it.

8—Dick stuck the bottle in his pocket until he could get a chance to test it, and he went merrily on his way, heading his ball against the wall.

9—But along came Peeler the Cop, a proper rotter who smacked boys' ears whenever he got the slightest excuse. He spotted Dick and gave a bellow of rage.

10—Dick took to his heels, and Peeler's feet were so big he was left far behind. But when Dick was about to join his pals, along came Peeler and copped them.

11—Peeler cracked their heads together nastily. "It's a blinking shame!" Dick told himself, and then he had a brainwave —what about Peg-Leg Pete's bottle?

12—Dick took a sniff at the bottle, then held up his hand and watched it. Sure enough his hand slowly faded away. "I'm disappearing!" he gasped. And he did!

13—" Now for Peeler!" Dick chuckled, and he set out to trail the big cop. Peeler halted at the next corner, and Dick began his tricks by shouting cheeky names.

14—Peeler whirled round to see where the voice came from. But Dick was quite invisible—and with his invisible hand he reached into an egg-box outside a shop.

15—It seemed to Peeler that one of those eggs sprouted wings and flew at him. Of course, the invisible Dick had thrown it, and it burst all over Peeler's face.

16—The cop was furious. He couldn't see anyone to lay his hands on, but he could hear a voice still shouting at him. So he chased that voice.

17—Round the next corner Dick was laying a trap. He had a tin of soft soap, and he poured it on the pavement. " Come on! Look slippy!" he shouted.

18—And that's just what Peeler did! He came round the corner like a runaway train, and when he planted his boots in the soap, he came down with a thump.

19—Peeler was wild, so he went on following the mocking voice. At last he lost it. But when he heard laughter behind a tree he thought he had found it again.

20—So he charged round the tree and hit out blindly with his baton. But instead of a boy he bashed the police inspector who was chuckling at a funny paper.

21—" What do you think you're playing at?" roared the inspector, flattening Peeler's nose with a bony fist. Peeler was so amazed that he could only gasp.

22—Then he tried to explain, but when he said he had been chasing a floating voice, the inspector thought he was off his rocker. So Peeler was arrested!

23—About this time Dick became visible again. As the effect of the bronze bottle's fumes wore off, his body began to appear, and soon he was as visible as ever.

24—" Oh, boy, what fun I'll have!" he chuckled. And he was right. Peeler the Cop was in a cell, and he couldn't stop the lads playing football now!

If you were invisible, just what would you do?
You'd do tricks that were tricky, and comic tricks, too.
    In " The Dandy " each week,
        You can all take a peek
At the new tricks young Dicky will bring to show you.

'Invisible Dick' champions **The Dandy** *spirit by using his power to take on the local bobbies! Drawn by George Ramsbottom.*   47

*Enterprising monkeys (just like the readers?) provide an energetic ending to the first **Dandy**, thanks to the wonderfully inventive drawing of 'Chic' Gordon!*

TEXT STORIES

*Popular text stories from the early **Dandy** years, with illustrations drawn by George Ramsbottom (right) and James Walker (below).*

The Bellhop left the reader with news of what to expect in next week's episode.

ROM THE outset of *The Dandy* until 1955, text stories formed a large part of the comic. The stories were a mix of adventure, comedy, magic and nature. Albert Barnes chose story tellers he had worked with in his days on *The Wizard* to provide the material. The Frost brothers, especially Kelman Frost, and the hugely talented and prolific Gilbert Dalton were the main authors.

A storyline synopsis would be discussed and worked up between the editor and author. The author would then produce weekly episodes of 2,500–3,000 words; some stories would last weeks, others would last many months and run to many series over a number of years.

A scene would be taken from the text and a heading picture drawn by the D.C. Thomson Art Department. Stalwart artists such as Toby Baines, George Ramsbottom, Fred Sturrock and Dudley Watkins produced the wonderful lead illustrations. A tailpiece hinting at what was happening in the following week's episode was illustrated by a little thumbnail sketch of *The Dandy* logo Bellhop.

The titles for the stories were not usually worked out

by the author. He would be writing the words under a general heading and it was not until the tale was ready to go in the comic that the title was decided upon. Titles took a lot of time and effort to get just right, input from all staff members was encouraged and great debates ensued. Arguments were the order of the day and the office could get quite heated over title decisions.

In the costings for the first *Dandy*, it is interesting to note that costs for text stories greatly outweighed the artwork costs. The most popular features in *Dandy* No.1 were the text stories of adventure and derring-do and it would stay this way for nearly a decade.

After the Second World War, *The Dandy* concentrated on humour and the most popular stories were the picture strip funnies like 'Desperate Dan'. By the end of 1955 the text stories were no more. Fittingly the last text story was a classic 'Black Bob' adventure.

Many of the popular text stories were converted into picture strips by *The Dandy* sub-editors. This treatment was given to favourites such as 'Black Bob', 'Our Teacher's a Walrus', 'The Ugliest Pig in the World' and 'Tin Lizzie'.

49

THE TWO BRAVE RUNAWAYS 1937

The Brook children, Jack and Betty, run away from their cruel aunt. Jack can make friends with any animal and Betty has a beautiful singing voice. During their flight Betty's voice brings them to the attention of a famous film director.

Trapped in a Secret Garage with Two Desperate Car Thieves.

THE TWO BRAVE RUNAWAYS

King Cole is No Leather Thumper—See Him Clout the Poor Old Stumper!

OLD KING COLE

Snooty's Knock-Out

OLD KING COLE 1938

Tales of the fun-loving King of Koronia, a country that lives for fun.

THE BLACK-STRIPED SWEETS THAT BILLY EATS 1939

Billy Parker is the son of the Sheriff of Hot Lead City, toughest town in the Wild West. Billy has a packet of amazing sweets that keeps anyone who eats them free from harm.

START THIS LAUGH-A-LINE FUN STORY TO-DAY.

He Can't Be Hurt, This Great New Friend—He Even Makes a Frying-Pan Bend!

THE BLACK-STRIPED SWEETS THAT BILLY EATS

The Sheriff's Soft-Boiled Son

STARTS TO-DAY! The Thrill Story of a Feud Between Penguins and Rats!

FREDDIE FLIPPER'S FIGHTERS

The Rat Army's Attack

FREDDIE FLIPPER'S FIGHTERS 1942

Freddie Flipper is the commander of a penguin army on an island which is under attack from hordes of rats.

CURLY'S TWO-TON KITTEN 1947

Curly's kitten, Snook, eats a fish that is under a spell and grows to an enormous size.

JAMMY JIMMY JOHNSON 1950

Jimmy Johnson stuck his hand into a magic bottle and ever since everything he touches turns to food.

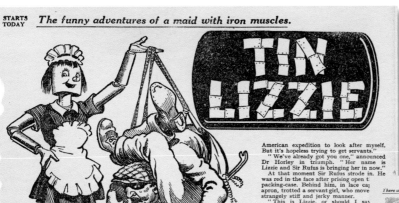

TIN LIZZIE 1953

The comic adventures of Professor Puffin and his robot maid Tin Lizzie.

PIE-FACE PETE'S SECRET PAL 1953

Martian Jek wants to test some Martian products on the people of Earth so he contacts schoolboy Peter Potter to help him.

BLACK BOB 1955

The last text story to appear in *The Dandy*.

THE ARTISTS
DUDLEY WATKINS

DUDLEY DEXTER WATKINS was born in Manchester on February 27, 1907. The proximity to ink and design was with him all his life. His father was a lithographic print artist, and his grandfather a designer in the lace industry in Nottingham, where the young Watkins moved at the tender age of three.

His talent was evident from a very early stage. At six years old his chalk drawing 'The Coming of the Mayor' impressed the education authorities of the day and not long after his twelfth birthday, work which he produced depicting 'The Nottingham Pageant' was exhibited at Nottingham Castle. Watkins started to attend evening classes at the Nottingham School of Art as a young teenager, and in the early 1920s he worked part-time with the window display department of the Boots the Chemist company in Nottingham.

Early examples of his contributions to *The Beacon* – Boots' staff magazine – demonstrate that he was by this stage an accomplished illustration artist and cartoonist. As a teenager with considerable artistic skills, Watkins was well aware of the boys' story papers then dominated by Amalgamated Press and saw the D.C. Thomson weekly *Adventure* come to the market in 1921, followed a year later by *The Rover* and *The Wizard*.

In 1925, after a year at Glasgow School of Art, Watkins' work caught the eye of D.C. Thomson, and he moved to Dundee to take up a staff artist position.

Dudley Watkins found himself working on the boys' papers under Managing Editor R.D. Low, with his contributions gradually increasing in importance from mastheads and title blocks to illustrating the growing number of boys' stories. He became the cover artist for *The Rover* and, as time went on, there was work to be done on *The Skipper*, and later, *The Hotspur*. He was one of many illustrators employed by D.C. Thomson and he also taught life drawing at Dundee Art School to bring extra income.

The first demonstration of Watkins' comic strip work was *The Rover Midget Comic* (1933), which was a promotion with *The Rover*, and *The Skipper Midget Comic*, which followed a year later. Although R.D. Low still saw the young Watkins as an illustrator of text stories rather than a comic strip artist, his first regular comic strip, about a clumsy and ineffective magician, 'Percy Vere

The Dandy's *most famous illustrator, Dudley Watkins, when a young man.*

Watkins produced 'The Broons' and 'Oor Wullie' strips for **The Sunday Post** *newspaper every week for 34 years.*

and his Trying Tricks', featured in *Adventure* in 1935 and ran for nearly two years before it was replaced by another Watkins' strip 'Wandering Willie the Wily Explorer'.

In 1935, a new project conceived by R.D. Low gave Watkins an additional opportunity. A supplement to *The Sunday Post* newspaper was to include two strips 'The Broons' and 'Oor Wullie' in a pull-out part of the paper which became 'The Fun Section', launched in March 1936.

These strips went on to become national institutions in Scotland. It was the success of 'The Fun Section' combined with the popularity of the 'Big Five' boys' papers that led to the idea of new weekly comics.

Young Dirky was a very popular text story illustrated by Watkins.

Desperate Dan.

Danny Longlegs.

The Amazing Mr X.

For the first issue of **The Dandy** (December 4, 1937), Dudley Watkins illustrated 'Desperate Dan', 'Smarty Grandpa' (with a character similar to Granpaw Broon) and 'Our Gang'. 'Our Gang' was based on the Hal Roach films and Watkins' interpretation ran in the comic for a decade.

The first 'Desperate Dan' was a short, half-page rough-tough-cowboy strip which started a process of evolution that saw Dan become one of the best loved comic strip characters of all time, drawn by the greatest-ever comic artists.

The Dandy was a hit and **The Beano** followed in 1938

and **The Magic Comic** in 1939. Watkins worked on them all – notably 'Biffo the Bear' and 'Lord Snooty and his Pals' for **The Beano**, and 'Peter Piper' in **The Magic Comic**.

As the Second World War brought paper and printing restrictions, **The Beano** and **The Dandy** were changed from weekly to fortnightly publications and **The Magic Comic** disappeared altogether. Watkins began working on a host of additional stories and strips, including 'Gulliver', 'Dick Whittington', 'Danny Longlegs', 'Tom Thumb', 'The Shipwrecked Circus', 'Jimmy and his Magic Patch' and others.

Peter Pye.

WATKINS' WORK in the comics was
eagerly awaited each fortnight as his
mockery of Adolf Hitler and Mussolini in
his strips added to the general propaganda
of the time. Such was Watkins' importance to the war effort
as an illustrator that he was excused War Service, but he
became a Reserve Police Constable in Fife in the war years.

His position within D.C. Thomson was unique, for he was
quite the most prolific of any artist of his time, and was the
first to be allowed by the firm to sign his work.

By late 1946, Watkins was living and working in Broughty
Ferry, by Dundee, and it was around this time that he
took on the task of illustrating a series of classic novels, or
'Famous Books In Pictures' which were to appear in **The
People's Journal** as serials. These included 'Treasure Island',
'Kidnapped', 'Catriona', 'Robinson Crusoe', 'The Three
Musketeers', 'Oliver Twist', 'Rob Roy', 'Prester John', 'The
Call of the Wild' and several others. Some later appeared
in book form as part of a series known as 'Told In Pictures'
and in a new tabloid comic brought out by D.C. Thomson
in 1953 – **The Topper**.

Dudley Watkins drew the cover story 'Mickey the
Monkey' and **The Topper** became established and was soon
joined by another great name in British comics – **The Beezer**
with Watkins once more responsible for the cover artwork –
this time 'Ginger'.

Watkins kept his regular weekly work going including
'Oor Wullie', 'The Broons' 'Desperate Dan', 'Biffo the Bear'
and 'Lord Snooty and his Pals', as well as taking on many
other assignments. He also had input to the annuals and
specials which became part of the ever-growing publication
programme.

He was a devout Christian and met his wife through his
work with the Church of Christ in Dundee. He lent his

*Robbie the
Bobby.*

Young Frankie Drake.

Our Gang.

*Dudley Watkins was working on this **Beano** cover when he died in August 1969.*

talents to the Church through many projects, such as mission calendars and religious illustrations, notably a comic strip 'William the Warrior' which appeared in a paper distributed by the Worldwide Evangelisation Crusade. It was always Watkins' unfulfilled intention to create an illustrated Bible, but he did produce two Bible story strips for ***The Sparky Annual*** in 1968 and 1969.

Dudley Watkins was at home at his desk on the morning of August 20, 1969 when he had a heart attack and died, with a 'Biffo the Bear' strip, a 'work in progress', on his drawing board. The strip appeared, completed by artist Dave Sutherland, as ***The Beano*** cover story on October 25, 1969.

THE ARTISTS

CHARLES 'CHIC' GORDON

Monkeys flying a plane. It could only happen in 'Bamboo Town', here shown as original artwork.

CHARLES ('CHIC') GORDON is worthy of a special mention as he illustrated the back cover of **The Dandy** from its birth, through the war years, until 1944 with 'Bamboo Town'. He made some of the most marvellous, complex, multi-character scenes look easy. During wartime his material was very patriotic with a strong anti-Nazi edge. He was never a prolific artist but important none the less. In total he drew only five series for **The Dandy**.

Bongo and Pongo from 'Bamboo Town'.

MUGG MUGGINS—THE CRAZY INVENTOR

THE ARTISTS
ALLAN MORLEY

Shaggy Doggy.

Hungry Horace.

Keyhole Kate.

'Charley Chutney the Comical Cook'.

'Old Ma Murphy the Strong Arm School Ma'm'.

'Freddie the Fearless Fly'.

ALLAN MORLEY started working for D.C. Thomson in 1925 and was well known to R.D. Low. He had worked on various strips in the Big Five and his distinctive style formed a large part of 'The Fun Section' in D.C. Thomson's *Sunday Post* newspaper. He drew 'Nero and Zero' in *The Wizard* and 'Nosey Parker' in *The Rover*. Allan Morley was so prolific that R.D. was on record as saying that if anything happened to the Morley fun-factory then the comics might close.

He was one of the initial team of artists on *The Dandy*. The first issue contained three of his most famous and long-lasting strips – 'Keyhole Kate', 'Hungry Horace' and 'Freddy the Fearless Fly'. Other Morley strips included 'Charley Chutney the Comical Cook' and 'Old Ma Murphy the Strong Arm School Ma'm', both of which started in 1944. His last new strip for *The Dandy* was 'Shaggy Doggy', from 1954 (this strip was reprinted in the 1970s as 'Waggy, the Shaggy Doggy'). He also contributed to *The Beano*, providing 'Big Fat Joe' for the first issue. In 1947 it was agreed that he, as well as Dudley Watkins, could sign his own work and this he did until he retired in 1958, after twenty-one years of drawing for *The Dandy*.

THE ARTISTS

RICHARD 'TOBY' BAINES

KNOWN BY his preferred name of Toby, Baines attended Sunderland School of Art before serving in the Balkans during the First World War. He joined the growing Art Department at D.C. Thomson on demob and worked on *The Rover*, *Adventure* and *The Hotspur*. Toby's speciality was animal and wildlife art and he was especially good at dog illustrations. Two of his lifelong interests were gardening and dogs.

Later, Baines' distinctive style would be put to good use working for *The Dandy* and *The Beano*. Two of his top stories for *The Dandy* involved animals: 'The Ugliest Pig in the World', who was a fabulous wild boar called Rip Snorter, and 'Dickey Bird', the boy who knew how to communicate to animals and birds by whistling.

In all Toby would do the illustrations for over twenty series in *The Dandy*, contributing greatly to its early success.

Examples of Toby's work for the comic and the annuals.

THE ARTISTS
JACK GLASS

'The Amazing Mr X' was the first British comic superhero (see page 90).

'The Crimson Ball'.

JACK GLASS worked from the D.C. Thomson Art Department when *The Dandy* was launched in 1937. His strong dark line gave him a very distinctive style that was very popular with the early comic fans.

Jack was a large jovial man, well-liked by the young artists who he would often treat to lunch. He lived in Dundee near to the Thomson offices and was a keen golfer and bridge player. *The Dandy* relied heavily on Jack's prodigious output in the early years and he was still drawing for the comic thirty years later.

On retiral, Jack moved south to Bournemouth.

'The Daring Deeds of Buck Wilson'.

'Never, Never Nelson'.

THE ARTISTS
FRED STURROCK

F RED STURROCK was a really popular, influential member of the D.C. Thomson Art Department. He joined the publishers in 1920 and made a name for himself as a sports illustrator. On *The Dandy*, Albert Barnes used him to draw many of the text story header pictures, and in his long career he drew more than thirty series of them. Fred especially enjoyed drawing all-action pictures, much loved and admired by his colleagues. His great sense of humour and infamous green eye-shade made him a target for the in-house cartoons that would circulate round the art department.

Lost on the Mountain of Fear.

THE ARTISTS
ERIC ROBERTS

Podge.

Dirty Dick.

LONDONER ERIC ROBERTS was a mainstay of *The Dandy* from the very beginning. He drew 'Podge' for the first issue and over the years his output went from strength to strength. His crowning glory was the fantastic public schoolboy 'Winker Watson' which he launched in 1961. 'Winker' was the only series in *The Dandy* that was more popular than the iconic 'Desperate Dan'. After a long, successful career, Eric drew his last series of 'Winker' in 1979.

Winker Watson.

Ginger's Super Jeep.

THE ARTISTS
JAMES CLARK

Jimmy and his Grockle.

JAMES CLARK illustrated the surreal strip 'Jimmy and his Grockle' in the first issue of *The Dandy*. Earlier, Clark had started work as an artist with D.C. Thomson's partner publishing house John Leng. Both companies were based in Dundee and Clark moved there from Glasgow in 1919. For *The Dandy* Clark drew more than twenty-five different strips, 'Jimmy and his Grockle' and 'Young Dandy', the 1957 story of a tame fawn, being the most popular.

Clark drew for many other D.C. Thomson publications, including *The Beano*, *The Topper* and the 'Towser' strip in *The People's Journal* weekly newspaper. However, many more pre-school youngsters knew of his work by following the adventures of 'Willie Waddle'. Willie was a comical dog and James Clark drew funny strips of him for more than thirty years, the work appearing in various publications and in his own books.

Young Dandy.

THE ARTISTS

GEORGE RAMSBOTTOM

Jungle Jake.

Barney's Bear.

GEORGE WAS a Lancashire lad, born in Salford in 1903. From school he joined the *Manchester Evening News* as a copy boy and it was during this period his artistic ability was noted. After a brief spell at an art agency George joined D.C. Thomson in 1936. His first series for *The Dandy* was 'Invisible Dick', which proved to be a very popular and ensured his future career in comics. He drew an amazing amount of work for *The Dandy*; two notable series were 'Little White Chief of the Cherokees' and 'Barney's Bear'. The 'Barney's Bear' story was written by *Dandy* editor Albert Barnes and the bear was intentionally named after him. George's career extended well into the 1970s and he was over seventy himself before he finally retired.

Invisible Dick.

63

THE ARTISTS
JAMES L. CRICHTON

Dangerous Duff – The Mouse Who's Rough and Mighty Tough.

Dandy *legend, Korky the Cat.*

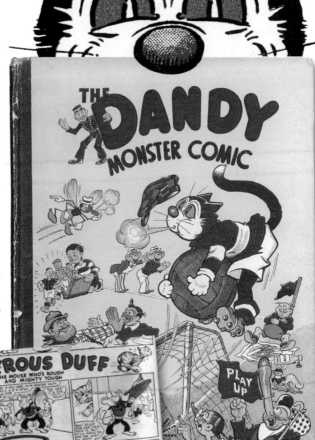

Crichton drew the cover for the 1944 **Dandy Monster Comic,** *as the annual was then titled.*

Raggy Muffin.

BORN IN Dundee in 1892 and educated at the local Morgan Academy, James L. Crichton was initially apprenticed at a firm of architects. He realised technical drawing was not for him and joined the art department of the *Dundee Advertiser* in 1913. After serving in the Western Front during the First World War, he returned to *The Courier* and his beloved drawing board. For the paper he created a rather unusual strip called 'Billy and Bunny'; the heroes were a teenage boy and his friend a humanised rabbit. It gained a cult following and ran daily for many decades, one art frame per day.

In 1937 he started drawing his most famous character, 'Korky the Cat'. He was the lead cover character for the bright new *Dandy* and within a few years was a household name. Man and cat remained together for almost twenty-five years and Crichton's *Dandy* covers became classics of the comic genre.

The Fiction Department hard at work creating stories for **The Dandy**.

The Art Department where the comics came to life.

THE DANDY

CHAPTER TWO

The War

1939–1945

*The war was a tough time for everyone – including all the **Dandy** characters.*

THE WAR

Jock MacSwiper had a new weapon to use against the Germans.

The Grockle manages to electrocute some inquisitive soldiers from a wartime 'Jimmy and his Grockle'.

IT MAY seem strange to some that *The Dandy* continued to pour out its fun-filled pages during the dreadful dark days of the Second World War. *The Dandy* team, however, saw their part in the war effort as being to brighten up the lives of their millions of young readers. The comic dropping through the letterbox would bring some light-heartedness to the youngsters enduring the worry and shortages of a country at war. These same shortages meant that *The Dandy* was reduced to twelve pages by 1942 in a number of stages from its original twenty-eight. In addition in August 1941 it started to come out on alternate weeks to its stablemate, *The Beano*. *The Magic Comic*, which had launched in late 1939, just before the start of hostilities, lasted only eighty issues before the scarcity of paper meant it had to close in January 1941. So it was that *The Dandy* changed to six pages of comic strips, two double pages of prose stories and one double page comic adventure/adventure strip. Fewer pages naturally meant less for your 2d in 1942 than you got in July 1939.

   The Dandy reflected the times by adding a huge dash of patriotism to the normal mixture of laughs and adventures. They mobilised a battalion of comic heroes to inspire British children.

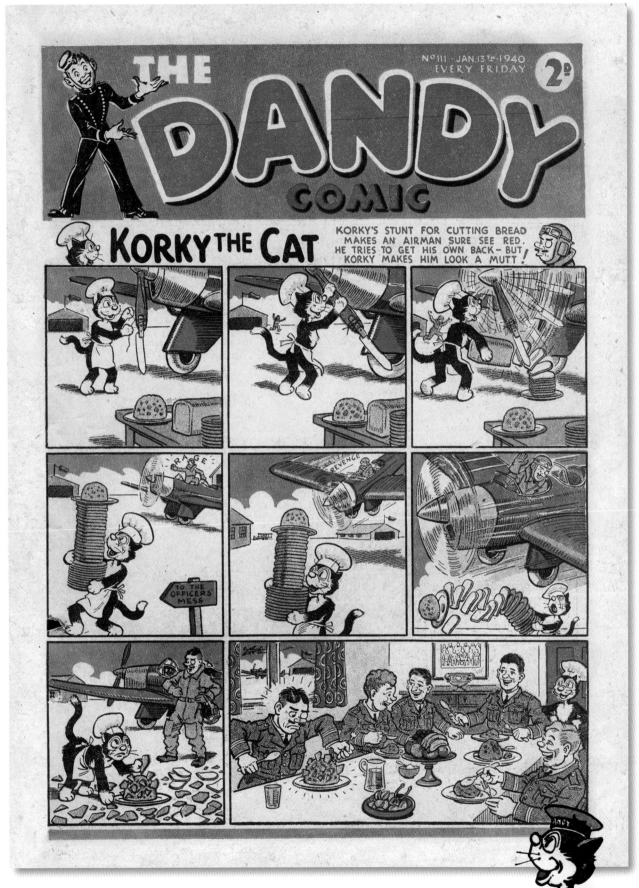

James Crichton drew a series of propaganda Korky strips for **The Dandy** *in 1940.*

The famous Nazi mice, one of the best 'Korky the Cat' strips ever produced.

Though the editorial office was run on a skeleton staff, with so many men going into the forces, ingenious scripts were still produced.

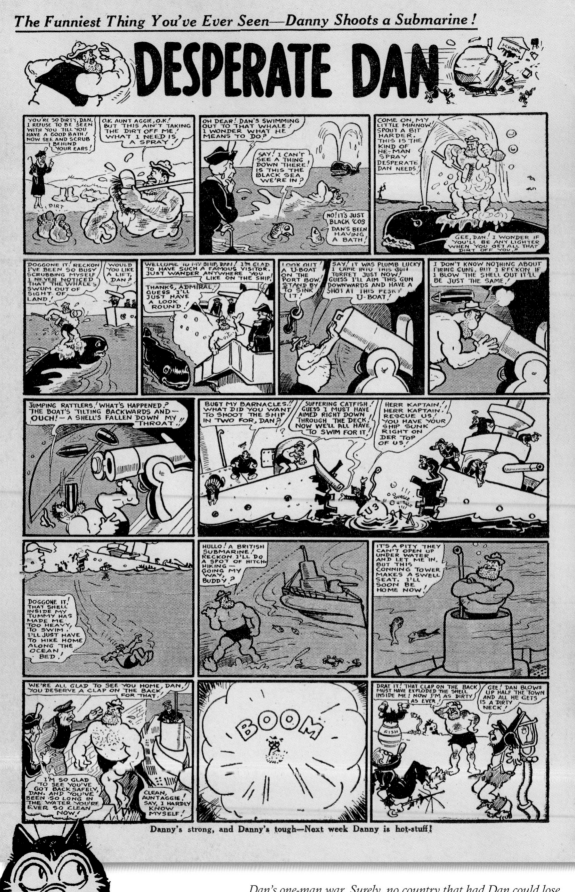

Dan's one-man war. Surely, no country that had Dan could lose.

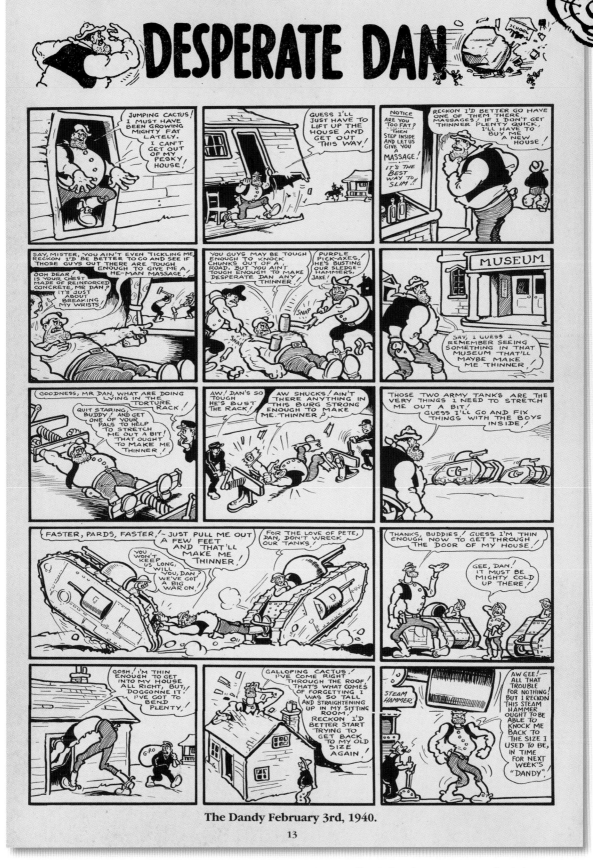

The Dandy February 3rd, 1940.

13

*Dan being a Texan meant that America had joined **The Dandy** war effort before the country actually did.*

Dudley D Watkins was not only producing magnificent pages for **The Dandy** *during the war, he was also lead artist for* **The Beano** *and drawing 'Oor Wullie' and 'The Broons' comic strips for* **The Sunday Post** *newspaper. Added to that he was a part-time Special Constable.*

No officer was a match for Desperate Dan in uniform.

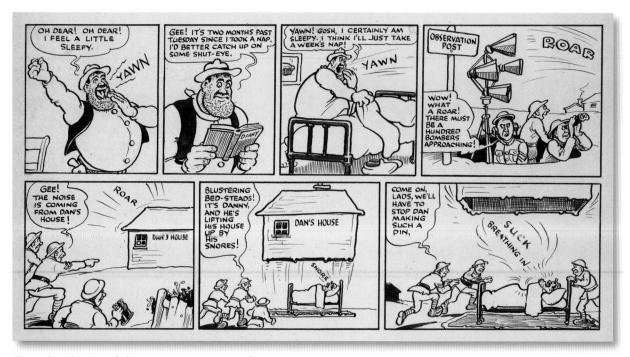

From the adversity of the times came some very funny scenarios.

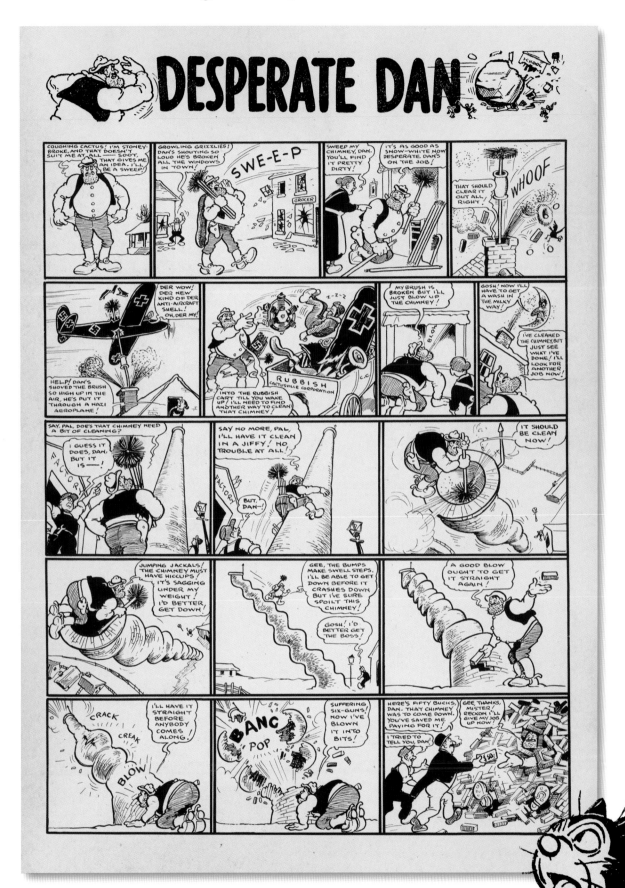

Only Dan could bring down a German aeroplane while cleaning a chimney.

Absurd, surreal and totally brilliant, 'Bamboo Town' takes on the Luftwaffe.

As the Blitz raged, Desperate Dan had the enemy on the run.

MOST OF ***The Dandy*** staff and a great many of its freelancers were off to war. Editor Albert Barnes was called up to the Royal Navy in 1940 and made only rare visits to the office in Dundee when he was on leave. For nine months his place was taken by George Thomson, a young ***Dandy*** sub-editor (later to become Lord Thomson of Monifieth). He was followed by John Low, former editor of ***The Rover*** and brother of R.D. Low. The day-to-day running of the comic was down to staff that were either too old, too young or not fit enough to be called up. ***The Dandy*** and ***The Wizard*** came out of a single office and all freelance artists were asked to try their hand at story writing too. Their great bulldog spirit meant ***The Dandy*** did not miss going to press.

Wartime suffering seemed to inspire Watkins to draw some truly awesome images.

The Dandy October 3rd, 1942.

21

Dan brings down two German planes with his bare hands after various circus adventures.

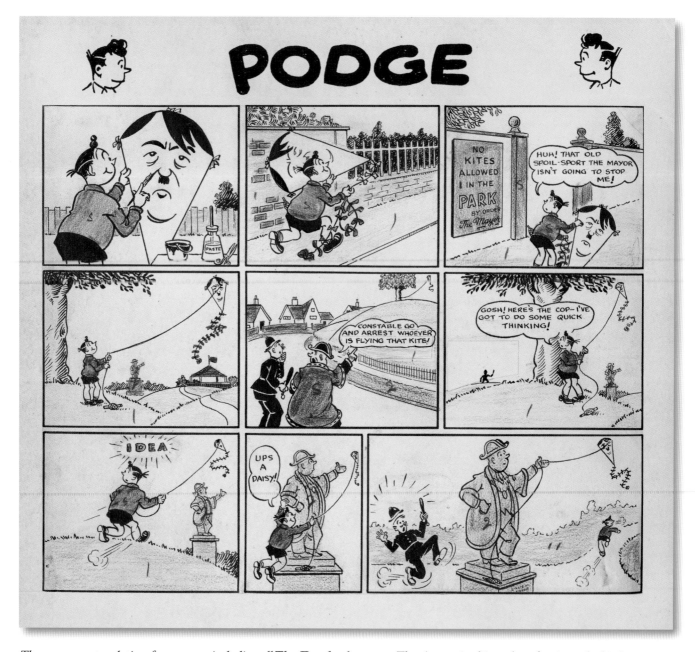

*The war was a tough time for everyone including all **The Dandy** characters. There's no mistaking whose face is on the kite!*

ARTIST ERIC ROBERTS who drew these wartime 'Podge' stories joined up with the RAF. One of his many tasks was drawing propaganda scenes that would be turned into leaflets and dropped over enemy territory (see page 84). Roberts continued to draw the occasional page for *The Dandy* while off duty during active service, as did several of the freelance brigade. This really typifies the spirit of Albert Barnes' wartime team.

Korky's smalls cause big trouble. Korky saw service with the Army, Navy and Air Force.

Wartime boys would have been envious of Podge and his Messerschmitt souvenir.

THE COMIC war continued and things got tougher for Nazi leader Adolf Hitler and Herman Goering, head of the Luftwaffe. In December 1939 artist Sam Fair started lampooning the two Nazis in the strip 'Addie and Hermy, the Nasty Nazis'. They were portrayed as a pair of bumbling idiots who spent their time trying to steal food, mostly from their own troops. The readers loved seeing them get trounced, the crueller the punishment the better.

ADDIE AND HERMY

Addie and Hermy get beaten up, the usual result of their incompetence.

With enemy leaders like this pair we were bound to win the war.

The remarkable imagination of comic artists brought fun to relieve the daily tensions that war brought.

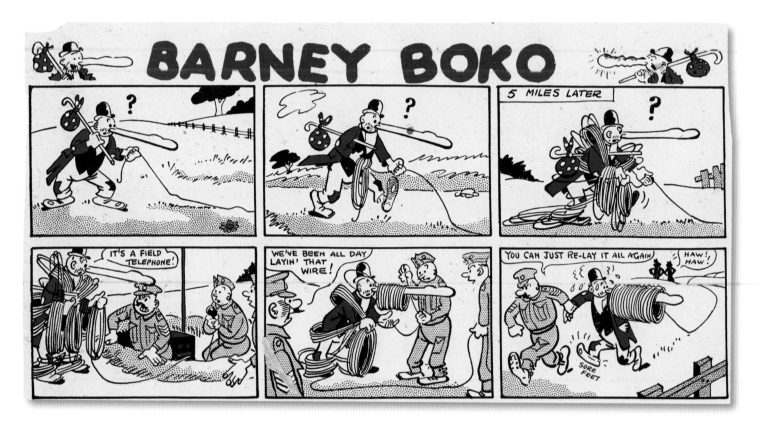

BARNEY BOKO'S monster snitch got him into all sorts of scrapes but during wartime it became an unusual weapon of war. The artist John Mason was an accomplished newspaper cartoonist and would script the sets that were stories without words. Barney was a 'gentleman of the road' and his military mishaps were often by accident.

In the studio John Mason kept spirits up by regularly doing in-house cartoons for his colleagues' amusement. The D.C. Thomson editors who set the artists' workload were the butt of most of the cartoons.

Nazi mice were a problem for Korky.

In fact, mice in general were a problem for Korky.

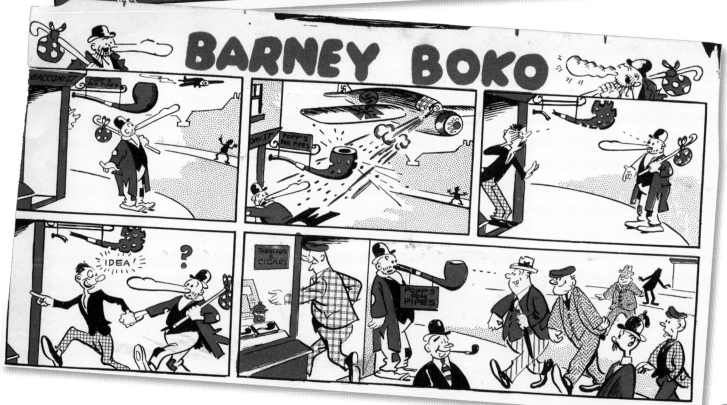

ERIC KNEW HOW TO MAKE THEM RAF!

DURING THE Second World War Eric Roberts served as a draughtsman in the RAF and kept the troops laughing during terrible times with his hilarious cartoons in the in-service publication *Tee-Hee*.

His drawings were so popular they even had the officers at London offices of the Ministry of Aircraft Production laughing, as you can see from this letter he received in January 1945.

TELEPHONE: FRANKLIN 2211
Extn. 1072

MINISTRY OF AIRCRAFT PRODUCTION,
S.O.(T)/D.Arm.D.
MILLBANK,
S.W.1.

Our Ref.....................

Your Ref.....................

16th January 1945.

Dear Roberts

    I have just received my January number of "Tee Emm" and am writing at once to say that I think that its brightest feature is your S.D.S.A.G.'s No.1. Please Keep "p the good work; I look forward, with many others, to seeing the remainder of the series.

    Please give my love to F/Lt.Watkins and F/O Bryant if they are still up there.

    Very best wishes and lots of success in the coming year.

        Yours very sincerely

Eric at his desk in the RAF.

Here are his 'Seven Deadly Sins of Wireless Operators' from **Tee-Hee**.

The SEVEN DEADLY SINS of W/OPS · Nº 3

— FAILURE TO WIND IN TRAILING AERIAL —

As well as technical drawings, Roberts' talents were put to use creating hilarious warning posters and health and safety instructions for the RAF. Here's a classic example discouraging officers from discussing top-secret information.

The SEVEN DEADLY SINS of W/OPS · Nº 4

— FAILURE TO ACKNOWLEDGE RECALL SIGNAL —

The SEVEN DEADLY SINS of W/OPS · Nº 5

"HELLO, SKIPPER, I'VE HUNG ON TO THE M/F PEOPLE FOR 25 MINUTES WITH OUR S.O.S. DO YOU THINK WE'LL MAKE IT?"

"YES, OF COURSE! I TOLD YOU TO CANCEL THE S.O.S. 15 MINUTES AGO!"

— MONOPOLY OF M/F SECTION FOR LONG PERIODS —

Eric drew this picture of his office in the RAF. It's signed by Eric and all of his colleagues.

The SEVEN DEADLY SINS of W/OPS · Nº 6

— FAILURE TO COPE WITH FAULT FINDING IN AN EMERGENCY —

The SEVEN DEADLY SINS of W/OPS · Nº 7

MY NAVIGATOR WOULD LIKE A FIX, PLEASE

— FAILURE TO SEARCH AND LISTEN BEFORE CALLING —

KEYHOLE COVER

AN UNUSUAL tale accompanies this rare copy of *The Dandy* from June 1945. The D.C. Thomson managing editor R.D. Low, who oversaw all comics during wartime, was taking a rare, well-earned break. He left *The Dandy* in the hands of youngster Johnny Hutton. Perhaps the young man was swept along in the euphoria that the recent winning of the war in Europe had produced for he decided to change the cover of the comic.

'Korky' was relegated to a half-page strip on the back cover and 'Keyhole Kate' was given star billing on the front. When Low returned he was furious. 'Korky' was immediately returned to the cover and harsh words were said to the would-be designer Hutton. This rare *Dandy* is very collectable and nowadays changes hands for more than any other 1945 *Dandy*.

Korky sitting unhappily at the top of the back page.

D.C. Thomson produced these magazines to tell the Dundee staff about those serving in the armed forces.

*During the war years, readers were spurred on to save paper, sometimes with the encouragement of **Dandy** characters.*

Rush round the houses,
From door to door.
Gather waste paper,
More and more.
There's plenty needed
To make shells,
Before we hear
The Victory Bells!

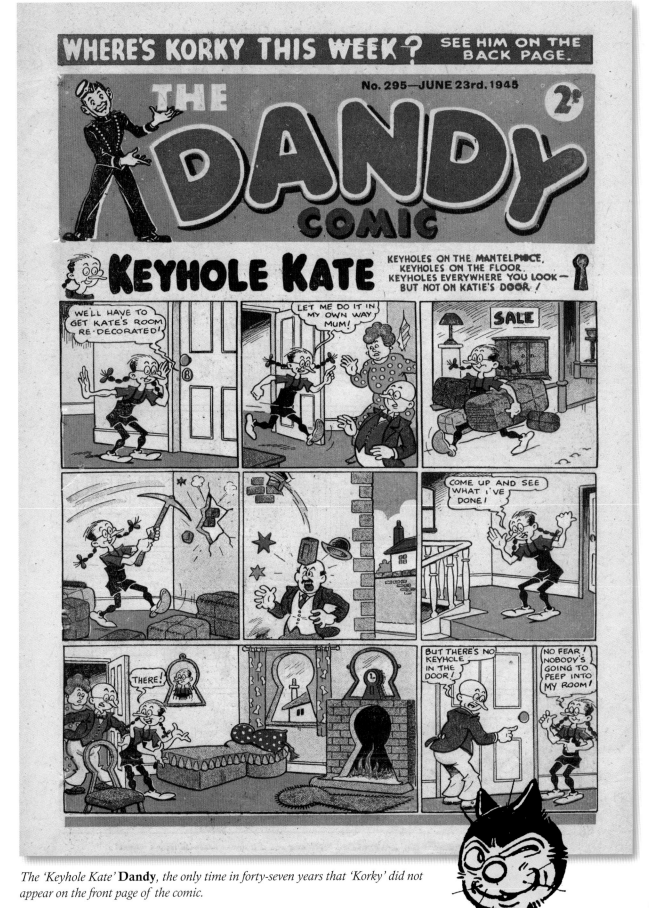

The 'Keyhole Kate' **Dandy***, the only time in forty-seven years that 'Korky' did not appear on the front page of the comic.*

87

BLACK BOB

'Black Bob', **The Dandy** *Wonder Dog, one of the most popular stories ever.*

AT THIS time the introduction of new stories to keep the comics fresh was down to group editor R.D. Low and *The Dandy*'s stand-in editor Johnny Hutton. They relied heavily on the talents of a small group of freelance authors to provide the fortnightly episodes that kept the pages filled.

Towards the end of summer 1944, one of *The Dandy*'s most prolific freelance authors, Kelman Frost, was visiting the offices in Dundee from his home in Hampshire. He and R.D. Low were good friends, having worked together on countless stories over the years. On this trip they took some time off to go walking in the Angus glens, to the north of Dundee, where R.D. had a house. They used this relaxed time to discuss new storylines and work out a timetable to provide the material the comics needed. R.D. would tell Kelman the type of series he was planning to run, working out a synopsis of how he saw it developing. Armed with this information Kelman would then produce the written stories that made up the series.

The discussions on this visit were around the great popularity of the MGM film adaption of Eric Knight's book, *Lassie Come Home*. It was released in 1943 and had been a huge success with both adults and children. R.D. was looking for a dog hero story that would also incorporate the beautiful scenery of the Scottish glens similar to the surroundings they were walking in. Within weeks of his return home to Hampshire, Kelman Frost had sent in the first three episodes of 'Black Bob'.

'Black Bob' first appeared in *The Dandy* on November 25, 1944. This first series of text stories contained eight episodes of approximately 3000 words each. A pen-and-ink illustration was used as a header to start off the story.

A new story coming in to *The Dandy* did so without much advertising, just a little mention in the previous issue and a topline saying 'Starts today'. Such was the popularity of this comic that stories became nationally known almost immediately.

On the week that 'Black Bob' launched in *The Dandy* sales reached 824,000 copies. Due to wartime paper shortages the Government only allowed 850,000 copies to be produced.

There are dozens of evil men in the circus—And they're all after Black Bob!

BLACK BOB

An Uneven Fight.

A STRUGGLE was taking place in a deep ditch at the rear of the circus ground on the edge of Galashiels. Black Bob was locked in a desperate fight with the India-Rubber Man from the circus, a short thickset fellow who shouted for help as he struggled.

Andrew Glenn and his cousin Tom came running up to the spot where the struggle was taking place. They had been lying in wait for this man to prevent him reaching the circus, for he had in his possession a very important letter belonging to Tom Glenn.

Behind them there were loud shouts from the Circus Americano as several of the circus men came running towards the spot to see what was wrong with the India-Rubber Man.

These men from the Circus Americano were at the root of all the trouble which Andrew and Tom Glenn had been having.

Their boss, Don Danli, was an evil rogue. He had found out that Tom Glenn possessed a chart showing where Captain Kidd, the famous pirate, had hidden a fabulous treasure and he was sparing no effort to lay hands on this chart. But Black Bob and the Glenn cousins were fighting back.

Their idea was to fight against Danli until Tom received word from his lawyers in London, who were trying to arrange with the Honduras Government for Tom to remove the treasure.

But just after Tom had received the letter, his pocket had been picked by one of the circus men. Now the two cousins and Black Bob were trying to stop the pick-pocket's companion from reaching the circus and handing Tom's letter over to Don Danli.

But Black Bob had never found it so difficult to hold anyone before. As fast as he gripped his opponent, the India-Rubber Man twisted in some extraordinary way and was free again. He held a thick stick and with this he kept trying to strike the sheepdog.

Andrew Glenn was the first to arrive, and as he looked down at the tussling pair he saw Bob grab one of the man's hands between his teeth. But the India-Rubber Man had been well named, for his skin was loose and rubbery—he slid his hand out of Bob's grasp.

Andrew Glenn waited his opportunity and jumped on top of the India-Rubber Man, crooking an arm round the circus man's neck and thus holding him in a stranglehold.

"The registered letter—where is it?" Glenn demanded.

Any other man would have been forced to give up under such a hold but the India-Rubber Man twisted himself right round so that he was facing Andrew Glenn, and drove his knee into the shepherd's stomach. At the same time he gave a yell, for Bob had seized him by the ankle.

The shepherd hung on as the man squirmed. He hoped Tom would go through the man's pockets, but Tom Glenn was already turning to face the first three circus men who had scrambled through the hedge. Don Danli was one of them, and he was red with rage.

"Settle them once and for all!" he was shouting. "There's nobody about to see what we do."

Tom used only his clenched fists, whereas Danli's two companions had clubs, and others were hurrying towards the fight.

Black Bob now had a proper grip on the India-Rubber Man and pulled his legs from under him. The man went down with Glenn on top of him, and as the circus man's breath was knocked from his body, the shepherd dived a hand into the man's nearest pocket.

Glenn was lucky. His fingers found the registered letter belonging to his cousin. He snatched it and stuffed it into his own pocket.

He scrambled out of the ditch, and saw Tom reeling under the blows of the two circus hands, while Don Danli ran towards the ditch, a knife in his hand. The shepherd crouched and waited for the attack, but Black Bob did not hesitate. He dived past his master and sprang at the raised knife hand.

Don Danli snarled and struck down at the dog, but Bob met the down-coming wrist and gripped with his sharp teeth. Danli screamed and dropped the knife, beating at Bob with his other fist to make him let go.

Andrew Glenn now had the thick stick which the India-Rubber Man had been wielding, and he saw his chance to run in and swing it at the South American's head. Down went Don Danli, and the shepherd raced to his cousin's aid.

Tom had been beaten to his knees by blows from his attackers' clubs just as Andrew Glenn arrived. Glenn lashed about so savagely with the stick that he drove the circus men back long enough for Tom to get to his feet.

"I've got it!" Gasped Andrew, grabbing his cousin by the arm. "Let's make for the main road and find the police. Hi, Bob!"

They ran for the road, but more of Danli's men came running up to block their path.

Andrew Glenn saw that they could not reach the lane and he swerved away from Danli's men, bursting through a gap in the hedge and into the field which was the circus ground. It was the only way open to them.

Behind, the pursuers turned back to help Don Danli to his feet. The circus owner was still shouting for the two cousins to be stopped, for by now he knew about the registered letter they had and he guessed its importance.

Panic In The Circus.

IT happened that most of the other circus men were at the far end of the ground, putting up a large canvas screen which had blown down during the night. They did not hear the shouts from the field, so the two cousins and Bob were able to make their way, unseen, as far as the big circus tent.

From inside came the crack of a whip, and the harsh voice of a man. Through an open flap Andrew Glenn saw the ringmaster rehearsing the troupe of trained horses.

Andrew Glenn glanced over his shoulder. Danli and his men would soon be in sight again, and there were an unknown number of men in front of them. The three would stand little chance of escape unless they did something to take attention away from themselves.

He stopped, grabbed Black Bob, and pointed through the flap of the big tent. "Scatter them, Bob!" he hissed, and gave a signal which Black Bob understood. He darted through the opening into the tent

---

Stranded on a rock, surrounded by the rising tide. What a fix to be in! But Black Bob is there.

Find out what he does in the

DANDY BOOK

These are only 2 of the hundreds of action, fun and thrill pictures in this bumper annual.

ON SALE NOW. PRICE 6/-

The prose style of 'Black Bob' with Jack Prout's artwork as the story title drawing.

A Thief Captured By The Mysterious, Breath-Taking Superman——
THE AMAZING **Mr X**

THE UK's FIRST COMIC SUPERHERO

Len Manners ,who transforms himself into The Amazing Mr X (below).

IN 1938, in the first issue of *Action Comics*, Superman burst onto the American scene, with the key elements of a super-powered hero in place, including a secret identity, a costume, and the battle for social justice. On seeing Superman's popularity, R.D. Low commissioned staff artist Jack Glass to try his hand at his own superhero and the result was 'The Amazing Mr X', Britain's first home-grown superhero!

'The Amazing Mr X' appeared in *The Dandy* for fourteen instalments between 1944 and 1945. It was conceived as a traditional adventure story with pictures and captions and did not adopt the pace and visual style of the American superhero comics. Mr X stood up for the oppressed, just like the first Superman stories, and he had an alter ego, Len Manners, who was a 'private inquiry agent' based in a 'large English town'. Like Superman he wore glasses as a disguise, and on spotting trouble donned a costume of black tights, a black cloak and mask, and a white woollen jersey with a red X. By tensing his muscles and taking a deep breath, his loose frame filled out with impressive muscles, enabling him to perform incredible feats. Like a true superhero he sought no reward for his actions, and, indeed, we are told, 'Mr X wanted no thanks or fuss.'

Some 'Amazing Mr X' stories followed Superman plots very closely, except that he pursued his enemies over rugged British landscapes, and the towns and cities he operated in were distinctly British in character. He dealt with criminals

3—Out of sight behind a large tree, Len changed into a queer costume, black skin-tight trousers, white jersey and black cloak and mask. Len Manners had transformed himself into the amazing, mysterious figure of Mr X.

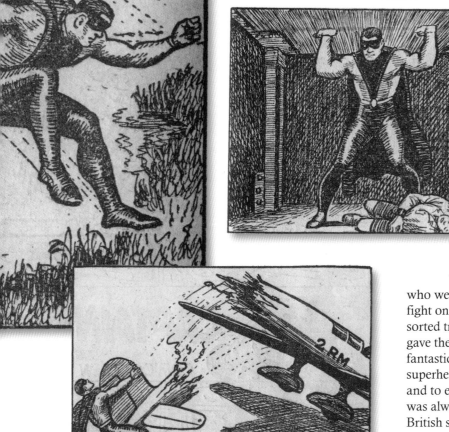

Mr X performed incredible feats of bravery and courage yet wished to remain anonymous, like many of the superheroes to come.

The strength, speed and agility of Mr X was truly amazing.

who were stealing from the Royal Mail, necessitating a fight on a moving train, solved a convoluted kidnapping, sorted trouble at a shipyard, and even wrestled a stag. This gave the stories a certain charm, but was not quite the fantastic excess commonly found in superhero comics. A superhero was supposed to soar between huge skyscrapers and to embody the ideals of the American Dream. There was always something a bit too down-to-Earth about the British superheroes, which is partly why they were never as popular as their American counterparts and why the series did not seem to have appealed much to readers.

'The Amazing Mr X' made one more appearance, in the 1962 **Dandy** annual, with more dynamic art by Dudley Watkins, but in this incarnation 'The Amazing Mr X' was less of a superhero, and his costume was a simple black bodysuit. It did not herald a return for Britain's first superhero, who was never seen again in the pages of **The Dandy**.

13—The Amaleks brandished enormous curved scimitars, while Mr X had no weapons but his bare hands, but the superman had no need of weapons. He dodged a sword-stroke, then leapt in. His arms encircled both of the seven-foot men, and then, thinking with hatred of the sacrifices these killers had thrown to their loathsome sacred crocodile, he exerted his amazing strength to its limit. The two men gasped, and there came the sound of ribs being crushed!

14—He flung the senseless natives from him, and in a few seconds had pulled little Jackie from his hiding-place. There was no danger now. As they set off for Algiers, each mounted on a camel, they looked back at the oasis with its smashed minaret. It was a job well done and worth doing. Mr X felt satisfied, for he had saved a young lad's life and had wiped out an evil thing from the earth. And as that is the last of his adventures meantime, we will leave Mr X to enjoy his African holiday.

In the next " Dandy "—DANNY LONGLEGS—a grand new fun story in coloured pictures.

DANNY LONGLEGS

DUDLEY WATKINS was responsible for two of the most popular strips in *The Dandy* during the late forties – 'Desperate Dan' and newcomer 'Danny Longlegs', the ten-foot tall medieval schoolboy whose great height got him into all sorts of adventures. Luckily for Danny his great height usually would rescue him also. This set showcased Watkins' great ability to design a scene. It is very difficult to scale a picture when the main character is twice the height of anyone else! The first *Dandy* strip that Watkins signed was the 'Danny Longlegs' strip of August 31, 1946.

*Danny Longlegs first appeared in **The Dandy** on February 3, 1945.*

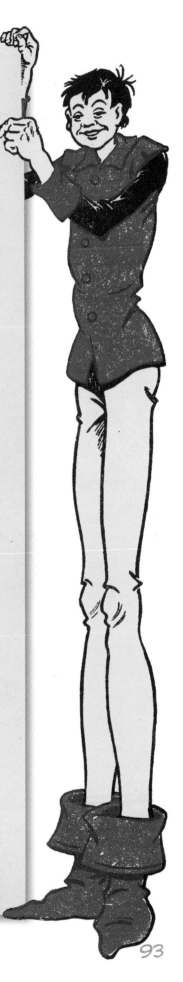

Great new story in pictures about the ten-foot schoolboy.

DANNY LONGLEGS

SLEEPY VALLEY was a very ordinary village, with lots of ordinary boys and girls. But there was one extraordinary schoolboy in Sleepy Valley. This was Danny Long, and although he was a mere schoolboy, he was nicknamed Longlegs—because he was more than ten feet tall! Now just a year ago, an Eastern prince called Ali Khan had come to England to kidnap Danny. The Prince had failed, but he hadn't forgotten. One day three strange men brought Danny a present.

2—Danny had watched the little procession draw near to his house, and he felt sure he recognised the little man in front. He was right. It was Tarbush, the dwarf from the Prince's court. The two black slaves unloaded their long package. "A gift from my exalted master," said Tarbush. Danny hastily set the gift against the wall of his house and started to unwrap it. "A mirror!" he gasped. "And it must have been made specially for me. That's good! I can see all of me!"

3—"Thank your master," he said, and he bent almost double so that he could talk down to the little man. "I will always remember him." Tarbush smiled a strange little smile. "You certainly will, O tall boy!" he replied. It almost seemed as though the dwarf expected something to happen—and it did. Suddenly Danny got a terrific kick in the pants, and the foot that kicked him was on a leg that came out of the mirror!

4—Danny whirled round, but saw no one who could have kicked him. Puzzled, Danny's glance fell upon his own image in the mirror, and he became even more puzzled. Danny felt sure he was frowning, but his reflection wasn't. Even as the giant schoolboy stared, his image in the mirror cheekily stuck out its tongue. Danny rubbed his eyes in wonder. Little Tarbush was chuckling fit to burst. He didn't seem surprised.

5—This cheeky, grinning image of himself got Danny thoroughly annoyed. It even blew a raspberry! "Magic Mirror from the East, eh!" howled the long schoolboy. "I should have guessed that Prince Ali Khan was up to some dirty work sending me this. Take that!" He swung his fist at the reflection, and the most amazing thing happened. Danny's reflection ducked, dodged the blow, and stepped clear out of the mirror.

6—Danny was absolutely flabbergasted by this image of himself. It was exactly like him, but it was completely flat and no thicker than the mirror from which it had stepped. What kind of Eastern magic was this? And what harm would the strange image do? "Catch it, Tarbush!" Danny yelled, breaking into a run. But Tarbush and the slaves were gone. Their job was done, and they were off to report to their master.

CHAPTER THREE

The Start of the Golden Era

1946–1959

A magical time in the comic world when the **The Dandy** *could do no wrong.*

THE GOLDEN LEDGER

ALBERT BARNES returned from the
Royal Navy to take the helm at the good ship
Dandy in 1946. Paper restrictions were still in
place, publication was still fortnightly and in
1947 the page count dropped to ten. Paper problems were
besetting all printers at this time but ***The Dandy*** was so
popular its huge circulation demanded lots of paper. The
circulation books show that every ***Dandy*** was sold.

The Dandy sales ledger tells an amazing story. This
page shows the entries for 1950. In total, sales that year
were 102,563,065, a truly astonishing circulation.

The Dandy was printed in Glasgow and Manchester.
Glasgow supplied Scotland and the north of England and
Manchester supplied England, south of Manchester.

The peak weekly sale of 2,035,310 was achieved for
the issue No. 439 on April 22, 1950. More copies were
put on the shelves that week to counteract a new-look
comic called ***The Eagle*** that launched that week. ***The
Eagle*** would go on to be a great comic, catering for a very
different audience than ***The Dandy***. From issue No. 447
on 17 June, 1950, the word 'Comic' was dropped from
the title – from now on it would just be ***The Dandy***.

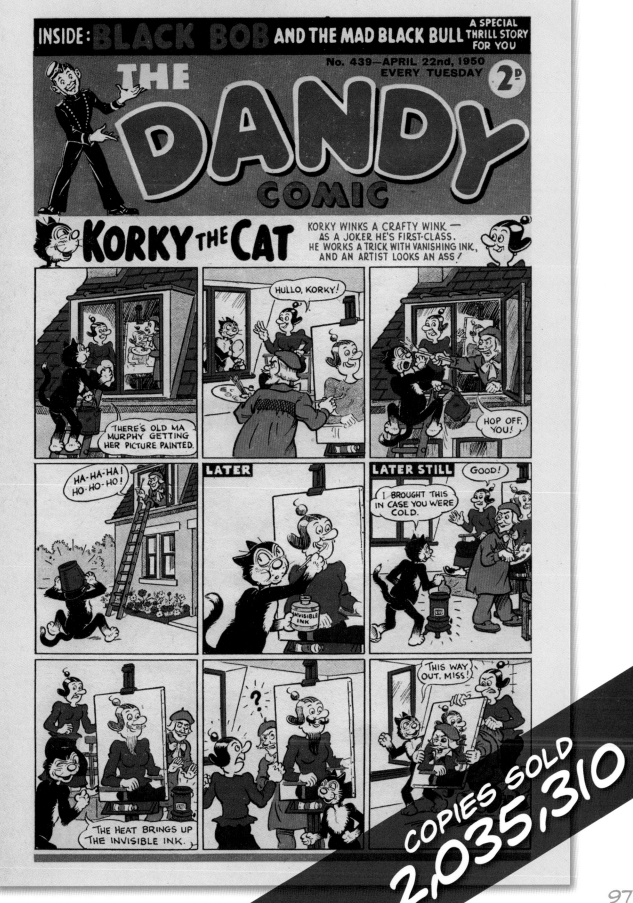

SCREWY DRIVER - 1955

DURING THIS golden era for the title Albert Barnes upgraded the content constantly. Picture strip adventure stories and cartoon pages replaced the text tales that were deemed to be old-fashioned by the bright young things of the 1950s.

Child inventor and great DIY fan, Screwy, loved to work with tools. Unfortunately, things rarely worked out as Screwy planned. Bill Holroyd was the artist.

THE SMASHER - 1957

THE DANDY'S answer to 'Dennis the Menace'. He was public enemy No. 1 to everything breakable. Whole cities of greenhouses fell to his catapult. He starred in *The Dandy* for almost fifty years. The original strip was drawn by Hugh Morren.

ADVENTURE STORIES

A SELECTION of the exciting adventure tales that *The Dandy* excelled in. The matching up of storyline to illustrator was done brilliantly. Of course Albert Barnes knew all about adventure stories, having started his editorial life on *The Wizard*.

TOMMY BROWN'S SLAVE 1950

Schoolboy Tommy Brown has a genie who protects him at all times. This classic set only ran for two months but was a massive success. Art was by Dudley Watkins and only his ever increasing workload stopped another series being done.

YOUNG FRANKIE DRAKE 1954

Seafaring adventures with a young Francis Drake. Dudley Watkins drew the first episodes then the story was picked up by Paddy Brennan.

TURTLE BOY 1956

London Kit, the shipwrecked boy, befriends a giant turtle. Together they look after each other and battle off treasure-seeking pirates. Again, this story uses Paddy Brennan's skill at action illustration.

The Invasion of Treasure Island: A story of London Kit, the castaway boy.

TURTLE BOY

WHAT a fearsome sight to see! In sheer surprise, London Kit, the castaway boy who lived all alone on Treasure Island, almost fell off the slippery back of his only friend, Shellback the turtle. For, climbing from the sea on to the reef that bordered the lagoon, was a crab—but such a crab as he had never seen in all his life before! It was a monster, with an immense body, huge eyes on the ends of thick stalks, and enormous claws that looked capable of nipping an iron bar in half. " Back to the beach, Shellback—quick !" gasped Kit.

A great story of THE DANDY'S famous Indian-fighter.

CRACKAWAY JACK

IN the pioneer days in the West, when waggon trains rumbled over the prairie to the golden lands of California, thousands of white settlers owed their lives to those fearless plainsmen who blazed the trails and fought off the savage Indians. Greatest of them all was Crackaway Jack, whose amazing exploit—the stealing of the Sacred Eagle Totem Pole of the Arapahoe tribe—had made him famous. The great Totem Pole was now held in Fort Resolution as a hostage for the good behaviour of the Arapahoes.

CRACKAWAY JACK 1955

Rip-roaring action Western with Crackaway Jack, the frontier scout. Paddy Brennan did the artwork and he relished *The Dandy Book* episodes where he would be given space for large and dramatic fight scenes, as shown here.

RUSTY - 1950

RUSTY WAS a cheeky little scamp who was quick with his fists or a catapult. The stories mostly revolved around home and school with parents and teachers the enemy. Very realistically drawn by Paddy Brennan, which seems a little at odds with the slapstick action in the storylines.

WILY SMILEY - 1952

MR MUTT - 1959

TWO NEW little strips from new artist A.G. Martin, always known to *The Dandy* editorial as George. He would become one of *The Dandy*'s stalwart artists and was the pen behind *The Topper*'s classic detective comedy 'Send For Kelly'.

In 'Wily Smiley the Jungle Joker', Wily Smiley uses his wits to put one over the jungle people and animals. Artist George Martin wrote a lot of the scripts himself, sending in beautiful little pencil sketches of his ideas which were stories without words. The strip ran for six years.

In 'Mr Mutt', the hapless teacher lives up to his name. The class put one over on Mutt on a daily basis. Pupil power from George Martin's brush in a strip that ran for nearly two years.

TIN LIZZIE - 1953

TIN LIZZIE was Professor Puffin's mechanical maid. She was joined in the strip by Brassribs, the robot butler. Both are the creation of the absent-minded Professor and instead of looking after him, they fight with each other. The strip started life as a text story but became an all-picture story in 1955. Jack ('Black Bob') Prout was the artist, with Charlie Grigg drawing a few of the later picture stories.

LITTLE ANGEL FACE - 1954

LITTLE ANGEL FACE is the prettiest, most demure, well-behaved girl anyone could imagine – until she is annoyed, that is. Boys especially find out the hard way that this little cutie is not at all what she seems. A strip that was ahead of its time and always looked a little out of place in *The Dandy.* Mind-boggling artwork from Ken Reid.

BING-BANG BENNY - 1956

THE DYNAMITE-HAPPY kid who uses explosives to protect his lawman father and their township. However, Benny's excessive use of dynamite usually brings everything down on his head. Hilarious stuff from the zaniest of all D.C. Thomson artists, the fabulous Ken Reid.

CHARLIE THE CHIMP - 1957

THE DESCRIPTION of the story went as follows 'Charlie the Chimp is a lovable imp – You'll meet him each week in this paper – He plays pranks galore and you'll laugh till you're sore – at every crazy caper.'

This pretty well sums up what went on in the strip. Charlie the chimpanzee becomes porter in the boarding house run by animal trainer Mr Marsden. Charlie is great friends with the son of the business, young Jack Marsden. Artist George Ramsbottom started the strip off but it is the sets by Charlie Grigg that most people remember.

CORONATION ISSUE

IT IS 2 June 1953, and a nation still in the grip of rationing finally gets the chance to let its hair down and party (a little)! The coronation of Queen Elizabeth II was, like her Diamond Jubilee earlier this year, a time for celebration and *The Dandy* was not about to miss the party!

Albert Barnes really pushed the boat out with this issue, in contrast with his stablemate comics. Where *The Beano*'s was a token effort at joining in the fun, Barnes's star characters are all enthusiastic participants in the celebration. 'Korky the Cat' made his way to London (with echoes of Dick Whittington played out in the introductory rhyme) to see the coronation procession, and 'Desperate Dan' made his way over the North Atlantic for the day.

The issue is full of the pageantry and colour of the occasion and, considering it was sent to the presses well ahead of the day itself, it is a remarkably accurate portrayal of the event! Perhaps the victory celebrations after the Second World War provided the inspiration: there is no doubt that the men who created it were truly proud to be British, and indeed they had done their duty in the war, fighting to preserve their nation for its new Queen.

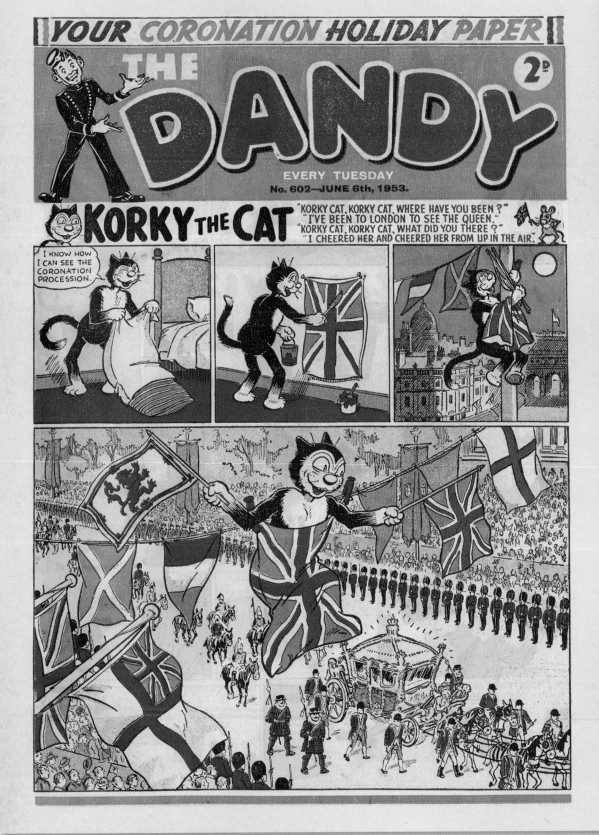

Flags aplenty wave as Korky the Cat bags the best 'sheet' in the house for the procession!

Hungry Horace gets his comeuppance for trying to take more than his fair share – a rationing morality tale? Freddy, meanwhile, finds a way to see the coronation procession.

Dan stops time in his efforts to see the coronation procession in London!

SNOW ! Yes, it is ! It's snow in the tropical Amazon jungle !

An Iced Drink.

IN his camp, deep in the thickly-wooded forest of the Amazon valley, Professor Puffin sat holding his nose. His mechanical maid, Tin Lizzie, was preparing a meal.

"You must have a bad egg there, Lizzie," gasped the Professor. "Something smells terrible !"

The Professor was in South America, leading an expedition in search of a lost Inca city. He was far from civilisation, but usually he never grumbled about his food.

Tin Lizzie was a super cook.

In fact, Tin Lizzie was super at every job she tackled, for although she wore a lace cap and apron, like an ordinary servant girl, she was really a robot.

She had been built by two of the Professor's inventor friends, who were anxious that he should have someone reliable to look after him on his dangerous expedition through the jungle.

Besides being able to do any job required, whether it was hacking down trees or fighting off wild animals, Tin Lizzie could think and talk, for she was fitted with a clever mechanical brain.

"It's not the eggs, Professor," she chirped in her shrill, tinny voice. "It's the cheese. It's gone a bit high, owing to the heat."

In fact all the food they had was suffering from the heat. The Professor lived mainly on tinned foods, which his native bearers carried for him, and it was all going bad. The tinned herring he had had for breakfast that morning had nearly walked out of their tin by themselves.

"It's you that's causing the trouble, Lizzie," muttered the Professor, glumly fanning his hot face with his hat. "Something's got to be done about you."

The terrific heat wasn't coming from the sun, although that was hot enough. Most of it was coming from Tin Lizzie.

A couple of days ago, because the cooking gear had been lost, she had turned herself into a walking stove and fried the Professor's eggs on her steel chest ! She had become red hot and she hadn't cooled down yet.

"I must look up the blueprints and instruction books that came with you, Lizzie," decided the Professor. "And in the meantime," he added hastily, "you'd better go and bury that cheese somewhere."

But Tin Lizzie didn't get a chance to do that. Just at that moment shrill cries of fear rose from the native bearers, who were camped beside the stores a few yards away.

They jumped to their feet, jabbering excitedly, and began climbing up trees in panic. The Professor looked round, startled, and then he saw the reason for their alarm.

Creeping out of the forest were dozens of lean, black shapes. Ugly animals with fierce, glittering eyes and sharp teeth.

"Giant rats !" yelped the Professor. "My goodness, there are scores of them ! If we don't drive them off, they'll eat up all our stores."

Tin Lizzie was already going into action against the rats. She hurled a bucket of water over them and then followed this by hurling the highly-smelling cheese into the middle of them. It was the cheese that stopped the rat invasion. The rats seized on it and carried it away into the forest with them.

"Thank goodness," panted the Professor, relieved. "We've got rid of the rats and the cheese as well. I don't know which was worse. But we shall have to move away from this spot at once. Now the rats know we have food here, they'll come back again."

"I'm not scared of rats," shrilled Tin Lizzie.

"I know," muttered the Professor. "But there's an Indian village not far from here. I don't want the Indians to know we are in their country. Any noise may attract their attention. And they may not be friendly."

The frightened bearers climbed down from the trees and started packing up the camp. It was while they were doing this that the Professor came upon the blueprints and instruction sheets that had been supplied with his mechanical maid. As he studied them, his frown suddenly cleared and he jumped up excitedly.

"Why, the whole thing's simple !" he exclaimed. "I should have studied this before. It says that in hot, tropical countries, your thermo-switch should be turned on."

"What's that ?" said Tin Lizzie.

"The book says it's a small switch behind your left ear for controlling your temperature. It cools you when you get too hot."

He peered behind Tin Lizzie's ear—or rather, the microphone that served her as an ear—and there was the tiny switch. He jerked it down.

At once he felt a wave of cool air.

"That's splendid," beamed the Professor. "Why, you're as good as a refrigerator, Lizzie ! Now perhaps you can fetch me a nice cold drink instead of the luke-warm stuff you've been serving up lately."

Tin Lizzie ambled off cheerfully and came back with a large jug of water. She tipped it towards the Professor's glass, but no water came out. She shook and banged the jug, but still no water poured out.

In desperation, she gave the jug a terrific wallop.

A big block of ice shot out and landed right in the Professor's lap.

"Ow !" howled the Professor, leaping up. He gazed at the ice in horror. "My goodness, I must have turned the switch too far ! Now you're freezing everything, Lizzie !"

The Retreat Of The Rats.

WAVES of icy cold air were coming from Tin Lizzie. Even the trees around her were withering and shedding their leaves. The Professor noticed that his hands were turning blue with cold and that the native bearers were shivering.

"D-dear me, this is t-too much of a good thing," mumbled the Professor, flapping his arms and blowing on his hands in an effort to keep warm. "We'll all catch colds. I'll have to turn that switch off again, Lizzie."

But when he tried to do that he had another shock. Tin Lizzie had turned so cold that the switch had frozen stiff. He couldn't shift it.

"M-my goodness, this is terrible," moaned the Professor, whose nose was turning blue now. "I've got to move that switch somehow. Hand me a hammer, Lizzie."

Lizzie cheerfully handed him one of the mallets used for knocking in tent-pegs. A few cracks on the head didn't worry her in the least. The Professor banged away furiously, but suddenly there was a sharp snapping noise and he paused in horror.

"Oh dear !" he howled. "Now I've done it ! I've broken the switch right off !"

There was no way of altering Lizzie's temperature now. She was getting colder and colder. Frost was beginning to form on her nose and eyebrows and the ground all around her was freezing hard.

"This is a calamity," gulped the shivering Professor. "You must keep in the sun, Lizzie. We'd better start marching. Perhaps that will warm you up."

But the native bearers had stopped packing the gear. They were building a huge fire and huddling round it in blankets.

"No can march," they mumbled. "Winter comes. We stay in camp."

"You can't stay in camp," howled the Professor. "What about the rats and the Indians ? And anyway it's not really winter !"

DANDY TWINS

The Editor expects to have the first list of prize-winners in the "Twins" competition ready for printing in THE DANDY two or three weeks from now.

'Tin Lizzie' would go on to be a picture strip, and run until 1960. Note the rather vague announcement about 'Dandy Twins' prizewinners.

Why did the penny stamp? —Because the threepenny bit.

But the natives refused to budge from the fire. The Professor was still arguing with them when there was a sudden scuffle in the undergrowth. Hordes of black shapes rushed towards the camp. It was the rats again.

"Lizzie!" howled the Professor. "Stop them! We won't have any food left if the rats get at it!"

Lizzie snatched up a bucket of water and charged at the rats. She hurled the water over them. But it had turned to a chunk of solid ice before it left her hands and nearly flattened the leading rats.

But that wouldn't have stopped them. It was the wave of freezing air coming from Tin Lizzie that stopped them. They skidded to a halt, shivering and sneezing.

Then they turned tail and bolted away from Tin Lizzie. But not before one of the boldest had seized a slab of bacon from the stores. It fled, carrying the bacon with it.

"Come back, you thief!" shrilled Tin Lizzie. "That's the Professor's supper!"

She charged after the fleeing rats. The Professor, in alarm, followed her.

"Never mind the bacon, Lizzie," he panted. "Let us get out of here!"

But Tin Lizzie was too far ahead to hear him. She clanked through the trees like a runaway steam roller, leaving a trail of withered leaves and frost.

Hurling rocks and chunks of frozen turf at the fleeing rats as she bounded along, she came over the crest of a hill.

Before her amongst the trees were palm-thatched huts. Outside one of them was a brown-skinned man with a spear. One of Tin Lizzie's chunks of turf caught him full in the chest and knocked him on his back.

"My goodness," howled the Professor, as he panted over the hill after Tin Lizzie. "It's the Indian village! And you've just laid out one of the Indians, Lizzie!"

The Snow Fight.

THERE was uproar in the Indian village. The sudden invasion of rats brought all the Indians scampering out of their huts. And when they saw it was Tin Lizzie who had driven the rats amongst them, they grabbed spears and went for her with yells of fury.

"Here's shelter," gasped the Professor, diving behind some big rocks.

The rocks stood at the base of a cliff, down which a small waterfall tumbled. Spray shot into the air as the torrent dashed down on the rocks.

Tin Lizzie ducked behind the rocks as spears came whizzing at them. And it was then that the Professor blinked up in amazement. Over Tin Lizzie's head the spray was freezing. It was turning into snowflakes!

"Good!" yelled Tin Lizzie. "That's just what we needed, Professor!"

She began scooping up the thickly-falling snow and rolling it into snowballs, she hurled the snowballs at the charging Indians.

Plonk! The leading Indian collapsed in amazement as a snowball burst in his face. He had never seen snow before.

The Indians halted, gaping. It was only around Tin Lizzie that the snow was falling. The rest of the country was still sweltering under the tropical sun.

Tin Lizzie bounded forward. Whizz! Smack! Plonk! More snowballs burst amongst the startled Indians. They prodded and goggled at the snowballs and then with yells of terror they fled into their huts.

"Now let's get out of here, Lizzie," gasped the Professor. "They'll soon recover from their fright. Then they'll come after us again."

He charged off, with Tin Lizzie clanking after him. When he got back to the camp, the bearers were busy preparing to march again. After Tin Lizzie's departure, the sun had warmed the freezing air and they had stopped shivering.

"You keep well in the rear, Lizzie," muttered the Professor. "I don't want you freezing up the bearers again or they'll refuse to march."

A few minutes later, with the Professor leading the way and Tin Lizzie bringing up the rear, the bearers resumed their march through the jungle.

And they were only just in time. Behind them they could hear a trampling amongst the trees and angry cries.

"It's the Indians," said the Professor. "They're after us again. Hurry!"

The bearers broke into a trot. The Professor pushed his way through the trees and then suddenly came to a halt with a yelp of dismay. Before him stretched a broad river.

"What's the hold up?" piped Tin Lizzie, clanking through the trees after him.

"This river," groaned the Professor. "How are we going to get across it? It's much too wide to make a bridge."

"We'll have to build a raft," chirped Tin Lizzie.

"There isn't time," moaned Puffin.

"Well, we'll have to swim," said Tin Lizzie.

But the Professor shook his head. He pointed across the water. Ugly, greenish-black snouts were breaking the surface.

"Alligators," he said. "The river is full of them. They'd tear us to pieces before we got halfway across."

There was still frost and snow clinging to Tin Lizzie. She strode forward and stepped into the water. At once the water around her began to freeze.

The ice spread farther and farther across. Soon it was thick enough to stand on.

"Get cracking, Professor," shrilled Tin Lizzie, up to her knees in ice.

The Professor wasted no time. He shouted orders and the amazed bearers crossed the ice to the other side of the river.

"Don't forget me," yelled Tin Lizzie after them. "You'd better fetch an ice-pick or something. I'm frozen in."

The Professor dashed back with a hatchet. He had to chop half a ton of ice away before he could get Tin Lizzie free.

But he succeeded at last and she clanked across the frozen river after him. Once she was on the other side, the heat of the sun began to melt the ice. By the time the Indians reached the bank, the ice had become water again.

The baffled Indians, unable to pursue the party any further, began to shoot arrows across the river. Tin Lizzie got caught in the shower and an arrow hit her behind the ear.

There was a sudden sharp click and immediately all the frost began to melt off Tin Lizzie.

"I'm cured, Professor!" shrilled Tin Lizzie. "That arrow's done the trick! It's worked the switch. I'm warming up again!"

She was right. The waves of freezing air were no longer coming from her.

When the Professor pressed on into the jungle a little later, Tin Lizzie was her old self again. She was quite warm. But fortunately she didn't get warm enough to turn any more food bad!

Next Tuesday in "The Dandy"— Tin Lizzie is in a bad way. Her body becomes so soft that even a baby could punch holes in her!

The Afghan with the iron will goes roaring along the iron way—

WILLIE THE WICKED

IT was holiday time, and Willie Wilson's Aunt Polly and Uncle Peter had decided that even a young rascal like their wicked nephew should have a few days at the seaside. Mustapha Kamel, the Afghan warrior appointed by Willie's Dad to protect people from the pranks of his awful offspring, couldn't possibly allow Wicked Willie off on his own, so he was going along, too. But the night before they left, Willie was busy with Musty's suitcase.

2—It was next day before the result of Wicked Willie's little job was known, and it was certainly a nasty piece of work! The young rascal had cleverly filed the hasp of Musty's case so that it would give way at a touch, and Willie gave it that touch just at the moment when the train was leaving! Walking alongside his guardian, whose hands were full of luggage, Willie stumbled against the Afghan. Musty's bag burst open, strewing his things all over the platform.

3—But that wasn't all, as Mustapha soon discovered. The scally-wag had tied bones and bits of sausages and old kippers to every one of the Afghan's possessions, with the result that every mongrel dog and stray cat within half a mile of the station came sniffing around. In two minutes, Musty's spare shirts and turbans were being carried to every quarter of the compass—and in less than two minutes the train to Bluepool was puffing out of the station!

4—Willie was safe in the last carriage with his aunt and uncle, and a great big grin appeared on his face when the train chugged off, for it left his guardian stranded without luggage, ticket, money, or even hope. "Musty won't be needing this," murmured the bad boy, and he calmly tore up the rail ticket that had been bought for Mustapha. At last he was free of the Afghan's eagle eyes and could do exactly as he liked! What marvellous fun he would have on his own!

5—But the courage of a hundred thousand fighting ancestors was in the blood of Mustapha Kamel, and with the tireless energy of a giant, he chased cats and dogs till he recovered his belongings. Then he tied up his case so that it couldn't burst open again, and hoisted it on his shoulder. Turning his bearded face in the direction of Bluepool, he set out along the railway, trudging in his bare feet from sleeper to sleeper for mile after mile. Musty knew his duty to Wilson Sahib. At all costs he must pursue the wicked one.

6—On and on, mile after weary mile, trudged Wicked Willie's guardian. Night fell, the sun went down, but Musty stayed on his feet and trod the sleepers. At last he came to Shrimpville Station. It was deserted. There were still many miles to go to Bluepool. Musty wasn't tired, but he had to hurry, for who knew what mischief Wicked Willie may have done by now? This was the station where "Puffing Percy," a historic old engine, was kept in a glass case, and when Musty saw it, he decided to speed up his long journey.

Willie is so naughty, his father hires an Afghan warrior to sort him out!

His iron steed is a century old—but it won't survive this day!

7—When the Shrimpville Station porters came on duty in the early morning, they were horrified to see that Puffing Percy's glass case was smashed, and the old relic stolen. They were mystified as well as horrified, for who would want to steal a hundred-year-old engine? Then Peter Postlethwaite, the booking-clerk, who read detective stories, looked for clues. "Ah! Tracks!" he exclaimed when he saw ruts in the platform made by the ancient wheels.

8—Mustapha Kamel was a powerful man. Alone, he had smashed the glass and pushed Puffing Percy along the platform and on to the rails. At that very moment, he was filling an old-fashioned coal-tender he had found in the engine-shed, and which he had coupled on to Percy. The fire under the boiler was lit, and Percy was puffing once more, although it was so long since steam had been raised in the ancient loco, that its puffing sounded more like wheezing!

9—Now, Peter Postlethwaite might have caught Musty if he hadn't got down on his knees to examine the ruts left by Puffing Percy's wheels. He was just rising, when a most unearthly wail rent the air and sent Peter flat on his back in surprise. The wail was the noise of Percy's whistle, unblown for a hundred years. Then to the ears of the railwaymen came a sound unheard for just as long— the rattle of Percy's wheels as the engine sped away into the dawn at a reckless ten miles an hour! "Get out a special!" yelled the station-master. "We'll catch that burglar, or my name's not Timothy Trout!" But this was easier said than done. Musty piled on the coal when he saw he was pursued. Puffing Percy groaned and moaned and crammed on speed till it was dashing on towards Bluepool at a speed far greater than it had ever reached before. For hour after hour it thundered on, crashing through level-crossings, and scaring dogs, cows and men just about out of their wits. But all this was too much for the old puffer. Disaster had to come.

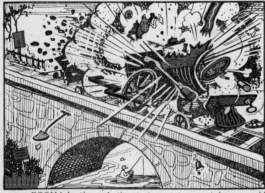

10—BOOM! In the end, the strain was too great for poor old Percy's rusty boiler. Just as Musty was crossing the bridge over the River Winkle, the explosion took place. Puffing Percy blew up, and scattered itself in little bits all over the landscape. Never again would it fill that big glass case at Shrimpville! Musty blew up with it, and it was lucky for him that there was a river underneath him to soften his fall. He hit it with a tremendous splash, and disappeared.

11—It was night before Musty reached Bluepool. He had got safely out of the river, but by the time he reached the Seaview Hotel, where the Wilsons were staying, the door was locked, and he had to climb all over the place before he found Wicked Willie's window. Ah! There he was at last, sleeping peacefully. Musty slid up the window and entered. As soon as he could lay hands on a cricket stump, he would be ready to wake up the wily wicked one!

Next week—Would someone be pulling Musty's leg?—For breakfast he gets a sea-serpent's egg!

The tremendous artwork is by Eric Roberts.

The deadly duel in the darkness of a ship's hold—
in a hanging forest of swinging chains.

CAT'S-EYE KELLY

Blackbeard The Pirate.

"PHEW! Isn't it ever going to stop raining?" asked Cat's-Eye Kelly as he clambered down into the hold of the old barge which served as a home for his gang. For the past few weeks there had been a continual downpour of rain in 17th century London, and it had made Cat's-Eye's job as a link-boy a very uncomfortable one. For Cat's-Eye had to guide the citizens of London through the pitch-dark streets.

The lad moved over to the glowing charcoal stove and started to peel off his wet garments. As he did so, the hatchway opened again to admit another lad with hair which was almost as red as Cat's-Eye's.

"Hello, Ginger," grinned Cat's-Eye. "Bringing your work home with you?"

The newcomer, Ginger Smith, was a gunsmith's apprentice, and he was carrying an armful of 17th century guns.

"I'm supposed to deliver these all around the town," confessed Ginger. "But it's so wet I'm going to leave them until morning. It may be drier then. But have you heard the news? Blackbeard Butcher has been captured and taken to Newgate Prison."

"Blackbeard Butcher?" echoed Cat's-Eye, his eyes widening in surprise. All England knew of the reign of terror which this pirate had brought to the high seas.

"Phew!" whistled Cat's-Eye. "What about his crew and ship?"

"Blackbeard was captured in Port o' Spain," said Ginger. "But his crew got away with the ship. I dare say by now they've elected another leader."

"Oh, well, there'll be some excitement in town tomorrow," declared Cat's-Eye. "But right now I'm for some sleep."

A chorus of agreement from the rest of his gang greeted this statement, and soon the dozen lads were curled up in their blankets. Dawn was breaking when suddenly Cat's-Eye sat up in his blankets. He had a feeling something was wrong. He glanced quickly up at the lantern in the ceiling and saw to his horror that it was swinging gently to and fro!

The barge was afloat!

"Hey! We're adrift!" he yelled as he flung his blankets to one side and bounded up the ladder.

Cat's-Eye half-expected to see the banks of the Thames slipping past, but he got a shock when he found that they were completely out of sight of land. The rain had at last stopped and a faint mist had come down, but as far as the anxious eyes of the boys could see there was nothing but water.

"She's never floated off before!" said Ginger. "She was securely tied."

"I expect it's all this rain coming downriver!" said Cat's-Eye. "It must have made the current so swift that it broke our moorings."

Some of the lads wanted to take to the water and strike out for land straight away, but Cat's-Eye would not allow this.

"We don't know in which direction land lies until this mist clears," he said. "And don't forget this barge is our home, and I for one am determined to get it back to the Thames."

Immediately there was a lot of excited discussion, but this was interrupted by an excited cry from Ginger Smith.

"Look!" he yelled.

The boys followed his pointing finger and saw a rowing-boat containing a slim figure.

"It's only a lad," said Cat's-Eye. "Let's get him aboard, gang."

They hailed the boy in the boat, and when he saw the barge he bent to his oars once more and rowed in their direction.

Willing hands helped him on to the barge, and Cat's-Eye saw that he was a thin, under-sized boy with pale, blue eyes.

Hardly had the newcomer's feet touched the deck before he blurted out—

"Quick! You must take me to London. I have urgent news."

"There's nothing I'd like better, friend," grinned Cat's-Eye. "But we can't steer this old barge. What's your name, and what is this news of yours?"

The boy sat down on the hatch-cover and buried his head in his hands.

"Too late!" he exclaimed. "He will get away now!"

"Who will?"

"Blackbeard Butcher! I'm the powder-monkey from his ship, the Black Maria. I was kidnapped from a British trader a year ago. A plot is afoot to rescue Blackbeard from Newgate. Some of his crew have smuggled themselves ashore with gold to

bribe the warders, and guns to fight with if necessary. They planned to get Blackbeard away from Newgate as soon as he arrived last night, and then take him to a hide-out they have in the Essex marshes."

"They'll never succeed," said Cat's-Eye.

"They have!" replied the boy. "During the night a pigeon brought news to the ship that the escape had been made. And even now the Black Maria is on its way to pick up its captain. There was so much excitement on board that I managed to lower a boat and escape. I had hoped to warn the Navy so that they could capture the pirate ship off the Essex coast."

Cat's-Eye's gang buzzed with excitement when they heard this news.

"With the fast tide that was running last night we should be off the Essex coast ourselves," said Cat's-Eye. "Maybe with luck we'll bump into an armed ship and can put them straight on Blackbeard's trail. And look! A ship! Coming our way!"

He pointed excitedly over the bow of the barge to where a big, three-masted ship was looming down on them.

The gang waved their arms and started to cheer, but the cheer died in their throats when they saw hanging limply from the topmast the dreaded black flag of piracy—the skull and crossbones!

"The Black Maria!" gasped Cat's-Eye.

Tom Jones, the powder-monkey from the pirate ship, went even paler when he saw the pirates approaching.

"They'll make me walk the plank if they get me back," he cried.

At once Cat's-Eye bundled the lad down the ladder and into the hold.

"Hide in here," he cried, pulling up some floorboards which covered the gang's food store. "You'd better take these, too. They're not much good without powder, but we'd better not let the pirates have them," and from Ginger Smith's bed he quickly collected the guns which the young gunsmith had brought home the night before.

Kidnapped.

BACK on deck, Cat's-Eye found the Black Maria hove-to alongside the barge, and grinning down from the ship's rail was a crowd of evil-looking pirates. But even as Cat's-Eye glared at them a voice thundered from the quarter-deck.

"Back to yer work, ye gang o' land-lubbers. D'ye think this is a pleasure cruise? Get every square inch of canvas up aloft, and look alive there."

"That will be Blackbeard," Cat's-Eye muttered to Ginger Smith. "They must have rescued him."

It was almost as if the pirate chief had heard Cat's-Eye speak, for in an instant he was bellowing again.

"Heave to, below there," roared Blackbeard. "We need another powder-monkey to take the place of Jones. Grab that red-headed lad. He looks a likely sort of rip!"

Cat's-Eye guessed that Blackbeard was referring to him, and at once he decided that he wasn't to be captured without a struggle.

"Keep your hands off me," he roared as half a dozen brawny pirates dropped down on to the deck of the barge.

"Yes, leave him alone!" echoed the gang. And in a few moments a pitched battle was raging on the barge. Cat's-Eye and his gang were so angry that their fury lent them strength, and the six pirates were having a tough time of it as they fought with the yelling, battling boys.

Two of the pirates were hurled bodily into the sea, and the boys might easily have won the battle had not more of the Black Maria's crew joined in. When these extra men arrived Cat's-Eye and his gang didn't have a chance. They were overpowered by sheer weight of numbers.

"You'll pay for this!" panted Cat's-Eye as he was carried struggling on to the deck of the pirate ship. "I'll never serve your guns!"

'Cat's-Eye Kelly' is another text story which went on to become a picture story, drawn by Jack Glass.

Who is given the sack as soon as he starts work?—The postman.

"Oh, won't you? We'll see about that, me hearty!" came a loud roar, and Cat's-Eye Kelly found himself face to face with the famous Blackbeard Butcher.

He was a big man with a chest like a barrel, and thin, cruel lips.

"When I want to make a boy my powder-monkey, he will be my powder-monkey!" thundered Blackbeard, drawing his huge cutlass. "Take him below, master gunner. Lock him in the hold for a bit. That'll cool his temper."

"This way," snarled the gunner as he dragged Cat's-Eye below decks. "By the time you've been in the hold for an hour or two you'll be hollering for mercy."

The gunner gave a nasty chuckle, and Cat's-Eye wondered just what was so horrible about the hold.

When he found out, his heart leaped with hope, for the chief danger about the hold was its darkness and the scores of heavy chains swinging from the ceiling.

"Ah! You can see to dodge the chains all right while I've got this door open," sneered the master-gunner. "But after the door is shut . . ."

Cat's-Eye's brain started to work like lightning. Clearly the magazine was used as a punishment-chamber where the members of the crew were put when they disobeyed orders. A couple of hours locked in the total darkness, with every movement of the ship bringing a chain clanking round about their ears would be enough to cool down the most angry member of the crew.

But Cat's-Eye realised that it would be no hardship for him. His strange, green eyes could easily pierce the darkness, and he would have no difficulty in dodging the heavy chains.

With an evil chuckle the master-gunner turned to leave the hold, but in a flash Cat's-Eye turned and gave the man a push.

"Hey! What——" spluttered the man, and he staggered sideways. But the pirate was a quick thinker. Even as he fell he pushed out his foot and slammed the door. And before Cat's-Eye could get it open the pirate was on his feet with cutlass drawn.

Bitterly disappointed that his bid to escape had failed, Cat's-Eye was forced to retreat. But as he did so he drew the little dagger which he used for trimming his link torch. Then the two stood facing one another in the blackness—dagger against cutlass and sight versus blindness!

Cat's-Eye's Gunpowder Plot.

THE ship gave a sudden roll, and Cat's-Eye saw his opponent stagger back as one of the swinging chains hit him on the chin.

Some empty kegs were stacked against the walls of the hold, and, reaching down, Cat's-Eye picked up one of these kegs and sent it rolling towards the man. The pirate heard it coming and made a blind swipe with his cutlass. With a ringing clang, the blade connected with one of the chains. The jar fairly jolted the gunner's arm, for he gave a cry of pain.

This was the moment Cat's-Eye was waiting for. With upraised dagger he dived forward, neatly side-stepping the chains, and closed with his opponent. The master-gunner gave a hoarse cry and tried to leap sideways—straight into one of the chains! Cat's-Eye crouched, ready to spring again. But there was no need for a further attack. The chain had done its work well, and the master-gunner lay unconscious on the floor.

"Phew! That was a risky business," panted Cat's-Eye. He opened the door, and glanced up and down the passageway. There was no one in sight, and just across the passage Cat's-Eye saw an open door leading to the ship's magazine. Here was

a chance to get even with Blackbeard.

He hurried into the magazine and quickly prised the bung out of a keg of powder. Then he laid a long trail from the door to the rest of the kegs. Next, with his tinder and flint, he set light to the powder trail.

"That should burn through in about five minutes," he murmured, eyeing the length of the powder trail.

Then he locked the magazine door and tucked the key in his jacket.

The pirates were so astonished at seeing Cat's-Eye that they just gazed in amazement as the lad tore across the deck and up on to the bridge.

"Where did you spring from?" howled Blackbeard as he turned to face Cat's-Eye with drawn cutlass.

"From the magazine," answered Cat's-Eye.

Scotland's Biggest Treasure

It is Prince Charlie's gold—and there's trouble in store for the two ship-wrecked guardians of it.

Their thrilling story, told in pictures, begins next week, under this title:—

Westward Ho With Prince Charlie's Gold

"Your master-gunner is unconscious below decks, and inside the magazine I've laid a burning powder trail. In five minutes this ship will be blown sky-high!"

The pirate's face turned purple with anger, and for a moment Cat's-Eye thought the man would burst.

"Where's the key?" howled Blackbeard.

"Here!" said Cat's-Eye, holding up the massive key. And then, before anyone could stop him, the lad drew back his arm and hurled the key far out across the sea, where it disappeared below the waves.

"I'll cut you in half for that!" screamed Blackbeard, hurling himself at Cat's-Eye. But the boy leaped lightly over the bridge rails and raced across to the ship's side.

"You've got four minutes to abandon ship!" he shouted, and then turned and dived into the water.

Once in the water Cat's-Eye struck out strongly for the barge, which was now some distance behind. Several times he heard bullets whistling over his head, but the pirates were not taking time to aim. They were panic-stricken at the thought of the smouldering magazine below them.

As he ploughed through the water, Cat's-Eye could hear the sounds of the pirates trying to break down the magazine door, but when he looked back and saw them lowering their boats he guessed the heavy door had withstood all their attacks.

"We thought we'd seen the last of you, Cat's-Eye," gasped Ginger Smith as Cat's-

Eye climbed on board. "What happened?"

Breathlessly Cat's-Eye poured out his tale, but before he had said many words a thunderous explosion echoed across the water. All eyes turned towards the Black Maria. The pirate ship was enveloped in flames, and a great cloud of black smoke was soaring skywards. Cat's-Eye's gunpowder plot had worked beautifully!

"That's the end of Blackbeard Butcher and his career of piracy," said Ginger Smith, but hardly were the words out of his mouth when a score of bullets whistled about the boys' heads.

"Not quite the end," said Cat's-Eye as the lads flung themselves to the deck. "Blackbeard is out for revenge."

Things looked grim for Cat's-Eye and his gang. The pirates were rowing in their direction and firing as they came.

"Wouldn't be so bad if we could fire back," muttered Cat's-Eye. "But all we can do is sit here and wait for the end."

"No, it isn't!" cried Ginger Smith excitedly. "I've got those guns I brought from the shop, and there's some powder and shot in my locker."

"Well, what are we waiting for?" cried Cat's-Eye, and in a few moments every one of the gang was armed.

Blackbeard and his crew were amazed to have their fire returned, and when one or two of them slumped at their oars, the remainder would have retreated had not Blackbeard himself urged them forward.

Brandishing a brace of pistols, the pirate chief threatened to shoot any of his men who stopped rowing, and the buccaneers had to bend to their oars.

Highly delighted at the chance of getting his own back on some of the pirates, Tom Jones, the ex-powder-monkey from the Black Maria, beamed all over his face as he rammed home powder and ball and fired as fast as he could.

"Make every shot tell, lads," cried Cat's-Eye. "Remember we've not got a lot of powder and shot."

The link-boy cuddled the stock of his gun well into his cheek and sighted along the long, engraved barrel. The pirates' boats, bobbing up and down in the water, made a difficult target, but Cat's-Eye's green eyes were as good in the daylight as they were in the dark. With finger tensed on the trigger, he waited until he saw the unmistakable figure of Blackbeard Butcher in his sights, and then he fired.

"You got him!" cried Tom Jones. "Blackbeard is down!"

A great cheer went up from the boys, and they started firing faster than ever. A few more pirates fell, then suddenly the boats swung round and began to row away rapidly.

"They're fleeing," shouted Tom Jones. "We've licked them."

"It wasn't only us," said Cat's-Eye, and he pointed astern. Bearing down on them was a frigate. It rapidly overhauled the pirates, and the wounded Blackbeard and his crew were taken aboard. Then the skipper steered alongside the old barge.

He explained that they had heard the big explosion, and had come to see what it was all about. He praised the boys for what they had done. And when, some time later, the frigate sailed up the Thames, she had

in tow the old black barge complete with flying colours—lent by the frigate's skipper.

Next Tuesday in "The Dandy" — Cat's-Eye's red hair gets him into trouble —but his green eyes get him out of it!

'Westward Ho With Prince Charlie's Gold', drawn by Paddy Brennan, is flagged up as a new story for the following week.

A brave girl's death-defying ride to fetch help for her father!

THE TICKLER TWINS on the REDSKIN TRAIL

POOR Tessie Tickler was just about all in. Here she was speeding on a stolen horse towards Fort Apache, with an arrow stuck in her shoulder and a pack of Indians chasing her. Things were looking pretty hopeless for Tessie, when suddenly a long, yawning crack in the ground loomed up ahead of her. Urging her mount into a furious gallop she made for the narrowest part of the gaping chasm. The horse made the leap of its life and landed safely.

2—Tessie had been sent by Steve Lundigan, the Pony Express rider, to Fort Apache for help when a troop of cavalrymen had been surrounded in a grove of trees by scalp-hunting Indians. Now the trail to the fort led Tessie down a steep-sided canyon which was joined now and again by smaller canyons. She was just passing the mouth of one when a bullet came from nowhere and brought her horse crashing down. Tessie fell to the ground like a stone.

3—Tessie hadn't seen her attacker, but it was Black Jack, the outlaw. He and his henchman had been led on a false trail by Steve's horse, Wildfire, for Steve had sent the horse away with straw dummies in the carrier baskets and saddle. Tessie lay there limp as a rag. She was weak from her wound and she had been knocked dizzy by the fall. Wildfire came charging towards her, then skidded to a sudden halt. He bent his head, gave a whinny of joy, and grabbed Tessie by the slack of her dress with his strong teeth.

4—Tessie was lifted from the ground, and Wildfire started to gallop off with his heavy mouthful down the trail for Fort Apache. But Wildfire wouldn't have got very far had it not been for the Indians who were after Tessie's blood! They ran smack into the two outlaws, when the latter came charging out of a side canyon. This was the start of a furious fight, outlaw guns against Red men's arrows, and, while it raged, Wildfire got clean away with his burden. The intelligent horse made off in the direction of Fort Apache.

5—Tessie soon recovered consciousness, but it took her a minute or two to fathom why she was hanging upside down. Pulling hard on the reins, she persuaded Wildfire to stop and set her down. She heaved the straw dummies on to the trail then dragged herself into the saddle. "Gee up, Wildfire," she muttered, and held on grimly as Wildfire sped like the wind over the dusty ground. Tessie was just about done for when at last she sighted Fort Apache.

6—Once inside the gates, she sought out the officer in charge and gave him Steve's message. Meanwhile, back at the scene of the ambush, Steve was already working on a plan to help the besieged cavalrymen. Using his knife, he had cut two rings in the thick bark right round the trunk of a tree. The rings were about seven feet apart. Drawing his knife downwards to form a slit, he and Tim then began to ease off the stout bark, using sticks as wedges.

'The Tickler Twins' was one of a long line of 'Cowboy and Indian' stories in **The Dandy**.

Two human tree trunks in a death or glory charge!

7—The bark was stripped off in one piece, which formed a hollow, pipe-like cylinder. With his keen-bladed knife, Steve divided the cylinder into two equal parts and scooped peep-holes in each. With these wooden "jackets" covering the top half of their bodies, the daring riders mounted, and sallied forth into the thick of the attack. Firing through slots on both sides, Steve took the Indians by surprise. They gaped in amazement at the horse with gun-turrets.

8—The Indians' surprise was short-lived. They soon saw that this was no new-fangled war-machine. Steve and Tim were struck by a hail of arrows—but they had no effect! The arrows just lodged in the bark like pins in a cushion. Their horse was brought down, but they landed on their feet and ran for the thicket. And now a surprise awaited Steve and Tim. There were only three cavalrymen left alive in the wood. The troop was all but wiped out!

9—"Tim, my boy," cried one of the men after Tim and Steve had taken off their masks. Tim did not recognise the battle-weary, blood-stained soldier, but he knew the voice—it was his father's! "Dad!" shouted Tim in excitement. He rushed over to his father's outstretched arms. "I'm sure grateful for all you've done, my man," said Captain Tickler, speaking to Steve. "But what's happened to Tessie? Did she not come with you?" The captain was a proud man when Steve told him how his daughter had gone off

on her own to Fort Apache for help. A loud whoop made the three look round. The Indians had banded together and were heading in a mass for the thicket. But neither Steve nor the Captain fired a single shot. Before the Indians were a hundred yards from the thicket the relief force of cavalry came charging along amidst the blare of trumpets. What a thrill it was for the watchers in the wood to see these cavalrymen sweeping along in a thundering charge that crushed the wild Indians and routed them completely.

10—Captain Tickler, Tim and Steve were soon taken to Fort Apache. Tessie's shoulder had been patched up by the doctor and she rushed out to greet her father. "Daddy! Daddy!" whooped Tessie. Captain Tickler scooped his little girl up in his arms and whirled her round like a roundabout. "Welcome to your new home, Tessie!" he cried. "You're a brave little trooper. I'm proud of you."

11—This was truly a red letter day for the captain. At last he had his family around him, and the perils of the Wild West were forgotten. At night, in the dining hall, a great banquet was given for the three adventurers. Even Wildfire was allowed inside, and he got a special cheer all to himself. The Tickler Twins were home at last, at the end of that long and dangerous Redskin Trail.

Next Tuesday in " The Dandy "—Great new story in pictures begins. It is WESTWARD HO WITH PRINCE CHARLIE'S GOLD.

George Ramsbottom, who drew this strip, was given a lot of Western stories to illustrate by Albert Barnes.

It's a calamitous coronation for Rusty, whose fireworks display goes with a real bang! The explosive art is by Paddy Brennan. Keyhole Kate makes a very personal flag, drawn by Allan Morley.

BLACK BOB

Drawn here with his master Andrew Glenn, from whom Black Bob is often separated. Many stories deal with dangerous, difficult, or unfortunate situations and Bob's need to be reunited with his owner.

ONE OF the foundation blocks in the success of 'Black Bob' was the wonderfully atmospheric artwork used in the story title drawings.

This was the work of Manchester-born Jack Prout, a D.C. Thomson staff artist who worked in the Dundee art studio. Jack joined the firm in 1923, aged twenty-four, and worked mainly for D.C. Thomson's women's magazines. His weekly workload would see him illustrating scenes from perhaps three differing stories. With such a high demand and emergency wartime staffing, the Dundee studio artists had to be flexible. However, in 1944, his talents as a dog artist were discovered by **The Dandy**.

Jack had served in the First World War, where he was wounded. During the Second World War he was in **The Courier** Home Guard Company which was made up entirely of D.C. Thomson staff including Dudley Watkins. After a day at the drawing board the men would leave the studio, get into uniform and turn out at company HQ. Much time was spent in exercises and in drills preparing for the defence of the town should invasion occur.

In 1946 everything changed for 'Black Bob' and his creators. D.C. Thomson's newspaper-come-magazine, **The Weekly News**, decided to run 'Black Bob' in a picture strip format every week. **The Dandy** editorial staff, now back to full strength after the war, reworked the prose stories into picture and text scripts. Jack Prout dropped his varied workload to concentrate on drawing the Wonder Dog.

BLACK BOB
THE WISEST SHEEP-DOG IN SCOTLAND !

Every boy and girl is sure to be thrilled by the amazing adventures of Black Bob as he finds his way through England to his home in the hills.

Black Bob will be the pet of every reader of " The Dandy."

His True Story Starts IN A FORTNIGHT !

He was now doing a **Dandy** heading plus a picture strip every week. Within eighteen months it was decided that Jack should stop drawing in the studio and work from home, where he could better concentrate on 'Black Bob'.

JUST STARTING—The Adventures Of Scotland's Wonder Sheep-Dog!

BLACK BOB

KIDNAPPED! BOB BREAKS FREE LOST IN LIVERPOOL ON THE WAY HOME

The Prisoner.

BLACK BOB poked his soft, black nose between the wooden bars and sniffed anxiously.

He could not tell where he was, or why he was there. He had never been shut in a box before and he did not like it. There was scarcely room for him to stand; across the top of the box had been nailed slats of wood. Black Bob pushed at these with all his might, but they did not budge.

His head ached and he was very thirsty. Some of the things that had happened to him recently were rather hazy in his memory, but he knew one thing for certain: His troubles were due to Jake Lang, the farmer who lived at the top of the lane from Black Bob's own home.

Black Bob was a sheep-dog, a Border Collie, sleek and shapely and five years old, ... jet black with a little . . .

thick stick in it and—Whang!—Black Bob had received a blow on the head which had knocked him senseless.

When he had recovered his wits he was in this box, with a strange collar round his neck and the feeling that he was being driven along in a motor-lorry. All night they had travelled southwards and all night Black Bob had tried to escape, without any success. Soon after dawn the lorry had stopped in a yard in a great city and the box had been lifted out by two strange men.

Bob had whined at them and had looked at them with his beautiful brown eyes, asking to be released, but one of the pair had growled:

"You stop where you are, laddie. Maybe they'll give you better quarters when you're on the ship bound for America."

That had been an hour ago and the box had been left ever since. Nobody had come near the imprisoned dog and nobody had offered to quench his thirst.

The poor sheep-dog could hear the rumble of traffic and the honking of motor . . .

Bob tucked his tail down and scampered on to the pavement. He had forgotten he was no longer in the country. The road was busy with traffic. There were lorries and cars, buses and trams, horses with carts and many other vehicles. There were so many whirring wheels that he got giddy looking at them and sat down on the pavement to steady himself.

The next moment he got a kick in the ribs and a man almost stumbled over him.

"Hey, get out of the way, you brute!" roared the angry human. "Where do you think you are?"

The dazed and bewildered sheep-dog got close to the wall and gazed about him in amazement. He had never seen so many people in all his life. They were pouring down the street in both directions. There were more people than he had ever seen at Selkirk market. Where they were all going and why they were in such a hurry, was marvel to him. People had never . . . such a hurry in the countryside. . . .

The MAD BAD DOG of Tinker's Hill

ON MAY 5, 1956 Black Bob's adventures in *The Dandy* were shown in picture strip for the first time. This was a resizing of first series from *The Weekly News* and was part of the trend that saw the text stories being phased out in all the comics.

The prose stories had run in *The Dandy* for eleven years, with twenty-one different series, all written

From prose style to picture story style. Black Bob's adventures were shown in **The Dandy** *in picture strip for the first time on May 5, 1956.*

by Kelman Frost. The prose format was deemed boring compared to the exciting graphics of the picture series. Now *Dandy* readers could get a better look at shepherd Andrew Glenn and his wonder border collie and they would be able to put faces to the various characters that inhabited the villages and glens in the Selkirk hills where Bob lived and worked.

Editor Albert Barnes and his sub-editors on *The Dandy* would all write 'Black Bob' storylines. Over the years Bill Swinton, Ron Caird, Jim Simpson, Iain Munro and Dave Torrie all contributed notable work to keep this magical series at the forefront. Jack Prout continued to do all the artwork which still appeared in *The Weekly News* first then in *The Dandy*.

Black Bob would find many unusual beasts and people in the Selkirk hills. In addition he would visit and have adventures in many different countries in North and South America, Africa and Australia.

THE WEEKLY NEWS was a top-selling publication. By the end of 1946, with paper restrictions lifted, it was selling over a million copies every week. It had a great name for light-hearted entertainment and 'Black Bob' shared his page with either a comic strip or a collection of cartoons. 'Black Bob' ran this way for an amazing twenty-one years, until September 1967.

Jack Prout did not draw his nine frame strip as a single page, like most strip artists did – instead Jack drew each frame individually, one single frame on his drawing board at a time. He said that this way he could do each as a single little masterpiece and not be distracted by the rest of the page.

He drew the frames slightly larger than the paper used them, and each week he would hand to **The Dandy** *editor an envelope containing nine beautiful eight-by-four-inch drawings.* **The Dandy** *staff would then put the strip together and do the write-up. The type was set separately and stuck with glue to the made-up pages by the cut-and-paste layout artist.*

Former chief sub-editor of **The Dandy**, *Dave Torrie, would marvel at the speed and rough hand Jack would use to do his pencil sketches, which he would then show to editor Albert Barnes for approval. If changes were to be made he would do them instantly as the editor watched. All the intricate detail and rendering was added when doing the final inking.*

WITH HIS terrific tales appearing in two national publications, the popularity of 'Black Bob' grew rapidly. It was no great surprise then that *The Dandy* editor Albert Barnes started to put together a collection of 'Black Bob' picture and prose stories for the Christmas market of 1949 (the book would be officially dated 1950) to join the very successful *Dandy* and *Beano* annuals that were much sought after as Christmas gifts. This 128-page book was titled simply **BLACK BOB *The Dandy Wonder Dog***, and was an unusual oblong shape which suited the proportion of *The Weekly News* artwork. Albert mixed text and strip stories, broken up with various doggy features. All the story artwork was by Jack Prout. This was the first of a series of books – in all eight were produced between 1949 and 1965.

In September 1967 the strip was discontinued in *The Weekly News* and Jack officially retired six months after this. He still did individual 'Black Bob' sets for *The Dandy Book* and *The Dandy Summer Special*. From time to time he would do a new character for Albert Barnes – his last one was the unusual 'Tomtin and Buster Brass'. Jack was drawing animals again but this time they were mechanical.

The old series were reprinted in *The Dandy* weekly until July, 1982 (see page 202).

'Black Bob' books, now very collectible, were produced for the Christmas market. (Eight were produced between 1949 and 1965.)

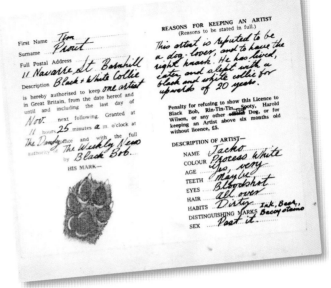

Jack with Timmy and the fake licence allowing the dog to keep Jack as a pet artist.

AFTER JACK PROUT put down his pencils for good *The Dandy* editor couldn't find anyone to fill his shoes. He had stamped his distinctive style on 'Black Bob' and no one else could draw it quite like him. In fact some even refused to try. Jack was so meticulous he would often draw three different versions of every single panel and give them to Albert Barnes to choose which one to use. It was a bit like putting a jigsaw together!

Prout's father lived until he was well over 100 years old and when Jack said he was considering retiring, Albert Barnes said 'What do you mean? You still have another thirty years of work in you!' He didn't want to lose one of his best artists.

When Jack retired he was given a black-and-white border collie just like Black Bob and on his last day the Art Department presented Jack with a licence for his dog Timmy, allowing the animal to keep Prout as a pet! It was signed by Black Bob himself with a muddy paw print. Unlike the champion sheepdog, however, Timmy wasn't so well-behaved. Some wondered whether it was Jack taking the dog for a walk or Timmy taking him!

Jack Prout drew this sketch as a joke for Albert Barnes showing how Black Bob would really look after all his numerous scrapes and adventures over the years.

127

BLACK BOB
THE ARTISTS

JACK PROUT
GEORGE RAMSBOTTOM
PETER FOSTER
KEITH ROBSON

JACK PROUT'S artwork never varied from its high quality. Some of his most beautiful scenes were taken from real life. An old bridge near Aberfeldy in Perthshire was the inspiration for the classic scene on the right. When Jack was unwell or swamped by his workload, only one other artist was regularly allowed to put pen to Black Bob.

He was another veteran D.C. Thomson staff artist, George Ramsbottom, 'Rammer' to his pals. On occasions, and these were very rare occasions, George would be called in to draw an episode. His period style, and that period was closer to the twenties and thirties than anything else, fitted with the classic 'Black Bob' look. Jack Prout approved of George's take on his beloved character. A complete strip of George Ramsbottom is shown over the page.

CONTENTS

A selection of 'Black Bob' drawings by Jack Prout and some sample pages from Ray Moore's **Dandy Monster Index** *recording specific appearances of 'Black Bob' over the years (see also the character index at the back of this book).*

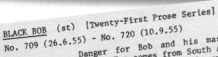

BLACK BOB (st) [Twenty-First Prose Series]
No. 709 (26.6.55) - No. 720 (10.9.55)

  Danger for Bob and his master Andrew Glenn, when Andrew's cousin Tom comes from South America to stay in the glen and is followed by his enemy, the evil lion tamer Salvador.

     Art: Jack Prout

129

Black Bob's battle in the swirling waters of the Black Pot.

PROFESSOR BURTON was a familiar figure on the hills near Selkirk. Every week-end he came to search for traces of Pictish and Roman dwellings. One day, Andrew Glenn and Black Bob found him digging beside the banks of Torry Water. He was very excited. " I've just found the site of a Roman camp !"

2—Glenn congratulated the professor then he and Bob went on their way. Later, however, Black Bob was near the river again. Suddenly he heard an excited shout. The professor climbed out of a hole holding a big earthenware vase. But in his excitement he missed his footing. He plunged into the river.

3—At once Black Bob dashed to the rescue, but the professor shouted to him, " Never mind me, Bob ! Save that vase !" The professor was more concerned about it than about his own safety. Black Bob saw that the professor was swimming quite well, so the collie leapt into the water and swam after the vase.

4—But what the professor didn't know was that the Black Pot lay just ahead. This was a whirlpool that sucked the water into an underground channel and emerged under the Falls of Torry, half a mile away. Black Bob had recovered the vase when he saw the professor being swept into the centre of the whirlpool.

5—The professor was not a strong swimmer and he was drawn nearer and nearer to the centre of the whirlpool. Finally he was dragged under the surface and whirled towards the hole in the river bed. Then he felt Black Bob's teeth grip his trouser leg.

6—Black Bob swam strongly away from the centre of the whirlpool, dragging the professor slowly behind him. It took the plucky collie a long time, fighting against the powerful current, but at last he managed to drag the professor ashore.

7—But instead of being pleased at his escape. Professor Burton could only sit and call himself stupid names for losing the vase. " It's probably smashed to smithereens by now," he groaned. But Black Bob had dived back into the river.

8—The collie emerged with the precious vase from the river, where it had sunk when he had gone to the professor's aid. The professor was overjoyed. Later, when he wrote a book about his finds, the professor presented a copy of it to Bob's master.

Next week—The start of an exciting new story. Three pages of Wild West adventure! Watch for CRACKAWAY JACK.

GEORGE RAMSBOTTOM   *George drew the 'Black Bob' strip when Jack Prout was unavailable.*

BLACK BOB

THE ARTISTS

The original 'Black Bob' strip did make it to full colour in the comic, but later some strips were coloured and had speech bubbles added, as in this example from the 1991 **Dandy Book**.

PETER FOSTER

WHEN MORRIS HEGGIE took over as *The Dandy* editor in 1986, he tried hard to recreate a modern classic 'Black Bob' series. He attempted to persuade Paddy Brennan, who was a wonderful animal artist, to accept the commission but after doing pencil sketches he never continued, saying he loved the original Bob and couldn't get close to it.

As Heggie said: 'For the 1989 *Dandy Book* I persuaded the talented Australian artist Peter Foster to do a "Bob" set. His work did not feel like Black Bob so I retitled the story "Rip". For the 1990 *Dandy Book* I got together with artist Keith Robson. Keith and I are old friends and he knew exactly what I was looking for, so he did not do it!'

'When an artist of the calibre of Keith says forget it you have to listen. We changed tack and did "Young Black Bob" who was from the same lineage as the original "Bob" and owned by Andrew Glenn's nephew. Good, but a compromise.'

KEITH ROBSON

NEW ARTISTS

BILL HOLROYD

BILL HOLROYD drew some of *The Dandy*'s best loved characters and was a very influential artist in the comic's development. He started working for *The Dandy* after the war, in 1948, drawing 'Plum MacDuff the Highlandman Who Never Gets Enough'.

His most popular character as far as *The Dandy* readers were concerned was the amazing metal boy, 'Brassneck', which started in 1964. The sets were always two pages and Bill packed them with crazy action. Bill's partnership with *The Dandy* chief sub-editor, Dave Torrie, who wrote the story ideas, produced some of the zaniest and imaginative comic strips seen during the sixties and seventies (see page 134). Bill drew many other characters for *The Dandy* and each one, from 'Wuzzy Wiz, Magic is His Biz' to 'Jack Silver' about an alien boy (see page 136), was a comic masterpiece.

The Tricks of Screwy Driver.

Willie Fixit

Brassneck.

At least that's how it seemed to the men in the Hovercar. But they reckoned without Jinky Baker. The fire engine had arrived outside the ground and, perched up on the big extending ladder, Jinky had seen what had happened. What could he do to foil the Hovercar Snatchers? His mind racing, Jinky yelled instructions, and the firemen fixed their high-pressure hose to the nearest water hydrant. Then, as the Hovercar headed for the gap in the fence, Jinky turned the hose on it!

WHOOSH! The powerful jet of water smashed into the windscreen of the Hovercar. The mystery car dipped violently as the water struck home. Blinded by the spray, the driver fought desperately to control the Hovercar. But it had been knocked off course—and it went hurtling straight towards the fence.

'The Hovercar Snatchers' had meticulously illustrated spreads by Bill.

The first instalment of the highly popular 'Jack Silver' series.

One of Bill's early strips, starting in 1949 – 'Wuzzy Wiz, Magic is His Biz'.

METAL MENACE

Brassneck kept cool. Head down, he charged the bull and butted it between the eyes!

GOSH! I HOPE BRASSNECK HASN'T INJURED THAT PRIZE BULL!

TAKE THAT, YOU BULLY!

Brassneck tackles a bull head on.

BRASSNECK

1964 SAW one of the great *Dandy* comic adventure strips make its debut, namely 'Brassneck'. The memorable strip was drawn by Bill Holroyd and the first series ran from December 5, 1964 (issue 1202) until February 24, 1968 (issue 1370). When Charley Brand visits his inventor Uncle Sam's house for a holiday, he gets into so much mischief, because he is bored, that his Uncle builds him a mechanical pal to play with.

And from that moment, young Charley Brand had a unique and very special friend, whom he named Brassneck – a pal made out of metal and electronic circuits – a walking, talking robotic marvel, so technologically advanced that he could think for himself and take part in all the activities that his close human friend Charley enjoyed. Together they were a sixties dream team, exponents of typical *Dandy* pranks and nonsense.

Brassneck was forever getting Charley Brand into bother, but always saved the day by rescuing him from whatever mess he had got Charley into, with his telescopic limbs proving useful in many difficult situations. The genius of Holroyd – fantastic artwork – gave this unlikely partnership a magical charm that captured the

OH GOSH! LET'S GET OUT OF HERE, BRASSNECK!

imagination of every *Dandy* reader, whether it was a tussle with the bully of a teacher called Snodgrass or overcoming the evil Swotty who kidnapped and dismantled Charley Brand's robotic chum. 'Brassneck' was the inspiration for *Viz* Comic's 'Tinribs' – a sign that a strip is truly a classic.

But Brassneck wasn't going to let the scallywag escape. Heaving Farmer Bennett up on to the cart, Brassneck grabbed the shafts and went hurtling after Tommy.

Teachers had a rough time of it in **Dandy** *comic strips.*

Bullies also had a tough time of it.

A bulldog's teeth go CRUNCH! — When it tries to have Brassneck for lunch!

135

THE FORCE IS STRONG IN THIS ONE

STARTS TODAY — The story of a funny-faced boy from another world.

JACK SILVER

A STRANGE LOOKING figure came bounding out of the woods towards the games park at Whitburn. The funny chap was a visitor to the town. In fact, he was a visitor to the World!

His name was Jack Silver, and he had flown to Earth in his space ship all the way from a far-off planet in outer space . . . .

THOSE MUST BE EARTH FOLK DOWN THERE. MY GOODNESS, LOOK AT THEIR FUNNY LITTLE EARS!

PASS TO ME, CURLY! — SHOOT!

Jack Silver's ears shone with rage. He pointed his gloved hand at the ball which had hurt him, and something like a lightning flash zipped from his fing—

Jack didn't know what the game of football was about, of course, and he wandered too close to the goal net as Curly Perkins let fly with a thundering shot.

WHUMP!

I'LL GET THEM TO STOP WORK FOR A MOMENT AND—

OOYAH!

GOAL!

WOW! I THINK YOU'VE HIT A CIRCUS CLOWN, CURLY!

I N 1973 an unidentified odd appearance was made by the first ever sci-fi story in **The Dandy**! 'Jack Silver' follows the adventures of Curley Perkins and his mysterious new friend from the distant planet of Marsuvia as they try to stop the evil Captain Zapp from taking over Earth.

There was a huge science fiction craze in the seventies with 'Doctor Who', 'Battlestar Galactica', 'Star Wars', 'Blakes 7' and 'Star Trek' coming on to the scene. **The Dandy** hoped to attract a new type of reader with 'Jack Silver'. Starting off as a red and pink inside page, it quickly grew a cult following and teleported to the prestigious centre spread in full colour.

In the story Captain Zapp has a machine called the Duplicator. All he has to do is simply feed in a picture of a strange creature and it is created, giving him an endless army of evil beasts to commit crimes. But unluckily for him, every week Jack Silver would use one of his alien gadgets to stop Zapp in his tracks.

Zapp met his match when he kidnapped Curley's grandmother. She made mincemeat out of him as you can see opposite and over the page!

Some of the menacing monsters Captain Zapp creates in his fight with Jack Silver.

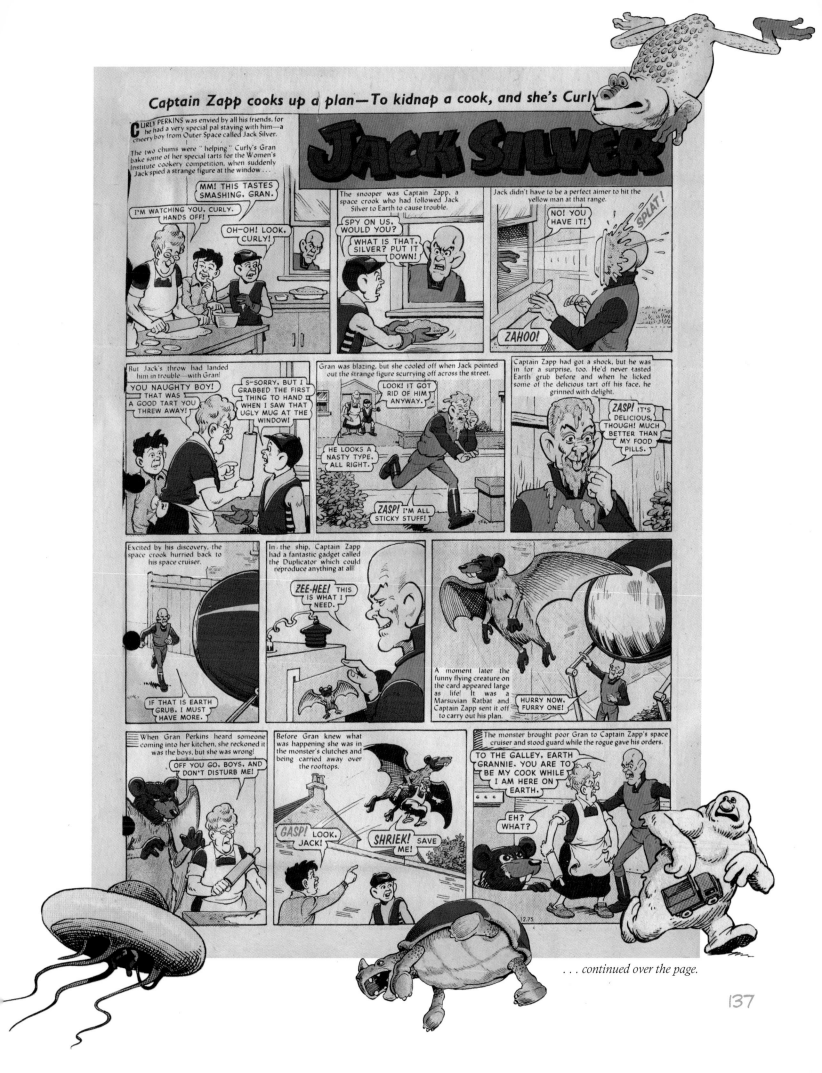

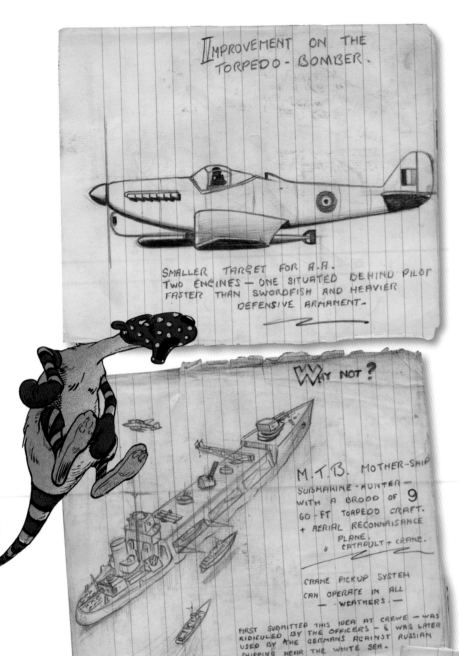

Bill Holroyd at work in his studio.

BRASSNECK ARTIST, Bill Holroyd, loved science so there was never any question as to who should create the futuristic story of 'Jack Silver'. Holroyd would drive his family nuts taking apart appliances at home and putting them back together again to create ingenious experiments. The combination of his imagination and amazing artistry made 'Jack Silver' truly out of this world.

Here are some excerpts from Holroyd's diary during the Second World War showing some of his ideas on how to improve the army's machinery.

Curley's Gran overcomes the evil Captain Zapp in this episode of 'Jack Silver', which starts on page 137.

NEW ARTISTS
KEN REID

The cowboys have the Injuns on the hop — Firing bullets that go off pop! 33

Big-Bang Benny.

Little Angel Face.

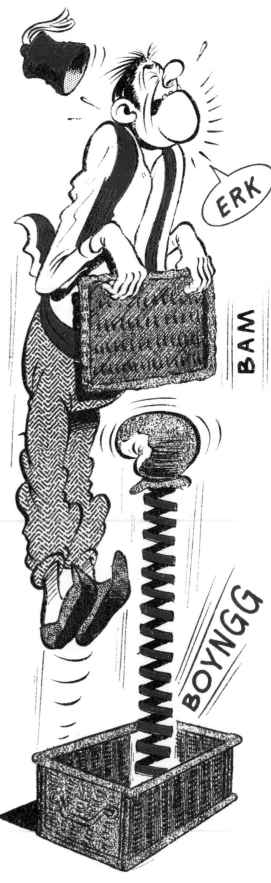

'Ali Ha-Ha and the Forty Thieves'.

KEN REID was born in Manchester and, by the age of fourteen, he had won a scholarship to Salford Art School. Ken then started work as a freelance artist. Over the next fifteen years he drew strips for the *Manchester Evening News*. By 1952, Ken was looking to move into comics and he finally secured work with Amalgamated Press, drawing his own creation 'Foxy' and ghosting another strip called 'Super Sam' in *Comic Cuts*. But, not long after he started working for them, Ken received a letter telling him that *Comic Cuts* was about to fold. Then came the turning point in Ken's career. His brother-in-law, Bill Holroyd, was an artist who worked for D.C. Thomson and he recommended Ken to R.D. Low. Low travelled down from Dundee to Manchester to discuss a new character for *The Beano* – a boy who was always concocting bizarre schemes to dodge out of things. Following Low's description, Ken pencilled several versions of the character and Low chose the one he preferred . . . and 'Roger the Dodger' was born. He also drew 'Jonah', perhaps the best work he did, for *The Beano*. For *The Dandy* his first strip was 'Little Angel Face' in 1954 and his most memorable 'Ali Ha-Ha and the Forty Thieves', a strip that made Albert Barnes laugh.

NEW ARTISTS
PADDY BRENNAN

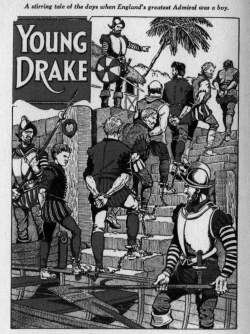

A stirring tale of the days when England's greatest Admiral was a boy.

YOUNG DRAKE

"MOVE, English sea-pup!" snarled the Spanish soldier. "Or are you afraid of the fate that awaits you in Puento?" But it was scorn, not fear, that showed on the face of the lad stepping ashore from the Spanish boat. For he was young Frankie Drake—the boy who, years later, was destined to smash the mighty Spanish Armada. At this moment, however, the future seemed black for the seven dauntless survivors of the crew of the trader *Devon Queen*, which had fallen into Spanish hands.

PADDY BRENNAN was born in Ireland and had his first work published while still in his teens. He worked for several minor publishers before undertaking work for D.C. Thomson in 1949 in response to an advertisement he saw in a Sheffield newspaper looking for artists. Paddy's first work for **The Dandy** was 'Sir Solomon Snoozer', which started in September 1949. Paddy was not quite 20 years old. He was a master of detail and composition and he flourished throughout the 1950s, producing hundreds of pages of top-quality artwork for adventure stories in **The Dandy** (including 'Rusty') and **The Beano** (including 'General Jumbo' and 'Red Rory of the Eagles'). Paddy was one of the few artists who successfully stood up to Albert Barnes, and he managed to stay a family friend. He remained a freelance artist and divided his time between Dublin and London. Described as urbane and cosmopolitan, Paddy was a lover of the theatre.

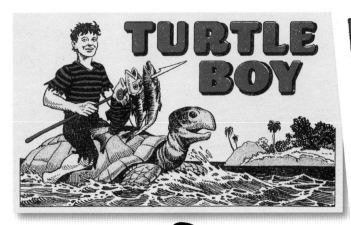

TURTLE BOY

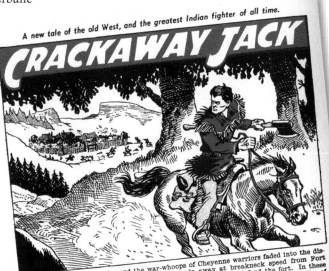

A new tale of the old West, and the greatest Indian fighter of all time.

CRACKAWAY JACK

THE crackle of musket-fire and the war-whoops of Cheyenne warriors faded into the distance as the buckskin-clad frontiersman rode away at breakneck speed from Fort Resolution. Behind him he left only a score of cavalrymen to defend the fort. In these days in the old Wild West, when Red men burned and killed to halt the westward drive of the white settlers, few dared ride the prairie alone. But this horseman riding furiously ... dependence for help was the great Crackaway Jack, hero of a hundred fights.

'Willie Willikin's Pobble'

NEW ARTISTS

CHARLIE GRIGG

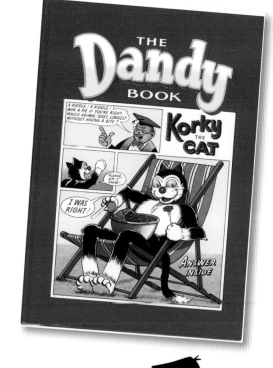

THE FIRST page Charlie had published in *The Dandy* was quite a memorable occasion, for it appeared in issue 500 which was a special edition. This was very fitting for Charlie was a very special artist. He began with a little strip called 'Sooty and His Shooter' in 1951. In 1962 he was given the prestigious job of doing 'Korky the Cat' for the cover of the weekly, replacing James Crichton, who was retiring. He made Korky a more lovable character and within a short while Korky's popularity soared. Charlie was good at producing human foils for Korky, often gamekeepers, fishmongers or policemen. The in-house colourists found his open style a joy to colour – during the sixties these *Dandy* covers were amongst the best in the field. Charlie did a lot of splendid adventure stories for *The Dandy* annuals, titles such as 'The Purple Cloud', 'The Umbrella Men' and 'Peter Potter's Otters'. He retired in the mid-eighties.

For his ninetieth birthday celebration, Charlie and his family visited *The Dandy* offices and he enjoyed looking back at original boards he had drawn forty years before. He still remembered all the difficult bits in each page.

Clanky – the Cast Iron Pup.

Korky the Cat.

Desperate Dan.

NEW ARTISTS
GEORGE MARTIN

Greedy Pigg.

Izzy Skint.

Claude Hopper.

GEORGE MARTIN, one of the best modern comic artists of his day, was brought to D.C. Thomson by Albert Barnes and R.D. Low in the 1950s and he made his debut in *The Dandy* in issue 554 with 'Wily Smiley the Jungle Joker'. *Hoot* comic often featured short, four-frame strips featuring D.C. Thomson characters from *The Topper*, *The Beano*, *The Dandy*, *Nutty* and *The Beezer*, mostly drawn by George Martin, and when *Hoot* merged with *The Dandy* he continued to produce them as 'Comic Cuts' for *The Dandy*.

George Martin wrote many of his own scripts, particularly for his work that appeared in *The Topper* and *The Dandy*. His other *Dandy* strips were: 'Ali Barber and the 40 Hee-Hees!', 'Robinson and his dog Crusoe', 'Sunny Boy – He's a Bright Spark', 'Mr Mutt', 'Jammy Mr Sammy', 'Greedy Pigg', 'Claude Hopper', 'Desperate Dawg', 'Jolly Roger', 'Izzy Skint', 'Hogg's Angels', 'Frogville Tennessee' and 'The Byrd Brains'.

NEW ARTISTS
KEN HUNTER

'My Pal Baggy Pants'.

13—But once again Baggy came to the rescue. "Wait," he said, at the foot of the hill. "Tie your sledges together." That done, he tied the front one to his magic carpet. I sat down behind Baggy. "*Abracadhingamybob*," muttered Baggy, and immediately the magic carpet started flying through the air, pulling the sledges up with it. "Hold on, lads," I called back, but my warning was too late for Skinny Craik. The sudden surge had left him hanging by his fingertips, and his pals had to hold him there by his jersey and his hair! Too bad for Mr Nash, for Skinny's flailing foot gave him a bash on the bean as old Nash was sledging down! The "airlift" was done many times that day, and we had oodles of fun, teachers and pupils alike —all thanks to my pal, Baggy Pants. But maybe it was just as well that the teachers remembered nothing about their day's sledging next morning after the magic effects had worn off!

KEN HUNTER, born in Yorkshire, was freelancing in London, doing work for **Radio Times** and **Picture Post** and teaching art at the Press Art School when he heard D.C. Thomson were looking for artists. He entered a competition the firm was running which offered cash prizes and commissioned work for the winners.

The outcome was favourable – Ken shared first prize and was invited to start work with **The Beano** in 1952. In fact, he was soon picking up so much work that he moved up to Dundee to be closer to the office, though Ken always stayed freelance. His first work for **The Dandy** was in 1956 ('My Pal Baggy Pants'). Over his long career, Ken would do classy illustrations for all the D.C. Thomson comic titles and was drawing sets for the **Comic Libraries** when well into his eighties.

'Buster's Battling Beetle'.

NEW ARTISTS
VITOR PEON

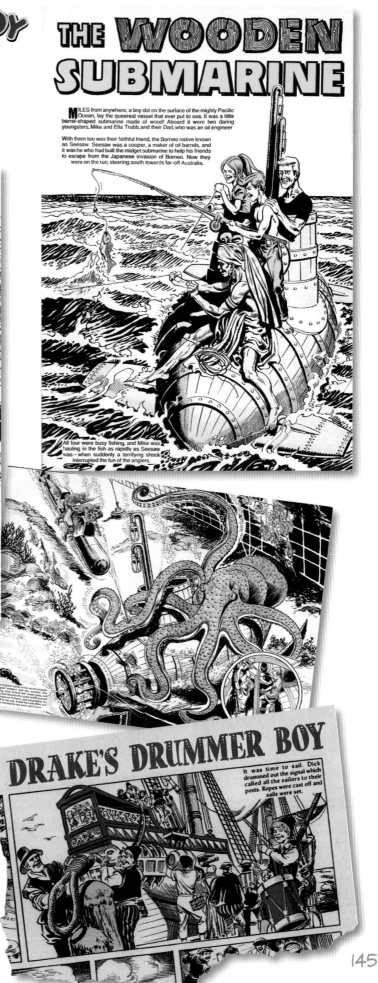

PORTUGUESE ARTIST Vitor Peon arrived at *The Dandy* in 1960. A lively, likeable character, he was a great favourite with everyone in the office. Albert Barnes, as an ex-Royal Navy man, was impressed by Vitor's ability to draw all things nautical, so he gave him mostly seafaring adventures to illustrate. These were mainly for the annuals and included large double page, single picture spreads that Vitor's flowing style suited well. The stories were 'Brave Ben Bold'(one story from this series 'Bold Ben's Boulder' is shown above), 'Drake's Gunner Boy', 'Young Rip the Startling Wrecker' and 'The Wooden Submarine'. Vitor's spell with *The Dandy* did not last long but produced some memorable tales. However, his best known work was 'The Laughing Pirate' for *The Beano* which he did around the same time.

HOW THE DANDY
WAS MADE

SO ... WHAT'S THE SECRET OF HOW WINKER AND HIS CHUMS AND MANY OTHER CARTOON CHARACTERS MADE IT ONTO THE PAGES OF *THE DANDY COMIC* EVERY WEEK? ...

THE JOLLY japes, wangles and comeuppances of a *Dandy* story all spring from the fevered imagination of the scriptwriter. Armed only with a pencil, notepad and his imagination, this intrepid soul must sally forth each day in search of nothing but fun.

Scriptwriters are fiercely protective of their craft. While anyone can write a comic script, it takes a special talent to do it time after time, year after year. Despite the breakneck pace of weekly comic deadlines, the scriptwriter retains an undiminished determination to improve – to make the next script even funnier.

...THE STORY LINE IS THOUGHT UP FOR THE CURRENT ISSUE, NORMALLY HAND-WRITTEN ON SCRAP PAPER.

IF THE SCRIPT MEETS THE EDITOR'S HIGH STANDARDS IT'S THEN TYPED CLEARLY AND ACCURATELY. THIS POLISHED VERSION IS SENT TO THE ARTIST ...

 FIND OUT ON THE NEXT PAGE!

THE ARTIST
READS THE
SCRIPT AND
A PENCIL
SKETCH IS
SUBMITTED
FOR THE
EDITOR'S
APPROVAL ...

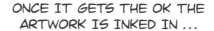

ONCE IT GETS THE OK THE
ARTWORK IS INKED IN ...

MANY ARTISTS USED BLUE PENCIL
FOR THEIR SKETCHES ...

THE SPEECH BALLOONS ARE THEN
ADDED TO THE FRAMES ...

EDITORIAL STAFF
WOULD THEN
MARK THE PAGE
FOR COLOUR TO
BE ADDED. IN THE
FRAME ABOVE
YOU CAN SEE SR
FOR SOLID RED
AND 440 FOR
A SPECIFIC
TINT ...

FINALLY, THE
PAGE IS SENT TO
THE ETCHERS'
DEPARTMENT
WHERE THE
ARTWORK IS
PROCESSED
AND MADE INTO
PLATES FOR THE
PRINTING PRESS.

ANNUALS

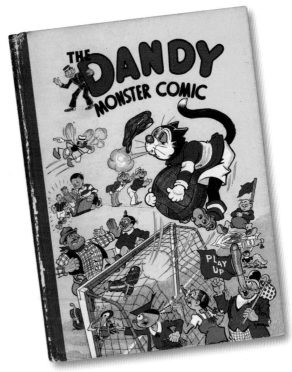

Montage cover by 'Korky' artist James Crichton appeared on the 1944 edition, bringing Christmas cheer to war-weary children.

Where it all started, the **Monster Comic** *of 1939, bringing new delights to children for Christmas 1938.*

THE DANDY ANNUAL has been a British Christmas favourite since the very first collection was published for Christmas 1938, the book being dated 1939. The early annuals were titled *The Dandy Monster Comic* – and were just that – a super-sized 128-page *Dandy* weekly. It contained the same mix of cartoons and text stories but there were many more cartoons in the *Monster Comic*. The same artists and writers did both weekly and annual strips.

The *Monster Comics* came out every year, right through the war. The 1941 edition carried a massive 144 pages, strange as the weekly comics were being reduced in page extent and going fortnightly because of lack of paper. These wartime books are very rare and very collectable.

The *Monster Comic* tag was dropped after the 1952 edition, the Christmas collection becoming simply *The Dandy Book* (and *The Dandy Annual* from the 2003 edition). During the fifties the massive weekly *Dandy* sales were not reflected in sales of the annual, which sold steady but relatively modestly. The high point in annual sales came much later in the eighties, when weekly sales were diminishing.

The artists and writers enjoyed producing the pages for the annuals as it gave them more space to showcase their work. Fashions change and longer individual stories were becoming the norm by the nineties, although the editors still packed the pages with fast action.

When the 1950 **Monster Comic** appeared in the shops **The Dandy** weekly was the country's most popular comic, selling two million copies per week.

Lovely Korky cover on the 1965 **Dandy Book**. *Artwork by Charlie Grigg.*

A big-selling book at Christmas, 1991, Ken Harrison produced the beautifully simple cover image.

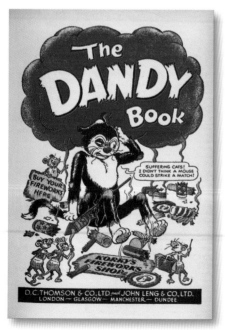

On the inside covers and title pages of many **Dandy Books** *a battle between Korky and the mischievous mice was waged . . .*

. . . although Korky didn't always come out on top against the crafty little mice.

Just as in the weekly **Dandy** *comic, Desperate Dan has featured from the beginning.*

SAY, YOU! BRING THIS DANDY BACK!

This Book Belongs To~

Dandy Annuals *proved to be massive sellers at Christmas time as gifts for children.*

THIS BOOK IS **MINE!** OR AT LEAST IT BELONGS TO MY PAL ....
ADDRESS ....
....

HANDS OFF!

SOOT

PEAS

The Smasher was one of the longest running strips in **The Dandy** *Annuals.*

Dan celebrated the Millennium in style on the year 2000 **Dandy Book** *cover.*

DAN RESCUE MISSION

THE **Dandy** ANNUAL 2013

75th BIRTHDAY

FUN FOR THE WHOLE FAMILY!

CELEBRATE BRITAIN'S LONGEST-RUNNING COMIC!

The 2013 **Dandy Annual**, *celebrating the 75th anniversary of the comic. Its traditional look shows some of* **The Dandy**'s *iconic characters, drawn by Nigel Parkinson, a great fan of* **The Dandy**'s *heritage.*

KEN. H. HARRISON.

153

CHAPTER FOUR

The Biff and Bang Years

1960–1969

Who was the mysterious Bellhop? See page 243. He stopped appearing in **The Dandy** *masthead in October 1960.*

The Dandy VERSUS The Beano

3ᴅ

THE DANDY and *The Beano* have always been talked about together. Sometimes it feels as if there is just one publication. But these two comics actually have a very different ethos and story construction style. The staff on *The Dandy* were very aware of this and would refer to their younger brother as being 'soft' though how anyone can call a comic soft when it has 'Dennis the Menace' in it, is a mystery. What they were talking about was the obvious way *The Dandy* use comic violence to make someone jump or to give them a surprise. The boxing glove on a spring catching someone in the face is very *Dandy*. *Beano* writers were more considered in their humour, it was thought.

The staff on both comics were great rivals and very proud of the traditions of each title. 'He's a good Dandy writer' meant that the author could come up with hard hitting 'robust' situations for whichever character he or she was writing.

The Dandy used more words than *The Beano*, certainly in the time of Albert Barnes as editor. Albert believed he was giving better value for money when there was more to read. *The Beano* saw this as cluttering up valuable space that could be better used with a comical drawing. *The Beano* accused *The Dandy* of being old-fashioned because of this and, undeniably, the sales of *The Beano* overtook that of *The Dandy*. You can just imagine how much crowing went on from *The Beano* the week that actually happened, no matter how small the margin was.

KORKY V BIFFO
The Beano *and* **Dandy** *were never closer in looks and style than when this pair of animated animals were on their covers.*

This girl's taking to cartie-making.

DAN V DENNIS

Top characters in each comic but they were like chalk and cheese in every way. Dan would kick Dennis's butt though Dennis would break Dan's windows.

TIN LIZZIE V MINNIE THE MINX

The Dandy *liked robots, they could wreak more havoc than a human. Minnie was the ultimate unruly tomboy. The two could not have been further apart.*

BASH STREET KIDS V THE JOCKS AND THE GEORDIES

The Jocks and Geordies were the hardest kids in any comic but they always fought amongst themselves. The Bashers targeted figures of authority, namely teachers, parents and police.

157

TOON TOWN

MY HOME TOWN was a remarkable feature page. Readers were asked to send in details and stories about the town they lived in. It was so popular that it ran from 1962 until 1970. Youngsters from John o' Groats to Land's End sent in amazing facts about their town, Purley being the first town to grace this page. Very few features lasted this long in a children's comic.

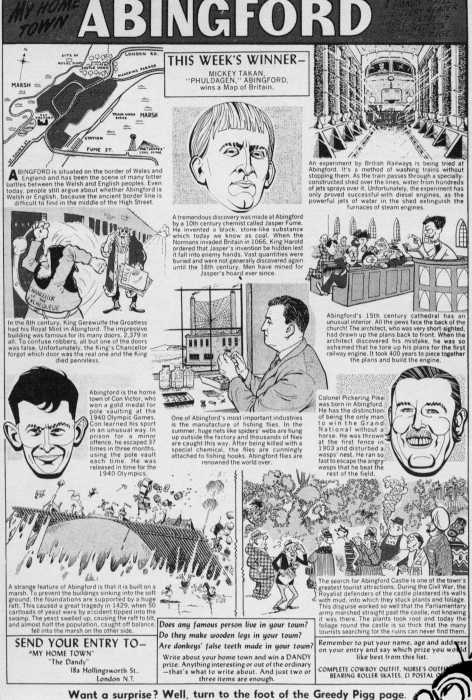

ABINGFORD

Young *Dandy* sub-editors Dave Robertson and Dave Marr did a spoof 'My Home Town' in 1967 for fictional Abingford – well, it was for the April Fool edition of the comic! Readers were fooled for a while but began to be suspicious when they saw who had sent the details in – Mickey Takan from Phuldagen, Abingford.

PAPER IS SILENT, but comics SNAP! CRACKLE! POP! and BANG! The art of comic lettering is often overlooked, but plays a huge part in conveying exactly the sound that, for instance, a snowball makes when it hits Mr Creep on the back of the head (see above). The SPLOSH! tells you it's soft, wet and probably freezing – perfect ammunition.

Every letterer had their own individual style, and matching lettering style to art style was an important decision. Also important was the choice of word – is it a THUD or a THUMP, a BIFF or a BOP? Try spelling out the sound a cricket ball makes as it passes through a greenhouse window, and you'll realise just how hard it is to get right!

COMIC GENIUS

*Boarding schools and their surroundings became a popular genre in the world of comics, as it had been in children's literature generally – for example, **Tom Brown's Schooldays** (1857) and Talbot Baines Reed's **The Fifth Form at St Dominic's** (1880), written for **The Boys Own Paper**. Also Frank Richards' **Billy Bunter** (which began in 1908) and later, the **St Trinian's** series of books (1948–53) by Ronald Searle. 'Winker Watson' followed in this tradition in the early 1960s.*

WINKER WATSON made his first appearance in a preview strip in ***The Dandy Book*** 1961, released for the Christmas market of 1960.

His first term in the Third Form at Greytowers Boarding School started on April Fool's Day 1961 – issue 1010 of ***The Dandy***, with the first story seeing him meet his best friend Tim Trott (nicknamed 'Trotty' by Winker), and arch adversary and authority figure Mr Clarence Creep, the crusty Housemaster, rarely seen in the early years without his bowtie, mortarboard and gown, with his pet bulldog 'Gruff' never far away.

The Headmaster often featured in the strips, but usually in scenes with Creep (often tucking in to a plate of something) rather than taking an active part. Creep was left to cope with the mayhem.

The setting probably took inspiration from Greyfriars School – a fictional English Public School used in the 'Billy Bunter' stories written by Frank Richards, which were popular from their first appearance in ***The Magnet*** in 1908.

Known as the Third Form's 'Wily Wangler', Winker Watson became popular very quickly and soon became an established, firm favourite with readers. Winker, one of the great comic adventure strip characters, would subsequently appear in numerous serials, drawn in the main by the stylish Eric Roberts until his retirement in 1980. Roberts' last published 'Winker Watson' work featured in the 1981 ***Dandy Book*** – 'Batty Books from Winker Watson's Library'. The serial aspect of 'Winker Watson' was unusual for a comic at this time – some stories are better described as long-running sagas.

Later 'Winker Watson' storylines were often reworked from the rich vein of early scripts, notably the tales of Winker's attempts to foil 'rich boy' Robin Boodle, renamed Darby Doshman, who in later adaptations was given the new identity of Jonathan Dosh.

Food was a theme never far from Winker Watson's thoughts, and pantry and larder raids were easy meat for Winker and his pals. Cookie the School Cook made occasional appearances, often armed with a massive rolling pin.

If Watson and pals couldn't dodge the exam altogether . . .

. . . the next best thing was to destroy the evidence!

The pupils of Greytowers often seemed to spend Christmas at school!

The strip also used the favourite **Dandy** *device – the boxing glove on a spring.*

The open coal-hole gag – always a winner!

Food and the Headmaster were never far from each other.

Out of a caning Winker wangled his way — By kidding that he was a casualty.

....EVERY SINGLE BOY HAS IGNORED THE RULE ABOUT BRINGING TUCK INTO SCHOOL, SO I SHALL CANE THE WHOLE CLASS!

PSST! OLD CREEPY MEANS IT THIS TIME, WINKER!

OH YEAH? NOT IF I CAN HELP IT!

FORM III

RED INK

WINKER WATSON and his classmates were on the carpet. They had stepped out of line by having a forbidden midnight feast. Now Mr Creep, their Housemaster, had brought them back into a line, ready for punishment!

BIFF!

WALLOP!

In the UK, in private schools where some of the funding came from government, corporal punishment was banned by Parliament from 1987. In other private schools in England and Wales, the ban took effect in 1999 – a year later in Scotland and 2003 in Northern Ireland. The implement used in England and Wales was a flexible rattan cane applied either to the student's hands or often at boys' schools to the trousered backside of the unfortunate miscreant. In Scotland a tawse, or leather strap, was more often used to administer punishment to the palm of the hand.

WINKER WATSON had a younger brother at school named Wallie and brotherly wangling warfare would break out – particularly when pocket money was concerned.

The Hoods (a group of white-coated, masked Sixth Formers) come on to the scene in the last few years of Roberts' work. Winker and his fellow third-formers are bullied by these older boys, and guile, quick thinking and ingenuity usually win the day.

After Roberts' death, the strips were reprinted for a number of years, with Tom Williams drawing some new strips for the 1980s *Dandy Books*, then Terry Bave took up the challenge. Bave followed Roberts' style initially, but gradually his own influence shaped 'Winker Watson' and the look of the strip continued to evolve when Stephen White took over in 2002 and on the occasions when 'Winker Watson' was brought back from retirement. A very contemporary 'Winker Watson' graced the pages of the 75th birthday edition of *The Dandy Annual 2012*.

The Hoods hunted and hunted, but their hut was so well camouflaged they didn't recognise it, even when they looked in the right direction.

But from inside, Winker and his chums had a great laugh at the puzzled rascals. The wangler had really put one over on the Hoods this time.

HEE-HEE!

SSHH! LAUGH QUIETLY, LADS!

HO-HO!

BISCUITS

Winker and his gang evade the Hoods.

CORPORAL CLOTT

THE COLONEL TOLD ME TO EXERCISE HIS HORSE, AND IT'S THE BEST JOB I'VE EVER HAD. CLATTERING CLOTT, THAT'S ME!

CORPORAL CLOTT first took the salute in *The Dandy* issue No. 990, on November 12, 1960. The strips featured the clumsy and incompetent Corporal Clott who innocently bungled his way through everything he did, often bringing chaos to the whole Army, much to the anger of the ever-suffering Colonel Grumbly, the officer in charge, who was constantly challenged by Clott's ineptitude.

Clott brought destruction and mayhem to every task he undertook on the Army base where the stories of the strips were generally set, or on manoeuvres, whether it was juggling with grenades or peeling potatoes. One episode in 1966, when Clott was stationed in Africa was criticised by some newspapers for being political and the strip for the following week, which continued the story, had to be pulled from the printers. Albert Barnes was not amused.

The strip was drawn by David Law until July 25, 1970, when it was taken over by Jimmy Hughes who guided Clott through five more disorderly years. Corporal Clott also starred in two *Dandy Comic Library* issues – in 'Taskforce' and 'Trouble Spots'. Clott returned in 1987 for a brief period, drawn by Steve Bright and appeared in several strips in the 75th birthday edition of *The Dandy Annual 2012*, portrayed in a very different style, drawn by Nigel Auchterlounie.

TWO SECONDS LATER—

UGH!

Few of Corporal Clott's bright ideas ever worked out the way they should have.

A familiar scene in a Corporal Clott strip – Colonel Grumbly with his fists in the air and Clott on the run.

Colonel Grumbly is the dominant figure of authority, constantly challenged by Corporal Clott.

An accident waiting to happen – Corporal Clott in his Jeep with his famous registration plate ICU2.

And as the saying goes – never work with animals, children . . . or Corporal Clott!

Only Corporal Clott could start with a ton of potatoes and peel them down to a small potful.

BULLY BOY

The disciplinarian Albert Barnes would surely have made Bully have his hair cut!

POETIC JUSTICE was rarely less poetic than in the thump-fest that was 'Bully Beef and Chips'. A simple tale of a boy and his bully, the strip saw poor Chips bullied in a remarkably inventive variety of ways, usually for no reason other than to satisfy Bully Beef's urge to hurt him.

Luckily, Bully Beef's brain did not match his brawn, meaning he always came off worst, in equally inventive reversals (often at the hands of his fearsome lookalike mother). Jimmy Hughes's pudding-bowled villain is surely one of the least appealing comic characters of all time.

As adults, we may have reservations about bullying in stories, but the readers disagreed: 'Bully Beef and Chips' ran on the back page of **The Dandy** for many years – an honour reserved only for the most popular stories.

The strip often ended with Bully seeing stars.

Surely it would have been less effort if Bully had just cut the grass himself?!

Bully might have benefited from some anger-management classes!

Unusually, Chips is allowed to exact his revenge first-hand in this story from 1967.

SPECIAL SUMMERS

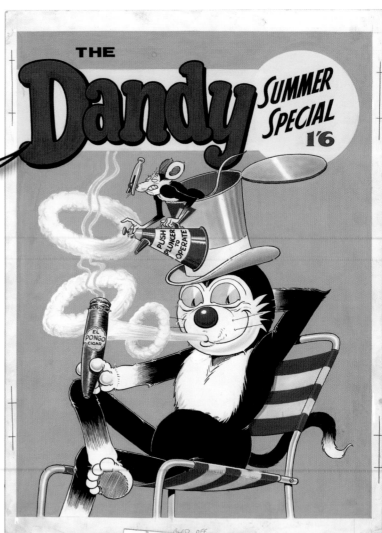

Forty five years ago having Korky smoking a cigar was deemed acceptable comic behaviour.

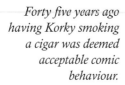

HE FIRST *Summer Special* to be published was a joint effort between *The Dandy* and *The Beano* which appeared in newsagents, especially at British holiday resorts, in the summer of 1963. It featured stars from both comics having summer holiday fun.

It was a large-format comic with lots of colour and 32 pages. It was such a success that the following year both *The Dandy* and *The Beano* produced their own *Summer Specials*. *The Beano* used the classic draughtsmanship of Dudley Watkins to do their bright Special covers which in the early years featured 'Biffo the Bear'. However, *The Dandy* had an ace up their sleeves in artist Charlie Grigg. Not only was Grigg marvellous at large-scale illustrations but he was also a seasoned seaside postcard illustrator who brought the British holiday scene to the covers of *The Dandy Summer Special*. They were some of the most brilliant covers done for any *Dandy* publication.

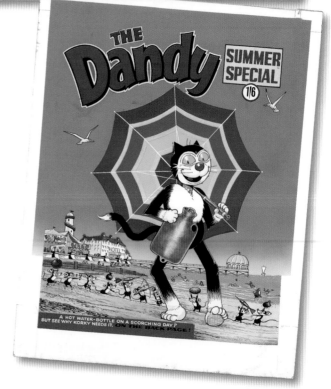

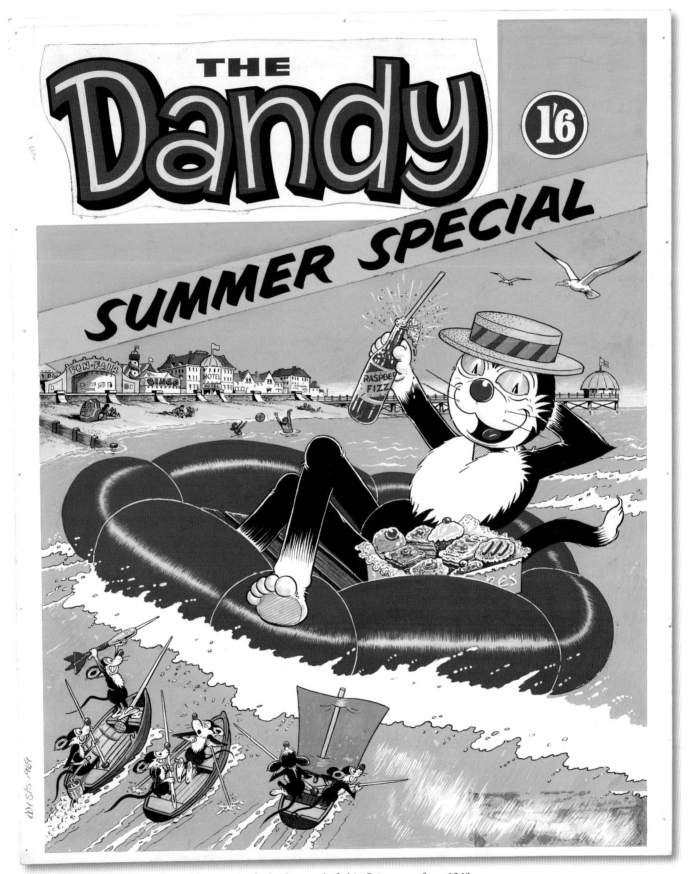

Look at the wonderful British seaside resort in the background of this Grigg cover from 1969.

Vibrant colours were a feature of the **Summer Specials** *as a result of being printed using the gravure process. This 'Korky' strip is very typical of the summer content.*

Bully on the beach. Our treasure hunter falls for a classic Dandy prank.

The superb back cover from the 1969 **Summer Special**. *It follows on from the large cover scene shown on page 179.*

*The black-and-white pages in the **Summer Specials** displayed extra quality with the use of a grey wash. This helped to give the pages depth and made them very different from the weekly line work.*

*A 'Black Bob' adventure drawn by Jack Prout. The freer layout of the **Summer Special** strip was welcomed by Jack who was always required to do his weekly 'Black Bob' strips in single postcard-sized frames so that the strip could be re-formatted in different sizes for use in D.C. Thomson's newspapers as well as **The Dandy**.*

Texan Desperate Dan always went on holiday to British-looking resorts, part of the quirky British / American world Dan lived in. This strip continues on the next page . . .

The gag of Dan lifting the stage of strongmen had been famously drawn by Dudley Watkins for a **Dandy** *annual. This illustration by Charlie Grigg is as good.*

Desperate Dan under full sail, revealing his collar size to be 25. Only rarely did Dudley Watkins draw Dan in colour and this example came from the 1969 **Summer Special**, *published shortly before his sudden, unexpected death.*

AND HERE'S DAN AT THE SEASIDE. HE DOESN'T BELIEVE IN WASTING MONEY HIRING A BOAT!

Charlie Grigg's colourful covers were a feature of **Dandy Summer Specials** *for decades, this one from 1971.*

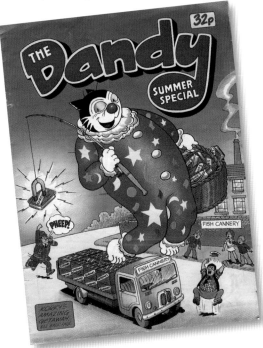

Still fresh, bright and popular in 1981.

185

FREE GIFTS

The cardboard Thunderbang was a really popular give-away and was repeated in many of D.C. Thomson's comics over a great number of years.

Morris Heggie can remember seeing a flock of Whirlybirds in the sky above his primary school playground when it appeared inside the comic.

IN 1960 *The Dandy* had a sales push which included free gifts for the readers. These were the first gifts since 1940. How things change, for today's comics have multi-gifts on every issue and would not sell without them. These gifts in 1960, combined with an increase in pages from twelve to sixteen, were to soften the blow of a price increase. Shock! Horror! *The Dandy* increased in price by one penny, for the first time in its twenty-three year life.

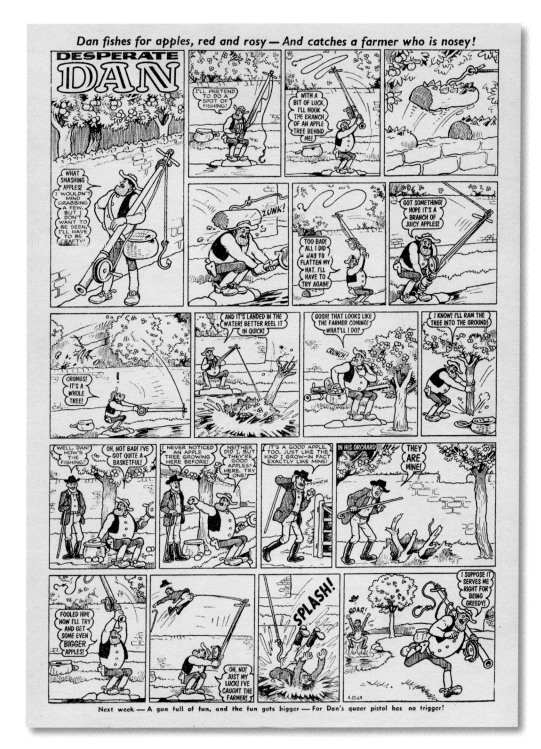

This is the last 'Desperate Dan' that Dudley Watkins drew. It, along with other strips, would be reprinted later in the 1970s.

A SAD END TO THE 1960s

THE LAST year of the 1960s ended on a very sombre note for editor Albert Barnes and his staff. Their great friend and colleague, not to mention leading artist, Dudley Watkins died suddenly at his drawing board on August 20, 1969. Albert did not try to replace him and instead chose to reprint 'Desperate Dan' stories in the comic from years past. He would carry on doing this for the next fourteen years.

THE DANDY

CHAPTER FIVE

Holding Course

1970–1979

*The many faces of Korky the Cat, the front-cover star of **The Dandy**.*
Korky stayed on the cover and there was little change within during the 1970s.

MAGIC MERCHANDISE

I N THE late 1970s various companies took out licences to produce a range of *Dandy*-based merchandise. The earliest products were mostly stationery and jigsaws although a bottle of 'Desperate Dan' bubble bath was produced – not that Dan was often seen using bubble bath! The illustrations for the products were drawn by Charlie Grigg. Looking at them now, they have a marvellous retro look.

DANDY BRANDS

Korky through the drinking glass.

When Dan tells you the time, no one argues.

Playing SNAP! with Dan cards could be mighty sore.

*Prompted by the 75th anniversary of **The Dandy**, the Royal Mail issued a set of comic character stamps in 2012, including one of Desperate Dan and **The Dandy**.*

MORE RECENTLY the gift market has looked to **The Dandy** and 'Desperate Dan' to provide fun products. Licences to use Dan's image has brought in important revenue in difficult trading times. Dan's super-human appetite made kitchen and cookware popular products for Dan to appear on.

You had to hit
Desperate Dan's
Bop Bag really
hard.

Colour a
cowpie.

*Tea cosy
and oven
gloves.* **The
Dandy**
*staff used
them as a
hat and
boxing
gloves.*

Hon-he-Hon! Monsieur Desperate en Paris.

A veritable traffic jam of Dandy delivery trucks.

193

PIE-EATER'S CLUB

Many students joined the club to get hold of the retro badges.

DESPERATE DAN started his Pie-Eater's Club in June 1978. For a 40p postal order, you were enrolled in the club and received two colourful badges, a sheet of club stickers, a secret password and the secrets of Desperate Dan's muscle building exercises. All this came in a swish plastic wallet. By 1980 there were nearly half a million members. In these times of diet and healthy eating, how many people would own up to being a member?

Charlie Grigg did the artwork for the amazing muscle building exercises.

Happy pie-eating chums! Ah, those wonderful days when we cared not a jot what was in our pies.

DUNDEE TRIBUTE TO DAN

The huge statue was sculpted in clay before being cast in bronze. It stands the best part of 3 metres high and is a landmark in City Square, Dundee.

The Colossus of Dundee strides across the cobbles.

N 2001 sculptor Tony Morrow was commissioned to create a larger than life bronze statue of Desperate Dan for the city of Dundee, the home port for D.C. Thomson and the comic capital of Britain. The whole bronze scene was to be Dan and his Dawg plus Minnie the Minx from *The Beano*.

You seem familiar.

*In **The Dandy** comic Dan has a stroll in Dundee and comes face to face with himself.*

CHAPTER SIX

All Change

1980–1989

Korky was pushed off the cover by Desperate Dan after forty-seven years in 1984, one of the many changes that followed the retirement of founding editor Albert Barnes in 1982.

HIGH NOON FOR THE TOUGHEST EDITOR IN THE WILD WEST!

ALBERT BARNES RETIRES 1982

AFTER 45 years as Editor of *The Dandy*, Albert Barnes retired in April 1982. The founder of the comic and inspiration behind Desperate Dan's signature chin would be a hard act to follow.

Shortly before he retired, Barnes was working on a secret project to create a new comic that even his staff knew nothing about! Albert thought the success of *The Dandy* came from Desperate Dan's big chin and decided the characters in the comic's lead story should all have one too. 'Dangerous Dumplings' were an anti-social family made up of Dad Dumpling, Ma Dumpling and the twins Pud and Pat who terrorised their poor neighbours.

Barnes was searching for an artist to draw 'Dangerous Dumplings' when a young school boy called Tom Paterson sent in some sketches and Albert was blown away. He took the sixteen-year-old novice under his wing and spent six months helping him develop the characters. Unfortunately for Albert, when Tom left school he was snapped up by the IPC before they could finish the project.

This never-before-seen 'Dangerous Dumplings' is the first professional work from the now legendary comic artist Tom Paterson.

Albert might have ruled *The Dandy* office like a navy commander but he was a perennial prankster. During the IRA bombings in the 1970s a fake bomb threat was called in to D.C. Thomson. After the all clear, Albert decided to wind up his office by painting a grapefruit black, writing 'bomb' on it and hurling it through the door at his Deputy Editor!

HEY, PARDNERS, MY CHEST-OF-DRAWERS CHIN'S MEANT TO BE MODELLED ON THAT OF ORIGINAL DANDY EDITOR THE LATE ALBERT BARNES. PITY HE HADN'T HAD A SHAVE FIRST BEFORE HE DID THE MODELLING!

Albert and the staff in **The Dandy** *office in the comic's prime..*

200

The first time Tom Paterson's artwork for 'The Dangerous Dumplings' has been seen. The strip was to have been the lead strip in a new comic Albert Barnes was considering before he retired.

BLACK BOB BOW-WOWS OUT

1982

In this episode reprinted in 1982, Black Bob travelled to Argentina. Unfortunately the series was running when the Falklands War started and worried readers actually wrote in to find out if Black Bob would make it home safely.

ALTHOUGH JACK Prout stopped drawing 'Black Bob' strips in 1967, *The Dandy* had been reprinting them since then. In those many adventures he travelled the world saving people from burning buildings, rounding up stampeding elephants, saving kidnapped kids and battling grizzly bears, but in July 1982 he hung up his collar forever when his last story was reprinted in *The Dandy*.

One of the last adventures that the comic ran was a classic 'Black Bob' series with the Wonder Dog in Argentina. Unfortunately the series was running at the start of the Falklands War between Britain and Argentina. *Dandy* chief sub-editor Dave Torrie recalls getting letters from anxious readers asking if Bob would be safe in that country while the conflict was going on. He replied that not to worry, Bob was a great survivor.

In the 1980s the cheeky writers at *Viz* ran a spoof of 'Black Bob' called 'Black Bag – The Faithful Border Bin Liner' about a posh toff and his pet plastic bag. Almost every episode ended with the bag meeting a sticky end.

The Viz take on 'Black Bob'.

BLACK BOB MEETS GNASHER

Stealthily, the two dogs entered the cab of the van— 37

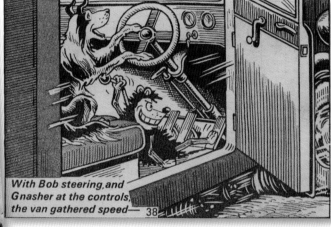

With Bob steering, and Gnasher at the controls, the van gathered speed— 38

QUICK, GNASHER! SLAM ON THE BRAKES!

TWO OF the best known dogs from the D.C. Thomson kennels came together in a *Comic Library* publication – Andrew Glenn's Black Bob and Dennis the Menace's famous canine sidekick Gnasher, drawn by David Sutherland.

Gnasher was originally created by writer Ian Gray and artist Davey Law and became one of the most recognisable support characters in **The Beano**. Sutherland's blend of cartoon style with the more traditional linework in this **Comic Library** story is a classic.

Details from Comic Library No. 33 in which Dennis and Gnasher enter the 'One Man and his Dog' competition after watching Black Bob on TV. Gnasher and Black Bob join forces to outfox a fox and some sheep rustlers. Dennis and Gnasher are, however, thrown out of the competition when they lead a flock of sheep through the refreshment tent.

LAST BELL FOR THE WILIEST WANGLER

ERIC ROBERTS RETIRES

IN 1980 Eric Roberts penned his final page for *The Dandy*. The Londoner had been with the comic since the first issue back in 1937 with his very first story, 'Podge', and was the last of the original artists to hang up his hat. Roberts created *The Dandy* classic 'Winker Watson' and worked his magic on Greytowers for over twenty-three years, his final strip coming out on September 29, 1979.

The only person who ever called him Eric was his close friend and editor, Albert Barnes; everyone else always called him Robbie. When D.C. Thomson decided to launch a new girls' comic in the 1960s, Albert suggested they name it after Eric's eldest daughter and the *Mandy* was born!

Eric grew up around the theatre and it definitely rubbed off, for he could do somersaults and stand on his head! His father was a stage manager and many of the actors and entertainers would board at their home.

Roberts was a night owl and used to sleep all day and work through the night. Once the ink was dry he would roll his work up into a spool, wrap it in thick brown paper, tie it with string and seal it with wax to keep it safe. He would never let anyone else post his work and if there was a postal strike he would hand deliver his work to D.C. Thomson's Fleet Street office.

Podge – Eric's first cartoon character from 1937.

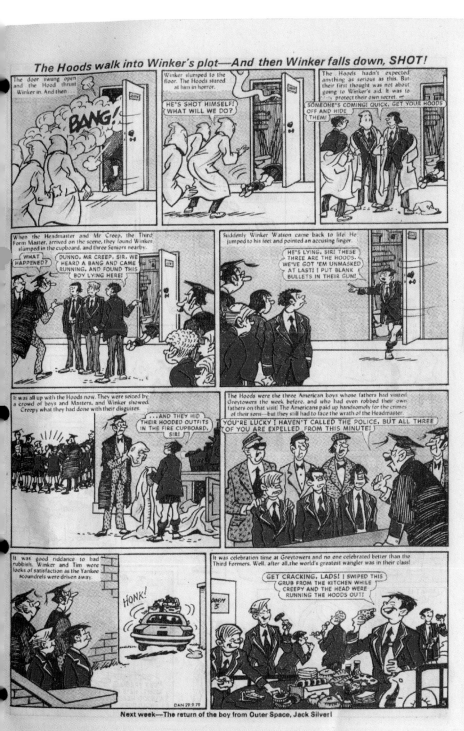

The Hoods walk into Winker's plot——And then Winker falls down, SHOT!

Eric's last ever 'Winker Watson' from September 29, 1979.

Eric and his daughter Erica.

This new D.C. Thomson magazine from 1967 was named after Eric's daughter Mandy.

THE TORR TAKES OVER!

Staff artist Jimmy Glenn drew this caricature of Dave Torrie after he won top bowler for Kirriemuir Cricket Club in 1985.

ALBERT BARNES handed over the editorial reins to Dave Torrie in 1982. Dave only had one job interview in his entire life and he didn't get it! Back in 1961 he applied for a position on the Dundee newspaper, **The Courier**, and was quickly told he hadn't been successful, but they did have a department more suitable for 'people like you'. Within the month he was writing comics alongside the wacky characters in **The Dandy**. He said it was the best second prize he ever won.

Under Torrie's new editorship, 'Korky the Cat' was finally ousted from the cover after forty-seven years in prime position – ever since the first issue. The company had tried in vain to get Albert Barnes to make 'Desperate Dan' the cover star for years but he refused, saying 'over his dead body!' Torrie gave Dan his first cover on

November 17, 1984, relegating Korky to an inside page in black and red.

Torrie had written thousands of scripts over the course of his illustrious career and kept every single one of them but there could only be one favourite. On Guy Fawkes Day back in 1966 Torrie wrote a 'Brassneck' script that caused a whole lot of fireworks when he included the recipe for dynamite in the story, incurring the wrath of the Home Office.

HOGG'S ANGELS

PORKY PERKINS → JASPER HOGG → BERT BACON →

ROAR!

Dave Torrie and his chief sub-editor John Methven came up with several great stories during their spell at the helm. 'Hogg's Angels' was never fully developed but was an excellent annual set, drawn by George Martin.

HAM and EGGHEAD

THIS JIGSAW'S VERY DIFFICULT BUT I'M DETERMINED TO FINISH IT!

KIDDIE'S JIGSAW
12 LARGE PIECES FOR A CHILD AGED 3

MAKING UP A JIGSAW, HAM?

YES! BUT IT'S FAULTY, EGGHEAD!

LOOK! I'VE BEEN SOLD AN UPSIDE-DOWN JIGSAW!

Here's a tale to turn you pale—About a spooky Jumble Sale! 77

Strange Hill School

This is Eddie Potter, an ordinary schoolboy. In fact he's the ONLY ordinary schoolboy at a very weird school!

THE SCHOOL'S HAVING A JUMBLE SALE TODAY, SO WE'RE ALL BRINGING ALONG OLD TOYS TO SELL ON THE STALLS!

SCHOOL

HI, VINCE. WHAT HAVE YOU GOT THERE?

HELLO, EDDIE!

OH, SOME OF MY OLD CLOCKWORK CARS! HAW-HAW!

WHIRR!

GASP! A HEARSE!

Then—

ER... WHAT HAVE YOU BROUGHT, HAIRY?

JUST SOME OLD CHAINS AND COBWEBS, EDDIE!

CLANK! CLANK! CLANK!

OO... ER!

'Ham and Egghead' was a modern version of 'Big Head and Thick Head', the 1960s strip which was drawn by Ken Reid. These new kids on the block were drawn by Steve Bright.

*'Strange Hill School' was inspired by the TV hit 'Grange Hill'. It became a **Dandy** classic with readers loving the bizarre and creepy school rooms and pupils. Matching up zany artist David Mostyn and the over-the-top scripts was a clever move by Torrie.*

*Dave Torrie and, in the background, sub-editor Iain McLaughlin, at **The Dandy**'s 50th birthday dinner in 1987.*

207

THE DANDY GOES NUTTY FOR

BANANAMAN

Here's Bananaman in his very first adventure in **Nutty** issue No. 1, February 16, 1980.

Steve Bright, who came up with the idea for 'Bananaman', is now a cartoon illustrator in his own right.

IN THE dizzy heights of **Dandy** Towers in the late 1970s, a superhero was born. A crack team of D.C. Thomson writers were sent to a top-secret office to create a new comic called **Nutty**. On the very first day Steve Bright was challenged to come up with a story about a boy who could turn into a superhero and he didn't need to be asked twice! Cheekily giving the boy the name Eric (his own middle name), Steve came up with a bumbling hero who always seemed to get it wrong but somehow got there in the end. The company loved it and quickly gave it the green light.

*Bananaman artist John Geering meets staff member Riona McElfatrick at **The Dandy** offices.*

Bananaman's arch enemies Skunk Woman (above) and Dr Gloom (below).

*An early episode of 'Bananaman' in **Nutty**.*

ROCKETED TO Earth as a baby, with a kryptonite-style weakness for mouldy bananas, the ability to fly and the superhuman strength of twenty men (twenty big men!), it's no surprise Steve Bright was a massive D.C. and Marvel superhero fan. 'Bananaman' was a wacky parody of 'Superman' with a touch of 'Captain Marvel'. Even the bad guys spoofed famous characters with homages to the Fantastic Four's Dr Doom and Batman's nemesis Cat Woman – Dr Gloom and Skunk Woman!

But who should draw Bananaman? Steve knew there was only one man for the job – 'Coronation Street' baddie and legendary artist, John Geering. The pair became an unbeatable team and it wasn't long before 'Bananaman' made his way from the back page to become the cover star, even getting his own TV series!

Geering loved a pint and it was common for him to drive all the way from Manchester to Dundee to enjoy a lunchtime drink with ***The Dandy*** office.

BANANAMAN

Bananaman's red gloves turned yellow for TV.

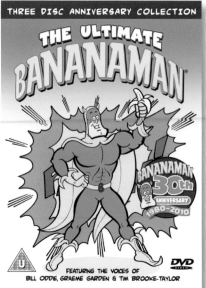

THREE DISC ANNIVERSARY COLLECTION

THE ULTIMATE BANANAMAN

The television antics of 'Bananaman' were spread over three series.

The Goodies (above) supplied the voices for the television series with Bill Oddie also doing the voice for Bananaman's sidekick, Crow (below).

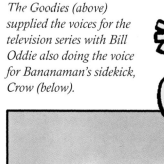

BANANAMAN WAS the first D.C. Thomson character to get his own television show. But with the show came a new look for the nana head. Gone was Eric's skinhead in favour of a new black hairdo in the shape of a banana and Bananaman's gloves changed from red to yellow. As well as a makeover, Eric Wimp received a new name, becoming Eric Twinge.

The Goodies did the voiceovers for the characters in the 'Bananaman' series with Tim Brooke-Taylor narrating, Graeme Garden as Bananaman and Bill Oddie playing Eric. The producers were so impressed with Oddie's bird impression they decided to use it in the show and hatched Bananaman's new sidekick, Crow!

MUNCH CHOMP! SHLURP!

The original drawing of Eric (above) and his makeover for television (right).

*In 1985 'Bananaman' was called on to join a whole host of **Dandy** cartoon legends.*

NUTTY LASTED for 292 issues but closed in September 1985. The advent of video games created a graveyard for comics as children spent less and less time reading and more time in front of the television. But you can't keep a good superhero down and when he got a call from Chief O'Reilly, 'Bananaman' blasted into *The Dandy* when it merged with *Nutty* that year, ever alert for the call to action!

Here's Steve Bright's all-time favourite 'Bananaman' baddie, Appleman, in action. Every week Bananaman faced a different villain but luckily for him they were even dumber than he was!

THE HEGGIE HURRICANE!

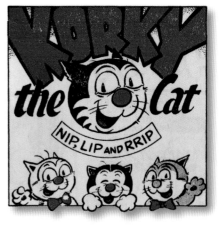

A new softer look for 'Korky the Cat'.

Morris Heggie at the editor's desk in the 1980s.

Readers complained that characters like 'The Smasher' were too violent.

IN 1986 *The Beano* was outselling *The Dandy* two-to-one and management decided it was time for a dramatic change. Dave Torrie was moved to *The Beezer* and the fiery-headed ex-lumberjack Morris Heggie took over with one mission – make it more like *The Beano*. Having spent seven years on *The Beano*, he was the perfect candidate and for the first time in fifty years he began to shake things up. A jab in the bum was the typical comical end to a *Dandy* story and by this time people were complaining that it was too violent and full of bullies with 'The Smasher', 'The Jocks and the Geordies' and 'Bully Beef and Chips' being the main offenders.

Morris decided to bring in *Beano*-style artists like Robert (Bob) Nixon and Brian Walker to take over the stories and draw them in a softer style. You can see the distinct difference between the old-style 'Bully Beef' and Bob Nixon's new softer style here. Heggie also used Nixon to give a fresh new look to 'Korky the Cat', replacing David Gudgeon.

'Bully Beef and Chips' from 1967 (above) and the late 1980s (left).

Dan illustrations with (left) and without (above) the distinctive flesh tones.

Like Morris, 'Spotted Dick' made the move from **Hoot** to **The Dandy**.

Morris felt 'Desperate Dan' had become dull with overcomplicated stories and decided to toughen him up and make the stories wilder. His new rootin', tootin' stories were given prominence in the comic with a rip-roaring three pages every week. Another noticeable change was the introduction of flesh tone to characters on the covers.

Morris introduced a new section in *The Dandy* called 'Comic Cuts' with mini-strips featuring the most popular characters in mini adventures. Another new addition was *Hoot*-escapee, 'Spotted Dick'.

CUDDLES AND DIMPLES

WHEN HE left *Hoot* to join *The Dandy*, Morris took one of his favourite characters with him, a naughty tot called 'Cuddles'. *The Dandy* already had a mischievous toddler called 'Dimples', so Morris decided to have them join forces as next-door neighbours – it was going to be double trouble.

In 1987 Morris decided the story would work better if Cuddles and Dimples were twins with the same parents. But he got a shock one Monday morning when Barrie Appleby sent in the first new strip with Cuddles' dad and Dimples' mum as the parents! He had no need to panic though, it was just Barrie playing a prank on Morris and it was quickly changed.

Barrie Appleby's sense of humour was legendary in the office. He often hid secret jokes on the pages to make *The Dandy* crew laugh. The poor art assistant and balloonist on *The Dandy*, Riona McElfatrick, used to spend hours changing the magazine the vicar was reading in 'Cuddles and Dimples' from a page three special to *The Dandy*.

A frame from the strip where Cuddles and Dimples' strips are merged.

The Vicar with his copy of **The Dandy** in a frame from 'Cuddles and Dimples'. Barrie Appleby's original illustration might have had the Vicar holding a less innocent magazine.

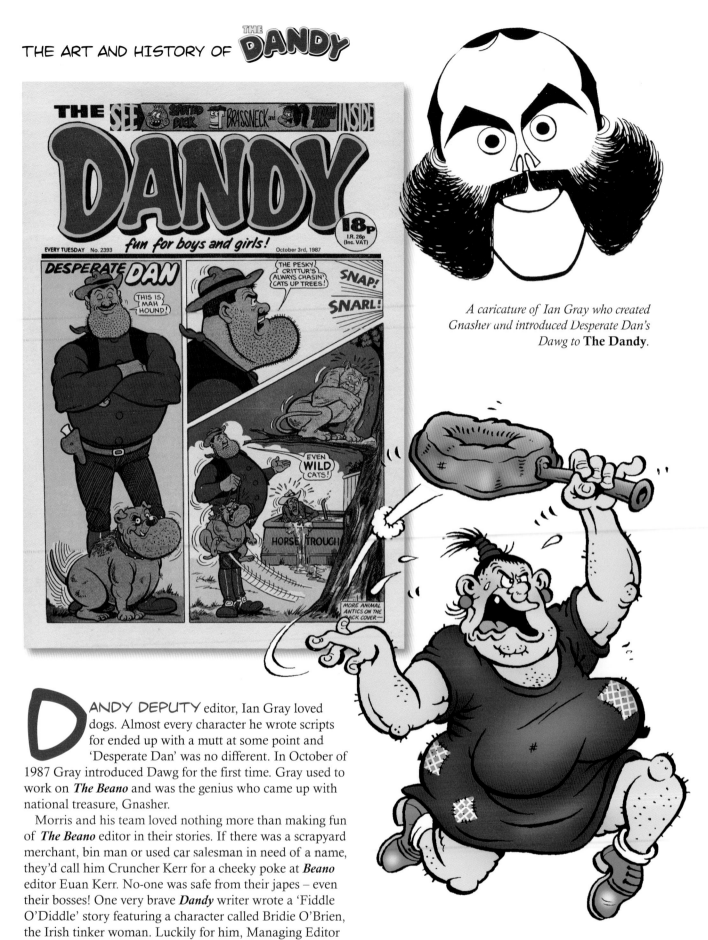

A caricature of Ian Gray who created Gnasher and introduced Desperate Dan's Dawg to **The Dandy**.

DANDY DEPUTY editor, Ian Gray loved dogs. Almost every character he wrote scripts for ended up with a mutt at some point and 'Desperate Dan' was no different. In October of 1987 Gray introduced Dawg for the first time. Gray used to work on *The Beano* and was the genius who came up with national treasure, Gnasher.

Morris and his team loved nothing more than making fun of *The Beano* editor in their stories. If there was a scrapyard merchant, bin man or used car salesman in need of a name, they'd call him Cruncher Kerr for a cheeky poke at *Beano* editor Euan Kerr. No-one was safe from their japes – even their bosses! One very brave *Dandy* writer wrote a 'Fiddle O'Diddle' story featuring a character called Bridie O'Brien, the Irish tinker woman. Luckily for him, Managing Editor Frances O'Brien saw the funny side.

Bridie O'Brien, a character in 'Fiddle O'Diddle'.

50 YEARS AND COUNTING

Riona McElfatrick was much more than the office art assistant. She was the main party co-ordinator and there were plenty of them.

CLUB
SWANKO
de
POSH
1937 - 1987

250 guests attended the 50th birthday bash at Dan's favourite Club Swanko de Posh.

invites you to a buffet-dance
in honour of
50 years of the Dandy Comic
The Scotsman, Gellatly Street, Dundee
Thursday, 3rd December, 1987

7 pm to 1 am

R.S.V.P.
M. Heggie, The Dandy
D. C. Thomson Ltd.
Dundee DD1 9QJ

Don't let looks fool you. Chief sub-editor Fred Crowe was a demon on the dance floor – and the rugby field.

*Craig Ferguson, brilliant scriptwriter for **The Dandy** and outstanding party animal.*

***The Dandy** gang at Club Swanko de Posh. The cowpie was pinched from the BBC Arena programme made about **The Dandy** and **The Beano** at the time.*

NEW ARTISTS
TOM PATERSON

Cartoon germs from an episode of 'Laughing Planet'.

Brain Duane.

TOM PATERSON was a stalwart of IPC's stable of comics and he had drawn for them for years, creating many characters, by the time *The Dandy* persuaded him to tackle a strip. His drawing style was based on the work of Leo Baxendale whose 'Bash Street Kids' he had loved as a boy. Tom's pages were crammed with hilarious little characters, signs and slogans which he would add to the background to embellish the actual strip he was drawing. Tom, however, was no stranger to *The Dandy*. As a schoolboy he had sent sample drawings in to editor Albert Barnes who was mightily impressed. Albert would drive down to Tom's home and encourage the budding genius – something he did with no other artist (see page 200). However, the Barnes–Paterson partnership did not flourish when Tom left school and he started work, aged eighteen, cartooning with IPC. His sets for *The Dandy* included 'Brain Duane', 'Fiddle O'Diddle' and the fantastic 'Hyde and Shriek'. Some of his best series were done working with *Dandy* scriptwriter Dan McGahey, whose zany stories appealed to Tom's sense of humour. Their 'Laughing Planet' series is a comic classic.

'The World's Daftest Discoveries' were hilarious, complex art spreads.

NEW ARTISTS
KEN HARRISON

'Rah-Rah Randall' was **The Dandy***'s answer to 'Dennis the Menace'.*

Ken took on the drawing of 'Desperate Dan' in 1983, after **The Dandy** *stopped reprinting classic Dudley Watkins strips.*

'Harry and His Hippo' was an annuals favourite.

KEN H. HARRISON was working in advertising when, on a job in Scotland, he met up with *Beano* artist David Sutherland. Their chat led to Ken sending in sample work to D.C. Thomson. Ken started his *Dandy* career drawing 'Sir Coward de Custard', the tale of a hapless knight who is saved by his smart young squire. He was the pen behind 'Mitch and His Mummy' and 'Rah-Rah Randall' before he took over as illustrator of 'Desperate Dan' in 1983, Ken was a classic Dan artist as one of the great influences on his drawing technique had been the work of Dudley Watkins. Later Ken would be asked to relinquish 'Desperate Dan' and take over on two other Watkins-designed strips 'Oor Wullie' and 'The Broons', the iconic Scottish characters that had been running in *The Sunday Post* newspaper since 1936. Ken did those wonderfully well also. His work on 'Desperate Dan' during the 1980s was one of the important milestones in the gradual modernisation of the title. Ken is held in the highest regard amongst his peers and at the time of going to press is still doing terrific strips of 'Minnie the Minx' for *The Beano*, working once again with ex-*Dandy* chief sub-editor Iain McLaughlin who wrote many of his 'Desperate Dan' stories.

Sir Coward de Custard was a real wimp.

219

NEW ARTISTS
BARRIE APPLEBY

ME'S DIMPLES!

ME'S CUDDLES!

THE DANDY ANNUAL 2003

ME'S FUNNY!

ME'S FUNNY TOO!

IT'S US, FOLKS!

BARRIE APPLEBY was an experienced cartoonist working for many titles with both D.C. Thomson and London-based IPC. He had worked on both *Nutty* and *Hoot* with Morris Heggie and came to *The Dandy* when Heggie was made editor. His characters 'Cuddles and Dimples', the terror toddlers, were amazingly popular. His trademark look was the bold line and ability to create radical layouts for this wildest of comic series. A spin-off from 'Cuddles and Dimples' was 'Ted Time Tales', a strip where the tots' vampire teddy bear came to life. It was obvious Barrie enjoyed drawing the selection of evil toys that inhabited the toy cupboard. Over the years Barrie encouraged many budding artists who were invited to visit his cluttered Suffolk studio, and he would gladly pass on tips he had picked up over the years. Barrie now works for *The Beano* drawing 'Roger the Dodger'.

NEW ARTISTS
NICK BRENNAN

Blinky and his sidekick,
Yellow Dog.

IN 1993 Nick Brennan arrived on *The Dandy* editor's doorstep with sample cartoon strips in his hand. He had never done cartooning before, and had been working in the drawing office of an aircraft manufacturer. The cartoons were rough, very stylised and not at all Dandyesque, however they made the editor laugh. They shrieked energy and fun. Nick was commissioned to do a series of 'Peter Piper', the old *Magic Comic* story – in his unique style which could not be further from Watkins, who first drew 'Peter Piper'. His most popular *Dandy* strip was 'Blinky' which the kids loved. 'Blinky' had his own fan club 'Blinky's Barmy Army' with crazy T-shirts and posters. Blinky's long-suffering sidekick, Yellow Dog, won a coveted Eagle award in 1997. Nick was helped immensely in his career by his artist wife Fran who often would colour Nick's drawings. She was no mean scriptwriter either, and the editor reckoned the best 'Blinky' strips were when Fran was scripting and Nick drawing.

COMPACT COMICS

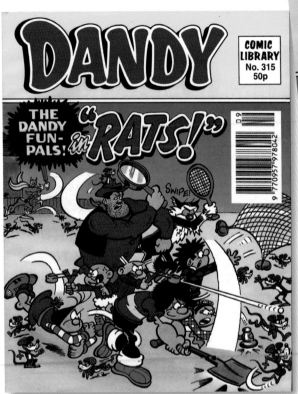

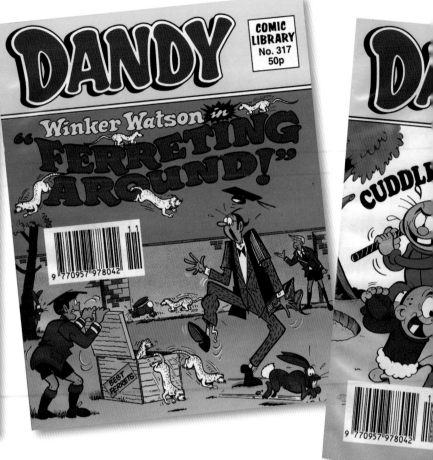

POCKET-SIZED comics called *Dandy Comic Libraries* appeared on sale in 1983. They contained one long sixty-four-page story featuring many of the *Dandy*'s top characters. The editor was Ian Gray, who would shortly become chief sub-editor on *The Dandy* weekly. The longer story gave more room for character development and could include some of the character's back story. The 'Desperate Dan' and 'Winker Watson' issues were the most popular but, coming out at the rate of two a month, they covered most known *Dandy* stars. *Dandy* editorial found them a good vehicle for trying out budding young artists, allowing their skill at drawing, say 'Beryl the Peril', to be honed in the little libraries before giving them a run in the weekly.

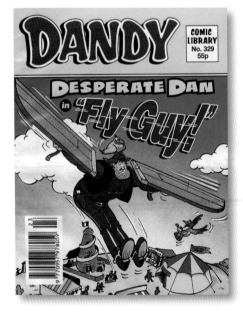

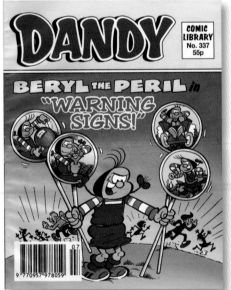

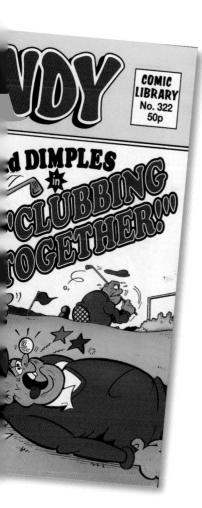

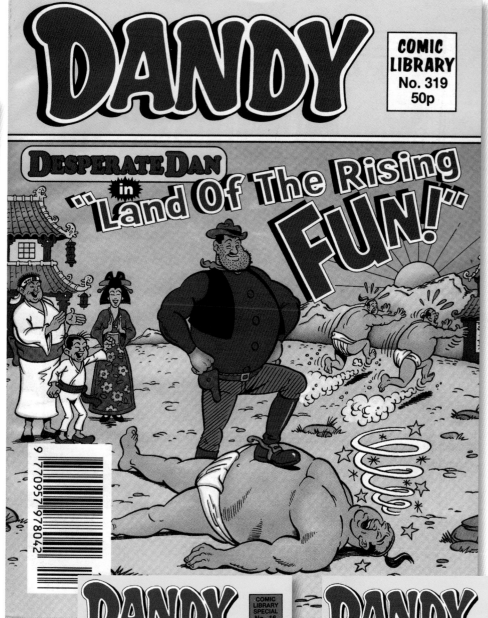

Nobody could write funny titles for the stories better than editor Ian Gray.

Dandy Cartoon Books, *featuring single-page cartoons, joined the series in 1985.*

THE DANDY

CHAPTER SEVEN

Goodbye Bullies

1990–2005

Bullying gets the boot as full colour brightens **The Dandy***!*

BYE BYE BULLIES

It was not only the unruly pupils who were violent in 'The Jocks and the Geordies'

N THE early 1990s some of the characters and storylines in **The Dandy** were perceived to be too violent, albeit comic violence. Political correctness was casting an eye at the fabric of the comic. 'The Jocks and the Geordies' story, which had been running since 1975, featured two gangs of battling schoolboys. The strip was the idea of Albert Barnes himself and even back at its start his chief sub-editor, Dave Torrie, had reservations about the level of comic violence it portrayed. It was drawn by Jimmy Hughes whose rough-hewn inking did give the story an angry look and the story was dropped in 1997. The other casualty was the 'Bully Beef and Chips' strip which like 'The Jocks and the Geordies', was drawn by Jimmy Hughes. The editor changed artists on the strip to give it a softer line but the spectre of bullying remained and it, too, was stopped in 1997. The friendly art styles of Bob Nixon and Sid Burgon had not saved it.

226

The final 'Bully Beef and Chips', drawn by Sid Burgon.

The final frame from 'The Jocks and the Geordies'.

227

FULL COLOUR COMIC AT LONG LAST

IN SEPTEMBER 1993 a cracking David Parkins drawn 'Desperate Dan' cover heralded the fact that *The Dandy* was increasing in pages and, more importantly, every page was now in full colour. Market research had shown that children perceived black-and-white pages to be old-fashioned. Well, if your parents were watching a black-and-white film, it was an oldie. The change was welcomed by editorial staff as it gave them another tool to play with when designing a page or writing a story. The in-house colourists, part of the Art Department at D.C. Thomson, were probably not so enamoured as their workload increased dramatically as many of the freelance artists continuing to draw in line only, leaving the colouring to the office.

Without doubt the most colourful Dan to date.

Artist Brian Walker who drew 'Barney', painted his strips in colour.

Black-and-white line drawings now looked unfinished. Compare these Pete Moonie drawings of 'Dinah Mo' in black-and-white and colour.

Tom Paterson's colourful 'Fiddle O'Diddle'.

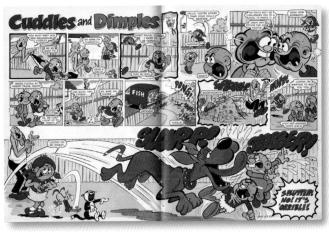

The 'Molly' artist David Mostyn liked doing colour work. He was one of the unsung heroes of 1990s **Dandy**.

'Korky the Cat' was back in full colour, just as he was at the start in 1937.

'Bananaman', the true-blue superhero was now blue, though seldom a hero.

At last, in this new 'Winker Watson' story, the Aliens really are as green as grass.

'Jonah' artist Keith Robson was a wonderful colourist. His sky effects were spectacular. 'Jonah' originally appeared in **The Beano,** *drawn by Ken Reid, as seen here in black-and-white.*

233

WORLD'S LONGEST RUNNING COMIC

THERE WAS a party in *The Dandy* office in June 1999. The staff, comprising of editor Morris Heggie, chief sub-editor Fred Crowe, Iain McLaughlin, Craig Ferguson, Andy Sturrock and art assistant Riona McElfatrick had just put to press issue No. 3007 which made *The Dandy* the longest running British comic, so securing a place in *The Guinness Book of Records*. The office received accolades from contributors and fans but not from their sister comic *The Beano*, rivalry between the two offices still being fierce. Ken Harrison would go on to draw a wonderful spread of characters from *The Dandy*'s back catalogue (shown below) to illustrate the entry in *The Guinness Book of Records*.

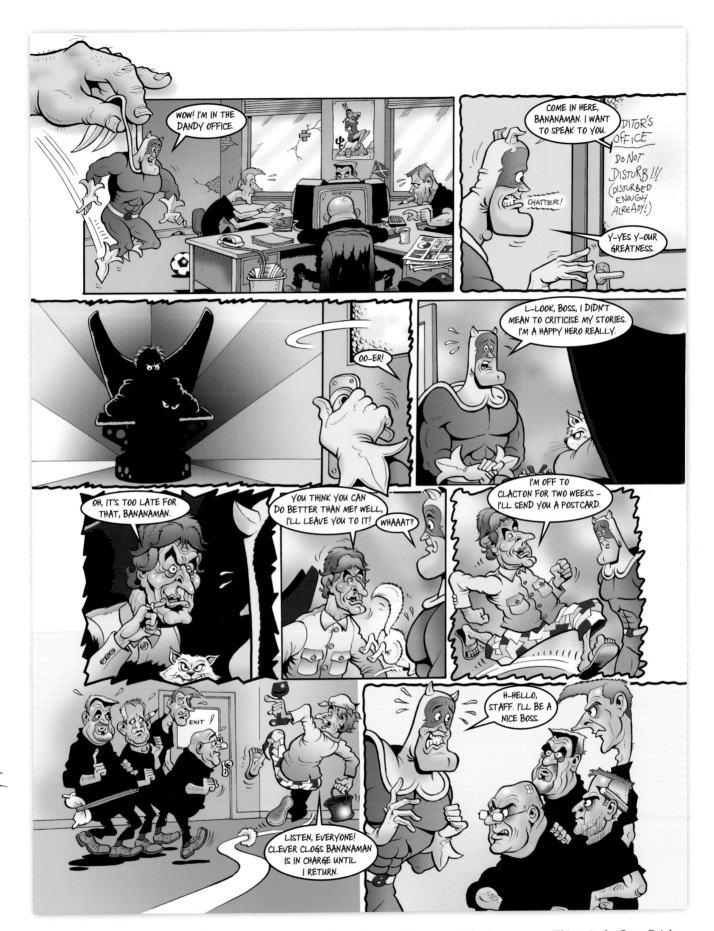

The Editor's job on the record-breaking comic was hard and he needed a holiday – a task for Bananaman. This strip, by Steve Bright, features Morris Heggie and the twenty-first century editorial staff, from left to right in the panel at the bottom left: Iain McLaughlin, Gordon Tait, Craig Graham and Al Bernard.

DAN GOES MISSING

A FUN story started in *The Dandy* on November 1, 1997. 'Desperate Dan' had struck oil while doing a bungee jump and become seriously rich. The wealth went to the big galoot's head and he resigned from the comic. A worldwide search began to find someone to fill Dan's boots and be the new star of the comic. Readers sent in the names of celebrities, sports stars, politicians and other comic characters who they felt might make a good substitute for Dan.

Oil rich Dan was not desperate now. He could afford anything he fancied. **The Dandy** and its readers were shocked.

The unthinkable happens. Dan had been in **The Dandy** *since 1937. The country's media were interested now and asking the question – is this the end of* **The Dandy**?

237

Dan sailing off with the Spice Girls was the front cover story on the tabloids.

On the pages of the comic Sir Trevor McDonald announces the demise of Dan on national news. Ken Harrison's drawing of Sir Trevor was absolutely spot on, a marvellous caricature.

FELLOW DANDY STARS, CUDDLES AND DIMPLES, HAD THIS TO SAY . . .

COO-EE, MUM.

USSES IS ONNA TELLY.

I'LL, ER, RETURN YOU TO THE EDITOR IN THE STUDIO.

LIVID RD.

Not all **Dandy** *stars were bothered about Dan going. Some fancied their cover character status.*

OI! WHO'S TAKEN THE **DAN** OUT OF THE **DANDY** ??

THE DANDY

EVERY MONDAY   *fun for boys and girls!*   No. 2922 November 22nd, 1997   45p

COULD *YOU* FILL DESPERATE DAN'S BOOTS ?

SITUATION VACANT

URGENTLY REQUIRED . Big, strong man with bristly chin and bulging biceps to star on pages of famous comic. Must like cow pie and owl-hoot juice and be adept at wrestling with grizzly bears. Apply to the Mayor of Cactusville

YIPPEE ! NO MORE SORE HEADS FROM DAN'S BIG BOOTS !

MR DANDY EDITOR IS HOLDING INTERVIEWS IN THE TOWN SQUARE.

WANTED ROUGH·TOUGH MACHO·MAN FOR DESPERATE DAN'S JOB APPLY IN PERSON

HOO-WEE! THIS IS GOING TO BE A LONG DAY.

The readers' favourite to take over from Dan was boxing champ Frank Bruno. He was certainly big enough. TV presenters Dani Behr and Chris Tarrant were also nominees. From the USA Arnold Schwarzenegger was the favourite candidate.

The mention of the 60th Birthday issue (right) was a clue that things would turn out well.

AUNTIE AND GENTLEMEN, WE HAVE FOUND NO REPLACEMENT FOR DAN. IT IS MY SAD DUTY TO CLOSE THIS COMIC STRIP.

BOO-HOO! AND IT'S OUR 60TH BIRTHDAY NEXT WEEK.

CHEER UP, AUNT AGGIE. THERE MAY BE NO DAN BUT THE DANDY IS A DOUBLE-SIZE BIRTHDAY SPECIAL NEXT WEEK.

The 60th Birthday **Dandy** *was a double-sized issue with a painted cover by Keith Robson. Keith also drew a picture story called 'Tricky Dicky Doyle' for this special issue, about a boy who owned his own practical joke factory. This tale had first appeared in* **The Dandy** *as a text story in 1943.*

Dan realises without him **The Dandy** *is doomed.*

Dan feels small as he sees The Dandy fall.

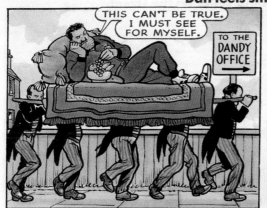

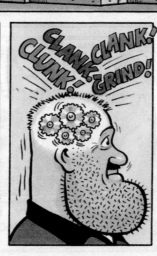

Sir Trevor McDonald was delighted when **The Dandy** *art assistant Riona McElfatrick sent him prints of his appearance in the comic.*

The happiest of endings for **The Dandy**'s *diamond anniversary.*

200 Gray's Inn Road
London WC1X 8XZ
Telephone 0171 833 3000
Facsimile 0171 430 4082

Ms Riona McElfatrick
The Dandy
D C Thomson & Co Ltd
Albert Square
Dundee DD1 9QJ

ITN

March 23, 1998

Dear Riona

I am writing to thank you most sincerely for all the help you gave in sending us the framed record of my appearance in The Dandy. You were very kind and patient through all the difficulties of getting the copy to us. It is now absolutely splendid and will, when we have decided where, occupy pride of place in our home. I am very delighted to have it and thank you most warmly for all the help you gave.

May I take this opportunity to send my kindest regards to all your colleagues who signed the letter to me and above all, Long Live Fun!

Best wishes.

Yours sincerely

Trevor McDonald

DAN'S BIRTHDAY MESSAGE

Hello,

Dear Dandy fans,

I hope you are enjoying this monster edition of your favourite comic. I apologise for the worry I've given you over the last few weeks. When I struck oil I guess I struck my head as well — how could I forget my pals just because of some dollars? Aunt Aggie will never let *me* forget — be sure. I've been trying to get back in her good books recently and offered to do her ironing. I guess it wasn't too smart to use a road roller — especially when I flattened her feet.

Aunt Aggie has often said I'm a little bit touched at times but I can tell you I was really touched by the letters and phone calls the Editor got asking me to come back. Thank you one and all.

I met an old pal on my travels. He was in the very first Dandy with me. I didn't recognise him at first but his face rang a *bell*. No wonder — he was the bell hop who told all The Dandy readers what was coming the next week. Cute little fellow, ain't he? You'll see him in quite a few of our pages this week.

Well, my fingers are getting sore now so I'll say cheerio.

See y'all next week.
Your pal for the next 60 years.
Desperate Dan

WHY THE BELLHOP?

FROM THE first issue of *The Dandy*, a mysterious figure was a constant presence on the cover: an unnamed hotel bellhop stood grinning by *The Dandy* masthead. Who was he? He never starred in a comic strip, although he did occasionally appear within, never speaking but carrying out normal bellhop duties. Mascots were not unusual for story papers, but in this instance his unexplained presence hints at a deeper meaning which may have been lost to us.

The best surmise may be that *The Dandy* was intended to be seen as a sort of hotel for kids, a house of fun, and that the bellhop was their welcome party and guide, a friendly face whose task was to ensure that his guests' stays were enjoyable. He also informed readers of what to expect in the next week's issue.

HITTING THE HEADLINES

The record-breaking Dandy did not go unnoticed either.

The tabloids loved the fact that The Spice Girls were on Dan's yacht.

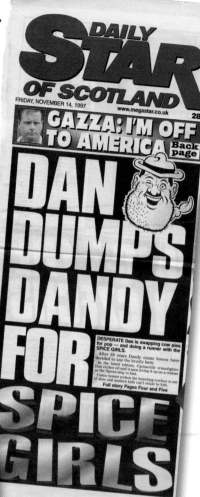

DAILY STAR OF SCOTLAND

FRIDAY, NOVEMBER 14, 1997   www.megastar.co.uk   28p

GAZZA: I'M OFF TO AMERICA Back page

DAN DUMPS DANDY FOR SPICE GIRLS

DESPERATE Dan is swapping cow pies for pop — and doing a runner with the SPICE GIRLS.

After 60 years Dandy comic bosses have decided to axe the bristly hero.

In the latest edition, Cactusville crimefighter Dan strikes oil and is seen living it up on a cruiser as the Spices sing to him.

Comic bosses reckon the brawling cowboy is out of date and modern kids can't relate to him.

Full story Pages Four and Five

THE EXPRESS, WEDNESDAY, JULY 7, 1999

New record

Scotland's best-loved comic makes history with 3,007 fun issues

BY BRIAN SWANSON

BREAK out the cactus juice and bring on the cow pie, the good folk of Cactusville are planning a high old time tonight, yessiree, indeedie.

If the above means nothing to you then you have never giggled at the antics of Desperate Dan, never grinned like an adolescent idiot at Korky the Cat, nor read The Dandy instead of doing homework.

Thankfully few other Scots have lived a similarly Dandy-free life.

And a good thing too because thanks to many generations of devoted readers, The Dandy enter the Guinness Book of Records as the world's longest running comic.

"Jings" as Oor Wullie, another favourite from the DC Thomson stable might say.

Saturday will see the release of its 3007th edition, finally beating the record held by the long defunct Comic Cuts since 1953.

Although sales have fallen from two million a week in the comic's heyday of the 1950s, to

SHAVEN: Desperate Dan could have missed the record-breaking issue if bosses had gone through with plans to scrap the character

As THE *Dandy* grew older its storylines were often picked up by the press. Amongst the headline makers was the lead-up to the 60th Birthday issue of *The Dandy*, with its great storyline of Dan leaving and running off with the Spice Girls. Other stories included the banning of cowpies due to mad cow disease, Dan losing his gun and becoming 'PC' and *The Dandy* being attacked by the millennium bug. Subsequent record-breaking issues and birthdays received good coverage. 'Desperate Dan' was also a tool for many of the political cartoonists working for the dailies.

Daily Record Tuesday, July 20,

CARTOON TIME: Artist Judi gets to work on the adventures of Keyhole Kate, right

Dandy draws on girl power

IT'S been around for 62 years, there have been 3007 issues and it is now the longest-running children's comic in the world.

But the Dandy has never had a female artist – until now.

Graphic artist Judi Mitchell created a bit of history yesterday when she finally breached the all-male bastion and started her new job drawing long-standing favourite, Keyhole Kate.

The 25-year-old, of Laurencekirk, Aberdeenshire, has been a Dandy fan since she was a little girl. But she's not

that bothered about striking a blow for sex equality.

She said: "It was a bonus to find out I was the first female to work here, but I've never been a feminist or anything – it's not a big deal."

Dundee-based publishers DC Thomson employ about 20 cartoonists on the Dandy and most work from home. Like the others, Judi will be given a script, and she reckons it will take her about a day to draw each Keyhole Kate page.

THE EXPRESS, SUNDAY, NOVEMBER 23, 1997

WANTED SOMEONE TO TAKE OVER FROM **DESPERATE DAN**

SEE! HIS HUGE APPETITE FOR EATING HUMBLE PIES

WINCHESTER

DESPERA
A DANDY NEW C

OOOPS! THERE'S ANOTHER SEAT GONE!

NEW-LOOK LINE-UP F
THE DANDY

ust Dandy

O WATCH THEIR WORDS, NOT LOOK AT PICTURES

or literacy
king at the
ks.
found factu-
venture sto-
mics were
a "face-sav-
te".
ear study of
-year-olds,
from the
outhampton
ys who are

weaker readers just tend to
look at pictures. It encourages
laziness and is no substitute
for spending time on a text."
The findings conflict with
Government guidelines recom-
mending boys — who lag behind
girls in reading — should be
given stimulating material.
Two months ago Education
Secretary David Blunkett told
teachers boys should read
exciting books so they would
think school was "cool".

COOL APPEAL: Blun

*Dan gets a makeover and makes
the centre pages.*

Holy cow pie

They took his cigs and his favourite
grub — now they've taken Desperate
Dan from us. But the
old rogue's still got
enough strength to
run off with the
Spice Girls ...

Dandy's desperate situation

THE EXPRESS SATURDAY, MAY 15, 1999

'Millennium
bug' may hit
record edition

(photo of man holding Dandy comics)

Dreadlock Holmes

The boy detective marking a new start for the Dandy

Daily Mail, Friday, September 24, 2004

INTRODUCING the boy detective
on a mission to bring the world's
longest-running comic up to date.
Dreadlock Holmes is the first ethnic
ity character to appear in the
's 67-year history.

By Michael Taggart

I'M FANCY DAN

Daily Record Friday, September 24, 2004   Page 41

'Dated' comic
gets revamp

By Craig McDonald
c.mcdonald@dailyrecord.co.uk

THE Dandy is getting a makeover in
an attempt to revive flagging sales.

NEW AGE:
Ollie Fliptrick,
Jak, and
Dreadlock
Holmes

Gun ban for Desperate Dan

Comic hero victim of political correctness

Daily Express Friday September 24 2004   31

FOR 70 years the adventures of
Desperate Dan have kept millions of children enthralled.

By Jo Willey

HECTOR BREEZE

"Oh, no! Desperate
Dan's joined the Lib
Dems!"

MAKEOVER:
The new Dan
has lost his
gun, circled,
and even his
spurs, a long
way from the
cowboy in his
glory days,
right

*Dan losing his gun was a
controversy. Was Dan being made
too 'PC' the media asked?*

*Will he, won't
he go? Desperate
Dan was the talk
of the town.*

BERNARD INGHAM

You may say I'm mad...

PEOPLE are beginning to talk. Readers think I
am "paranoid" about Tony Blair. I would put it
differently. While I acknowledge he was a gracious
host at the Queen's golden wedding lunch, I am
disappointed and disturbed by his leadership. I
had better explain myself.

THE SUN, Friday, September 24, 2004   45

SEE!
HIS TOUGHER
THAN TOUGH
HIDE —
HE'LL SURE
NEED IT!!

LASSIC SCOTS WEEKLY

oes PC ...that's Politically Comic, folks!

Sun

Saturday, November 15, 1997   20p   MADE IN SCOTLAND FOR SCOTLAND

IT'S A
DANDY
READ

10 FREE
GOES
ON TONIGHT'S
£10 LOTTO

DAN'S
A FAN
He loves today's
FREE
TV mag

PLEASE
DAN'T GO!

THE DANDY

CHAPTER EIGHT

A New Editor

2006 . . . and into the future

Preparing for the next seventy-five years.

A NEW EDITOR

WITH A DIFFICULT TASK...

Editor Craig Graham hard at work.

WHEN MORRIS Heggie moved on in 2007, taking over D.C. Thomson's comic archive, that rarest of things was required . . . a new *Dandy* editor, only the fourth in its history!

The man to take on that honour was Craig Graham, a *Dandy* staff writer. After joining *The Dandy* in 2001, he became 'Spokesman' for the comic in 2004. In a previous life, he had also 'done time' on *The Beano*. Nobody's perfect.

The new editor's most pressing concern was the changing way that comics were bought and sold.

The heyday of comics coincided with the age of the newsagent. Children could pop into the corner shop on their way to school and buy a new comic every day. Most didn't have the means to do this, so comics were swapped and traded, becoming a sort of playground currency.

But at the start of the twenty-first century, the newsagent at the bottom of the street had largely been replaced by the supermarket on the edge of town, and ever more kids were being driven to school instead of walking.

How would *The Dandy* deal with this shift in shopping habits?

THE DANDY ETHOS IN A TIME OF CHANGE

WHILE THE DANDY had its share of iconic characters, it had always been an anthology comic: a collection of disparate stories, albeit with a common ethos. This was the norm with British humour comics, but a new kind of children's magazine had appeared in recent years. Based on characters from television or films, these magazines relied heavily on browsing children or parents recognising the cover star. Free gifts added to the appeal, often resembling toys you could actually buy.

The Dandy responded by challenging its competitors

The Dandy *had to change, but the essential, cheeky fun of childhood was never likely to be replaced.*

head-on. For the first time, characters from outside the D.C. Thomson stable would star on the cover. Inside, as well as the traditional *Dandy* comic strips, there were features on video games, movies and television shows. There were competitions, puzzles and games.

It was a long way from the old *Dandy*, but the new *Dandy* was still cheeky, anarchic and fun-loving. To highlight the changes made to Britain's longest-running comic, its name was changed: *The Dandy* was about to become *Dandy Xtreme*.

DANDY XTREME

DANDY XTREME launched in August 2007 as a fortnightly publication. With a free gift on every issue, and the biggest movie stars on the front cover, it was well placed to fight against the new pretenders to its throne. Readers loved it. They loved to see their idols in the comic, the games and film reviews, the competitions, the humour and, of course, the comic strips, too, in a sixteen-page pullout *Dandy Comix* section

Traditionalist comic fans were less enthusiastic. 'It's not *The Dandy* we know and love,' they cried, and they were right . . . up to a point.

Craig Graham maintains that upsetting older readers in order to please new readers is part and parcel of editing a national institution like *The Dandy*.

'The best *Dandy* is always *The Dandy* you grew up with,' he explains. 'People cherish their memories of comics, and when things change it can feel like an attack on their childhood.'

'I think it's great that people care enough about *The Dandy* to tell me when they like – or dislike – it and comment on what we're doing, and I enjoy a good-natured debate with our older readers who don't see why change is necessary. They usually vent their ire at me for a minute or two, but then they usually talk themselves round to my point of view!'

Dandy Xtreme *looked at changing to an A5 'schoolbag' size in 2009, but the comic would have been hard to find on crowded shop shelves.*

BACK TO THE FUTURE

IN EARLY 2010, *The Dandy* team presented their vision for the future of Britain's longest-running comic to the D.C. Thomson management. It was a big change from *Dandy Xtreme*, and as they waited for the verdict on their efforts, the team held their breath. They needn't have worried as their proposals were accepted

The 'new' comic harked back to its roots, but it was new and fresh. It looked modern, but hand-crafted. It was easy to read, but had laughs for adults as well as kids. It had classic comic characters and bang-up-to-date celebrity spoofs. In short, it was a modern version of the original *Dandy*, full of wisecracking irreverence and whimsical silliness. It seemed only right to lose 'Xtreme' from the title – *The Dandy* was back to stay.

THE HUNT FOR FRESH CARTOON TALENT

THE RACE was on to get the new *Dandy* ready to launch in October 2010. There was a serious amount of work to do, and very little time, considering that *Dandy Xtreme* also had to carry on until the launch.

'The first thing we did was set about finding some new artists,' said Craig Graham. 'Although we knew we already had some of the best illustrators in the business working for us, there was no way they could produce enough strips to fill the new comic. For a start, each issue would need twice as much artwork as *Dandy Xtreme*, and we were going back to weekly publication too – it was going to be a mammoth task!'

'We already had a few suitable artists on file, but we put out some emails to clubs and forums and asked our regular contributors if they knew anyone who could help out. In the end, we were delighted to find that there were many really talented cartoonists out there, and even more delighted that they wanted to join our team.'

254

OLD FRIENDS AND NEW RECRUITS TOGETHER

THE ARTISTS OF THE NEW

GRADUALLY, THE roster of artists for the first revamp issue was decided. Chosen because of their diverse styles and somehow complementary senses of humour, the roll of honour (in no particular order) was: Nigel Parkinson, Wayne Thompson, Duncan Scott, David Mostyn, Lew Stringer, Nigel Auchterlounie, Chris McGhie, Jamie Smart, Alexander Matthews, Andy Fanton, Phil Corbett and Garry Davies.

'The thing we really wanted was for the comic to feel like it was drawn by hand,' said Craig Graham. 'We had all these great artists producing brilliant strips, and to make the comic feel glossy and precise like a normal magazine would have ruined that.'

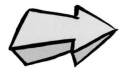

'Scratch of the Week' by Garry Davies.

'Doctor, Doctor' by David Mostyn.

'Professor Dandy' by Nigel Auchterlounie.

'Robot on the Run' by Alexander Matthews.

WE PUZZLED over the use of computers for ages because, at the end of the day, you do actually need them to make comics these days. Finally, we made a list of all the things that might ruin the effect we were looking for (like page numbers, text boxes, empty panels, etc.) and had Jamie Smart draw them for us. That way we could be sure everything would look like it had been drawn by hand – because it was! We really wanted kids to be inspired to think they could draw their own comics, and it worked – they sent in loads to us!'

'We were so pleased with the result that we went a bit nuts and asked Jamie to complete a style guide of widgets which would cover everything we needed. It's a great bit of work: really funny, unique and inventive.'

'Pre-Skool Prime Minister' by Jamie Smart.

'Count Snotula' by Duncan Scott.

'Postman Prat' by Lew Stringer.

RETURN OF THE CARTOON STRIP!

THE DANDY has always been home to some of Britain's greatest comic strip creations. Can you imagine a discussion of British comics without mention of 'Desperate Dan', 'Korky the Cat' or 'Winker Watson'?

It was this proud heritage which *The Dandy* turned to in 2010. But rather than rely on those great names from the past, *The Dandy* was determined to come up with some new and fresh ideas to sit alongside the classics of the past.

In the timeless spirit of sticking one's tongue out at authority, the new *Dandy* took on boring politicians, teachers who wanted to be 'down with the kids' and meddlers who wanted to take the fun out of childhood.

It also poked fun at consumer goods, movies and advertising in its inspired 'Madvertisements', in which absurd, made-up products were offered for sale.

In returning to its cartoon roots, *The Dandy* did not offer an escape from modern life, but celebrated it in the best way possible – by laughing at it!

'Kid Cops' made sure the Law of **The Dandy** was upheld.

Classic characters, such as 'Bananaman', were given a new look to bring them up-to-date.

'Madvertisements' poked fun at popular products.

*'What's in Cheryl's Hair Today?' was just one of the daft things that appeared in **The Dandy**!*

Even the Queen was featured, begging your pardon, Ma'am!

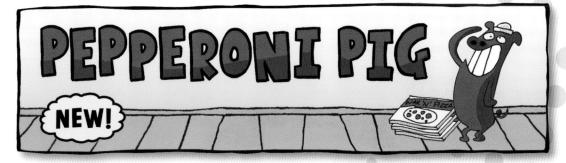

BRING ON THE CELEBS

Harry Hill burst into **The Dandy** *in October 2010.*

IT'S NO secret that 'celebrity' culture has exploded in Britain in the last few years, and children are just as interested in 'celebs' as adults are. Knowing this, *The Dandy* team decided they wanted to have some fun. So the comic began to poke gentle fun at the great and the good, like Jeremy Clarkson, Stephen Fry, Cheryl Cole, Lord Sugar and, of course, Simon Cowell.

The Dandy's resident celebrity was Harry Hill, of 'TV Burp' and 'You've Been Framed' fame. Harry was delighted to be asked to star in his very own comic strip, and even roped in some of his 'TV Burp' writers to chip in some ideas. Beautifully executed by Nigel Parkinson, 'Harry Hill's Real-Life Adventures in TV-Land' is one of the highlights in *The Dandy*'s long and much-loved history.

To be caricatured in *The Dandy* is very much an honour, and most celebrities featured get in touch to say how delighted they are – often asking for a signed print for their dressing-room wall!

Celebrities were cast as junior versions ('Little Simon' for Simon Cowell) of their adult personae.

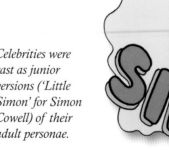

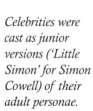

Chris Evans' appearance featured one of his beloved Ferraris as a pedal-car!

Gordon Ramsay took on the dinner ladies at his school.

Lord Sugar's grumpy 'Apprentice' face made him a natural for inclusion.

Who knew! Lord Sugar is played by Sid James and the others are Kenneth Williams and Barbara Windsor from the 'Carry On' films!!

It explains a lot! I had thought *The Apprentice* was a serious show, but now I know it's a *comedy* --

Just a minute and I'll soon have you done! It's a *sign of the times* how much work you three need!!!

Lord S, matey, I've got a *sales* problem here!

Ah well, that's something you need to work hard at!

Hard work never hurt anyone!

Wayne Rooney's hair transplant was ripe for **Dandy** treatment!

The Queen, this time doing Olympic duties.

Yes, that **is** Simon Cowell dressed as Michael Jackson!

TAILPIECE

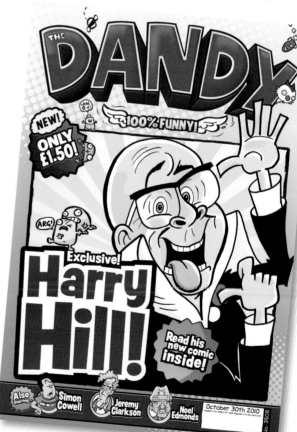

AFTER seventy-five years, four editors and more than 3,500 editions, does *The Dandy* of today have anything in common with its groundbreaking ancestor? Well, a surprising amount!

TODAY'S **DANDY** lampoons authority and celebrates the anarchy of childhood – as it did in 1937.
TODAY'S **DANDY** is surreal and surprising, but also rooted in the everyday – as it was in 1937.
TODAY'S **DANDY** is funny – just as it was in 1937.

How can this be? Well, *The Dandy* has never forgotten who reads it: children. For children, there is nothing to say that a cowboy can't go to the Moon, or that a cat can't talk. In *The Dandy*, the normal rules of life are there to be bent . . . in the readers' favour.

Comics are an escape from rules, from authority, and there are just as many rules to be bent today as there were seventy-five years ago – maybe even more!

The Dandy is and always will be thoroughly, defiantly, magnificently NOT for grown-ups – exactly as it was in 1937!

THE *DANDY* INDEX OF STRIPS AND STORIES

This index provides much information on The Dandy and is divided into three sections. The first section is organised chronologically. For each year up to 1986 there is a summary of publishing details (price, number of pages, free gifts) and then a listing of the characters that first appeared in that year, including how long the strip ran for (not always continuously), the artist and, in most cases, a synopsis. From 1986 there is just a listing of new characters.

After each strip there is a symbol which identifies the type of strip (from 1986, all strips are comic strips):

(C)   Comic strip
(A)   Adventure strip
(CA)   Comic adventure strip
(S)   Prose story

The second section is an index of artists active up to the end of 1985, listing, for each artist, the strips worked on. The third section is an alphabetical index to the book.

The material up to the end of 1985 has been taken from *The Dandy Monster Index*, written by Ray Moore. We are most grateful to Ray Moore for his permission to reproduce his work and offer our sincere thanks.

1937
Price: 2d.
Page count: 28; published every Friday.
Free gifts: No. 1 (4.12.37) – Express Whistler; No. 2 (11.12.37) – Jumping Frog.

KORKY THE CAT (C)
No. 1 (4.12.37) to date, with gaps 2005, 2007-10
Art: No. 1 (4.12.37) – No. 1051 (13.1.62), James Crichton
No. 1052 (20.1.62) – No. 2116 (12.6.82), Charlie Grigg

No. 2117 (19.6.82) to 1986, mostly David Gudgeon 1986-99, Robert Nixon 1999-2007, Dave Sutherland, Steve Bright, Lesley Reavey, Dave Windett, Henry Davies, Andrew Painter 2010 to date, Phil Corbett
Cover: No. 1 (4.12.37) – No. 2242 (10.11.84), except No. 295 (26.6.45)

KEYHOLE KATE (C)
No. 1 (4.12.37) – No. 721 (17.9.55)
Art: Allan Morley
Cover: Appeared as cover strip in No. 295 (26.6.45)

DESPERATE DAN (C)
No. 1 (4.12.37) to date
Art: No. 1 (4.12.37) – No. 1454 (4.10.69), Dudley Watkins
No. 1455 (11.10.69) – No. 2148 (22.1.83), Dudley Watkins reprints, with a few by Charlie Grigg and one by Bill Holroyd
No. 2149 (29.1.83) to 2007, Ken Harrison (John Geering, 1994-7; also David Perkins) 2008 to date, Jamie Smart
Cover: No. 2243 (17.11.84) – to 2007
Desperate Dan Books: 1954, 1979, 1990, 1991, 1992, 1997

JIMMY AND HIS GROCKLE (CA)
No. 1 (4.12.37) – No. 106 (9.12.39)
Young Jimmy Johnson receives the present of a huge egg from his Uncle Bill in South America, from which emerges a dragon-like creature which breathes fire and emits a strange 'grockle' sound.
Art: James Clark

THE TRICKS OF TOMMY (S)
No. 1 (4.12.37) – No. 10 (5.2.38)
Fun with a lad called Tommy Payne, a joker who gets up to mischief by imitating other people's voices.
Art: Fred Sturrock

OUR GANG (C)
No. 1 (4.12.37) – No. 340 (29.3.47)
Featuring all the kids (Alfalfa, Spanky, Darla, Buckwheat, etc.) from the 'Our Gang' film shorts produced by Hal Roach for MGM. Due to copyright restrictions the 'Our Gang' strip never appeared in the yearly Dandy Monster Comics.
Art: Dudley Watkins

RED HOOF (S)
No. 1 (4.12.37) – No. 38 (20.8.38)
Ian Duncan, the son of a stalker in the Highlands of Scotland, adopts an orphaned deer fawn as a pet and is told by his father that his fawn 'Red Hoof' may grow up to be a rare 'King Stag'.

LOST ON THE MOUNTAIN OF FEAR (A)
No. 1 (4.12.37) – No. 38 (20.8.38)
Major Bryant, his two children and his man-servant Handy Clark, crash-land their plane on a strange mountain plateau in the Andes. After Major Bryant parachutes from the plateau to seek help Handy and the children have some hair-raising adventures whilst awaiting his return.
Art: Fred Sturrock

THE MAGIC SWORD (S)
No. 1 (4.12.37) – No. 18 (2.4.38)
The adventures of Kelman the fair-haired boy and his magical singing sword. With the help of Omar the Wise Man he must undertake a number of terrible tasks in order to topple the tyrant King Jask from the throne of his homeland Shirak.

BARNEY BOKO (C)
No. 1 (4.12.37) – No. 258 (22.1.44)
Art: John R. Mason

SAMMY AND HIS SISTER (C)
No. 1 (4.12.37) – No. 10 (5.2.38)
Art: Frank Minnitt

HUNGRY HORACE (C)
No. 1 (4.12.37) – No. 860 (17.5.58)
Art: Allan Morley, although latterly some by George Drysdale.

FREDDY THE FEARLESS FLY (C)
No. 1 (4.12.37) – No. 667 (4.9.54)
Art: Allan Morley

MAGIC MIKE AND HIS MAGIC SHOP (C)
No. 1 (4.12.37) – No. 10 (5.2.38)
Art: Sam Fair

SMARTY GRANDPA (C)
No. 1 (4.12.37) – No. 125 (20.4.40)
Granpaw Broon by any other name!
Art: Dudley Watkins

THE TWO BRAVE RUNAWAYS (S)
No. 1 (4.12.37) – No. 38 (20.8.38)
Betty and Jack Brook are two children who run away from the house of their cruel Aunt. Jack, a cripple, has a strange empathy with all kinds of animals while his sister Betty has a beautiful singing voice. Betty's singing brings them unknowingly to the attention of a renowned film director.

THE DARING DEEDS OF BUCK WILSON (A)
No. 1 (4.12.37) – No. 38 (20.8.38)
The adventures on the prairie trail of Buck Wilson the singing cowboy and Snowfire his wonder horse.
Art: Jack Glass

WEE TUSKY (S)
No. 1 (4.12.37) – No. 40 (3.9.38)
The thrilling jungle life of Tusky the baby elephant and Minbu his Mother.

JOKES AND

JOKES AND JOKES (feature)
No. 1 (4.12.37) – No. 131 (1.6.40)

BOASTER BILLY (C)
No. 1 (4.12.37) – No. 10 (5.2.38)
Art: Fred Sturrock

WIG AND WAM THE SKOOKUM TWINS (C)
No. 1 (4.12.37) – No. 77 (20.5.39)
Art: Sam Fair

PODGE (C)
No. 1 (4.12.37) – No. 290 (14.4.45)
Art: Eric Roberts

MUGG MUGGINS (C)
No. 1 (4.12.37) – No. 10 (5.2.38)
Art: Charlie 'Chic' Gordon

WHEN THE WEST WAS WILD (S)
No. 1 (4.12.37) – No. 16 (19.3.38)
Young Jack Ryan, his pony named Star and the prairie wagons are on the danger trail which leads to the Golden West.

INVISIBLE DICK (CA)
No. 1 (4.12.37) – No. 96 (30.9.39)
The comic escapades of young Dick Brett, who becomes invisible every time he sniffs the liquid contained in a strange bronze bottle.
Art: George Ramsbottom

BAMBOO TOWN (C)
No. 1 (4.12.37) – No. 153 (2.11.40) [First Series]
Art: Charlie 'Chic' Gordon

1938
Price: 2d.
Page count: 28; published every Friday.
Free gifts: No. 11 (12.2.38) – Dainty Dandy Nougat; No. 12 (19.2.38) – Dandy Tasty Toffee; No. 39 (27.8.38) – Red Indian bow and two

arrows; No. 40 (3.9.38) – Dandy Nougat Bar; No. 53 (3.12.38) – Dandy Fruity Lollipop.
Annual: The first annual, *The Dandy Monster Comic*, published in September, and annually thereafter.

FLIPPY THE SEA SERPENT (C)
No. 11 (12.2.38) – No. 38 (20.8.38)
Art: Frank Minnitt

TEDDY BEAR (C)
No. 11 (12.2.38) – No. 38 (20.8.38)
Art: Sam Fair

LATE AGAIN LARRY (C)
No. 11 (12.2.38) – No. 38 (20.8.38)
Art: Fred Sturrock

SLEEPY GUS (C)
No. 11 (12.2.38) – No. 38 (20.8.38)
Art: Fred Sturrock

THE HOUSE THAT JACK THE JOKER BUILT (S)
No. 11 (12.2.38) – No. 55 (17.12.38)
A young lad named Bobby gets up to all kinds of tricks when he is asked by Jack the Joker, a retired conjurer, to look after his house.
Art: Fred Sturrock

BAD-LUCK BILLY (S)
No. 17 (20.3.38) – No. 24 (14.5.38)
Bad-luck Billy Johnson is given a bit of string by a sailor who acquired it in the Far East. Billy soon finds that the person who owns the string has only to wish a wish and he gets whatever he asks for.
Art: Fred Sturrock

BUFFALO BOY (S)
No. 19 (9.4.38) – No. 38 (20.8.38)
Set over a hundred years ago in the American Wild West, a white boy, unsure of his identity, becomes the master of a thundering buffalo herd.
Art: Jack Glass

7 TERRIBLE TASKS FOR THE 7TH SON (S)
No. 25 (21.5.38) – No. 38 (20.8.38)
Sir Arthur Belmore is killed by order of the wicked King John. His six sons are imprisoned and his lands and castle are given away to the evil Baron Gorman. Sir Arthur's wife and their youngest son Erik, escape to the Welsh border. Erik is brought up to seek his lost brothers and regain his father's property.
Art: Dudley Watkins

HANDY CLARK ON THE TREASURE TRAIL (A)
No. 39 (27.8.38) – No. 77 (20.5.39)
In this sequel to 'Lost on the Mountain of Fear' Handy Clark and Peter and Patricia Bryant discover a parchment which leads them on the trail of hidden treasure in the wilds of Africa.
Art: Fred Sturrock

THE SMASHER (A)
No. 39 (27.8.38) – No. 52 (26.11.38)
Glasgow Harry, the site engineer of a railway construction crew in South America, is aided and abetted by young Ralph Barclay, the site manager's son, when the railway is attacked by a mysterious seven-foot tall metal monster.
Art: James Walker
See also 1957

DOPEY DINAH (C)
No. 39 (27.8.38) – No. 178 (26.4.41)
Art: Sam Fair

SIMPLE SIMON (C)
No. 39 (27.8.38) – No. 120 (16.3.40)
Art: Hugh McNeil

MEDDLESOME MATTY (C)
No. 39 (27.8.38) – No. 226 (31.10.42) [First Series]
Art: Sam Fair

BUSTER BILLY (THE PRIDE OF THE REGIMENT) (S)
No. 39 (27.8.38) – No. 70 (1.4.39)
Jerry Richards, an orphan who lived with his aunt and uncle on their farm, reared a billy goat called 'Buster Billy' from a kid. His uncle cruelly sells the goat as a mascot to an army regiment which is set to go to Africa to fight the Zulus. Unable to control its new mascot, the regiment allows Jerry to join it and to go with them to Africa.
Art: James Walker

WILD YOUNG DIRKY (S)
No. 39 (27.8.38) – No. 77 (20.5.39) [First Series]
During the 1745 Jacobite rebellion a young Scots lad, famed for his accuracy with dirks and dagger, helps to defend his homeland from the invading Redcoats.
Art: Dudley Watkins

THE PLUCKY LITTLE PETERSONS (S)
No. 39 (27.8.38) – No. 56 (24.12.38)
The Peterson family strive to keep their home together when their father is wrongly imprisoned for a crime he didn't commit.

THE SIGN OF THE RED RAVEN (S)
No. 39 (27.8.38) – No. 52 (26.11.38)
Robin Redford is kidnapped by a hunter of the Kanaka tribe. At first he is terrified, but he soon realises that the strange mole on his chest is thought to be the sign of the Red Raven. As the legend goes, whoever wears this mark will one day lead the Kanaka tribe to great victories.
Art: Jack Glass

THE THREE BEARS (S)
No. 41 (10.9.38) – No. 80 (10.6.39)
The adventures of Pa

and Ma Bear, plus Little Snoop the smartest baby bear in the world, in the Andes mountains of South America.
Art: James Clark

NEVER, NEVER NELSON (A)
No. 53 (3.12.38) – No. 106 (9.12.39)
Bill Nelson, a circus scout, has the job of tracking down animals from all over the world for circus acts. Irrespective of how dangerous an animal might be, Bill never fails to deliver.
Art: Jack Glass

WHISTLING JIM (S)
No. 53 (3.12.38) – No. 84 (8.7.39) [First Series]
Whistling Jim learns to speak to the birds and gets them to do his bidding by whistling to them. With this unusual ability Jim tries to help people in trouble.
Art: James Walker

OLD KING COLE (S)
No. 56 (24.12.38) – No. 120 (16.3.40) [First Series]
Misadventures of the rascally and fun-loving King of Koronia.
Art: Fred Sturrock

LOST IN THE LAND OF BAD KING JOHN (S)
No. 57 (31.12.38) – No. 72 (15.4.39)
In the time of wicked King John, Danver Castle is attacked. Hal and Joan Armstrong, two youngsters, escape from the castle but they do not know the whereabouts of their parents' house and so their only hope is to travel through many towns singing the 'Armstrong Fighting Song' in the hope that someone will recognize it and guide them to their destination.
Art: James Walker

1939 ....
Price: 2d.
Page count: 28 to No. 96 (30.9.39), then 24 from No.

97 (7.10.39) on; published every Friday.
Free gifts: No. 78 (27.5.39) – Korky balloon; No. 90 (19.8.39) – Flying balloon and prop.

STRAIGHT FROM THE JUNGLE TO MAGIC LAND (S)
No. 71 (8.4.39) – No. 90 (19.8.39)
In Africa a white boy, unaware of his origins but named Raboo by the natives, has a lion called Rajah as a pet. This brings him to the attention of an unscrupulous circus scout, who kidnaps the boy and his lion and sends them to a circus in the USA. Once in America Raboo and Rajah escape and try to find their way back home from the new and strange 'Magic Land'.
Art: Jack Glass

THE MAN FROM LAUGHING MOUNTAIN (S)
No. 73 (22.4.39) – No. 82 (24.6.39)
Long Tom Piper, the man from laughing mountain (so named because of its fierce echo), rescues young black slaves from the cotton field plantations of the Southern States of America and takes them to a secret valley.

SACRED BULL OF BATMANDU (A)
No. 78 (27.5.39) – No. 89 (12.8.39)
On the north-west frontier of India, British Secret Service Agent Captain 'Tiger' Hart and his Afghan companion Gunga Dar must rescue the sacred bull of Batmandu from the clutches of Sind tribesmen in order to prevent an Afghan war.
Art: James Walker

JUMPING JIMINY (THE KANGAROO WHO'S ALWAYS ON THE HOP) (C)
No. 78 (27.5.39) – No. 131 (1.6.40)
Art: William Ward

WHO'S TO WEAR THE KING'S BOOTS? (S)

No. 78 (27.5.39) – No. 89 (12.8.39)
The King of Slovania, having no heirs, fears civil war will erupt after his death if a suitable successor cannot be found. In desperation he orders the royal cobbler and his apprentice to take a pair of his boots into the streets and let everyone try them for size. Whoever can wear the boots with ease shall be the next King.
Art: George Ramsbottom

THE UGLIEST PIG IN THE WORLD (S)

No. 81 (17.6.39) – No. 106 (9.12.39)
The adventures of Moog, the big Indian boar who is the ugliest pig in the world.
Art: Toby Baines

JAK, THE DRAGON KILLER (S)

No. 83 (1.7.39) – No. 121 (23.3.40) [First Series]
The adventures of a roaming dragon slayer in ancient Greece.

THE MAN WHO OWNS AN ALI BABA CAVE (S)

No. 85 (15.7.39) – No. 96 (30.9.39)
Peter Pym, the owner of Fursehill Dogs' Home, teaches children to be kind to animals. There is a special reward waiting for anyone who mends his or her ways – the Ali Baba cave of wonders!
Art: Toby Baines

THE BOY WITH IRON HANDS (A)

No. 90 (19.8.39) – No. 144 (31.8.40)
The boy David with the powerful 'Iron Hands' is told by his mentor 'The Master' to gather together a band of knights to rid their homeland Caledon of the tyrant King Roderick the Red.
Art: Fred Sturrock

THE BLACK-STRIPED SWEETS THAT BILLY EATS (S)

No. 90 (19.8.39) – No. 102 (11.11.39)
In Hot Lead City, one of the toughest towns in the Wild West, Billy Parker, whose father is the sheriff, has a packet of sweets which contain a secret chemical that keeps anyone who eats one of them free from harm in any way.
Art: James Walker

OUR TEACHER'S A WALRUS! (S)

No 91 (26.8.39) – No. 133 (15.6.40)
Mr. Brown, the village schoolmaster, doubting the power of a magic wishing pill given him by an old gypsy woman, makes a rash wish and is transformed into a walrus!
Art: George Ramsbottom

HIS DAD WOULDN'T BUY HIM A BIKE (S)

No. 103 (18.11.39)
A one-off story of Peter Pym, the man who owns the Ali Baba cave. A boy wants a bike for his birthday but gets a dog instead.
Art: James Walker

DRAKE'S DRUMMER BOY (S)

No. 104 (25.11.39) – No. 126 (27.4.40)
The adventures of a small boy on board the 'Golden Hind' during the war with Spain.
Art: Jack Glass

LITTLE WHITE CHIEF OF THE CHEROKEES (A)

No. 107 (16.12.39) – No. 170 (1.3.41)
Harry Martin is heading west across the prairies in a covered wagon, with his mother and sister, when the wagon is attacked by a band of Cherokees. They are saved from death by the raven-shaped birthmark on Harry's chest which the Indians recognize as their tribal symbol. They make young Harry their Chief, but will not allow him or his mother or sister to continue on their journey.
Art: George Ramsbottom

ADDIE AND HERMY (THE NASTY NAZIS) (C)

No. 107 (16.12.39) – No. 169 (22.2.41)
Art: Sam Fair

THOSE BLINKING VACCIES AGAIN! (S)

No. 107 (16.12.39) – No. 126 (27.4.40)
'Real-life' stories of a crowd of big-town boys and girls who have been evacuated to the country.
Art: Toby Baines

1940

Price: 2d.
Page count: 24 to No. 131 (1.6.40), then 20 from No. 132 (8.6.40) to No. 153 (2.11.40), then 18 from No. 154 (9.11.40) on; published every Friday.
Free gifts: Nutty Nougat Bar – No. 121 (23.3.40).

WILD MAN OF THE WOODS (C)

No. 121 (23.3.40) – No. 174 (29.3.41)
Art: Sam Fair

JIMMY'S POCKET GRANDPA (S)

No. 121 (23.3.40) – No. 154 (9.11.40) [First Series]
Jimmy Bruce's Grandpa, a scientist, has discovered a liquid that will make people small. Having first tried it on himself he is delighted with the results. The only trouble is that he forgot to formulate an antidote! [The comic strip 'Peter's Pocket Grandpa' (1975–83) bore more than a passing resemblance to this story.]
Art: Fred Sturrock

THE UGLIEST PIG IN THE WORLD (S)

No. 122 (30.3.40)
Single adventure of Moog the Indian boar.
Art: Jack Glass

SWALLOWED BY A WHALE! (S)

No. 123 (6.4.40) – No. 147 (21.9.40)
Tom and Tilly Wallace along with their favourite boatman, Jonathon, are swallowed by a gigantic whale whilst out fishing in their boat. Finding themselves still alive in the whale's stomach they live as best they can.
Art: George Ramsbottom

HAIR OIL HAL (C)

No. 126 (27.4.40) – No. 204 (27.12.41)
Art: John Brown

CRIPPLE CHARLIE (S)

No. 127 (4.5.40) – No. 135 (29.6.40)
In the little township of Long Gulch in Eagle Canyon lives Cripple Charlie, a lame boy who is the youngest deputy sheriff in the Wild West.
Art: Toby Baines

HI! HERE COMES THE DOG MAN (S)

No. 127 (4.5.40)
A complete one-off story of Peter Pym, the man who owns the Ali Baba cave.
Art: James Walker

WHISTLING JIM (S)

No. 128 (11.5.40) – No. 139 (27.7.40) [Second Series]
Whistling Jim, now in the army, gets to grips with war on the home front.
Art: James Walker

THERE'S A CURSE ON THE KING (S)

No. 136 (6.7.40) – No. 166 (1.2.41)
King Valdemar of the Northland has a curse put on his right hand, making everything he touches with it become giant size.
Art: Toby Baines

THE DOG MAN IS A DIRTY DOG (S)

No. 140 (3.8.40)
Another one-off Peter Pym adventure.
Art: James Walker

BASH HIM! HE'S THE UGLIEST PIG IN THE WORLD (S)

No. 141 (10.8.40)
Another one-off Moog adventure.
Art: Jack Glass

BRITISH BOYS AND GIRLS GO WEST (S)

No. 142 (11.8.40) – No. 164 (18.1.41)
Twenty-two British boys and girls go to live on a Canadian ranch for the duration of the war.

WILDFIRE, THE WAR HORSE (A)

No. 145 (7.9.40) – No. 167 (8.2.41)
Wildfire, a British gun horse, searches for its master Tim Holt in war-torn France.
Art: Jack Glass

DRAKE'S DRUMMER BOY (S)

No. 148 (28.9.40)
Complete one-off story of young Rob Drury aboard the 'Golden Hind' during the war with Spain.
Art: Jack Glass

THE DARING DEEDS OF THE SHERIFF'S LITTLE SISTER (S)

No. 149 (5.10.40) – No. 160 (21.12.40)
When fighting Bob Green, the sheriff of Red Gulch, breaks his leg, his thirteen year-old sister Susie has to help him keep the peace to prevent him from losing his job.
Art: George Ramsbottom

OLD KING COLE (S)

No. 155 (16.11.40) – No. 178 (26.4.41)
More adventures with the wily old King of Koronia.
Art: Fred Sturrock

1941

Price: 2d.
Page count: 16 from No. 162 (4.1.41) on; published every Friday to No. 195 (23.8.41), then fortnightly.

THE ADVENTURES OF DICK TURPIN'S KIDS (S)

No. 165 (25.1.41) – No. 176 (12.4.41)

The children of Dick Turpin, the famed highwayman, hear that the Bow Street runners are planning to take them into custody in order to trap their father when he comes to rescue them. To avoid this the children run away from home in Highgate and try and find their father to warn him of the runners' plan.
Art: George Ramsbottom

BRAVE LITTLE COMRADE OF THE COWARDLY LION (S)

No. 167 (8.2.41) – No. 174 (29.3.41)

The evil princess of the Dark Lands wishes to kill the prince of the neighbouring land, Prince Victor, who is always guarded by his friend a lion. The princess takes away the lion's courage with the help of a magic mirror and then believes Prince Victor will be an easy target but she reckons without the lion's friend, a mouse called Sammy Squeaker, frustrating her evil plans.
Art: James Clark

JAK, THE DRAGON KILLER (A)

No. 168 (15.2.41) – No. 193 (9.8.41) [Second Series]

More adventures with the dragon killer of Ancient Greece, this time in picture form.
Art: Fred Sturrock

BOOMERANG BURKE (A)

No. 171 (8.3.41) – No. 206 (24.1.42)

Adventures of Bill Burke the 'No-gun Mountie' as he rounds up outlaws in North-West Canada with the aid of his boomerang.
Art: Jack Glass

CENTIPEDE PETE (C)

No. 171 (8.3.41) – No. 204 (27.12.41)

Art: James Clark

JOCK MacSWIPER (C)

No. 174 (29.3.41) – No. 199 (18.10.41)

Art: R. MacGillivray

YOUNG HUSKY

No. 175 (5.4.41) – No. 191 (26.7.41)

By accident a husky pup wanders away from his mother's sledge team and gets lost in the forest. In the forest the young pup is adopted by a family of wolves.

THE CHIMNEY-TOP TEACHER (S)

No. 177 (19.4.41) – No. 191 (26.7.41)

Everyone in the town of Telford Green looks upon the local mill with its chimney stack as the mainstay of their lives. So when wealthy Reuben Corder buys Telford Hall and wishes to pull down the mill with its chimney stack as it spoils his view, the local school teacher Leslie Adams climbs to the top of the chimney in order to save it and the mill.
Art: James Walker

GRANDMA JOLLY AND HER BROLLY (C)

No. 179 (3.5.41) – No. 199 (18.10.41)

Art: John R. Mason

JIMMY'S POCKET GRANDPA (S)

No. 179 (3.5.41) – No. 196 (6.9.41) [Second Series]

More adventures with Jimmy Bruce's midget Grandpa!
Art: Fred Sturrock

THE TWINS DARE THE REDSKIN TRAIL (S)

No. 192 (2.8.41) – No. 207 (7.2.42)

Davie and Effie Lee face dangers as they journey west to join their father who is the cavalry officer in charge of Fort Grange.
Art: Toby Baines

HASSAN AND HIS FLYING CARPET (S)

No. 192 (2.8.41) – No. 208 (21.2.42)

Hassan is the adopted son of Abu the carpet weaver and rights the wrongs of the evil Caliph Sammara of Bagdad with the help of his magic carpet.
Art: James Walker

BLACKHAWK'S BOY (A)

No. 194 (16.8.41) – No. 203 (13.12.41)

In the 16th century young Peter Bartley, the son of an abducted fisherman, becomes cabin boy aboard the ship of Blackhawk the infamous English privateer. Peter hopes that Blackhawk will help him find his missing father who is a galley slave aboard a Spanish galleon.
Art: George Ramsbottom

YOUNG KING COLE (S)

No. 197 (20.9.41) – No. 211 (4.4.42)

Fun when Old King Cole retires as King of Koronia and he makes Peter the page boy the new monarch.
Art: Fred Sturrock

MICKEY'S MAGIC BOOK (C)

No. 200 (1.11.41) – No. 377 (28.8.48)

Art: James Crichton

BAMBOO TOWN (C)

[Second Series]
No. 200 (1.11.41) – No. 258 (22.1.44)

Art: Charlie 'Chic' Gordon

BIG STARR (A)

No. 204 (27.12.41) – No. 211 (4.4.42)

An 18 year-old blacksmith, Tim Starr, becomes sheriff of the western cow-town of Three Pines.
Art: Jack Glass

1942

Price: 2d.

Page count: 14 from No. 205 (10.1.42) on, then 12 from No. 212 (18.4.42) on;

published fortnightly on Friday.

WATCHFUL WALLY (C)

No. 205 (10.1.42) – No. 224 (3.10.42)

WILLIE WOODPECKER (C)

No. 205 (10.1.42) – No. 277 (14.10.44)

Art: John R. Mason

PETER PYE (CA)

No. 207 (7.2.42) – No. 226 (31.10.42)

The story of a small boy in medieval times who with the help of his friends the dwarfs and their magical cooking equipment hopes to become personal cook to the King.
Art: Dudley Watkins

THE TWO TOUGH LAMBS (S)

No. 208 (21.2.42) – No. 213 (2.5.42)

The story of two children left in the care of a cruel grocer when their mother dies.
Art: Toby Baines

FREDDIE FLIPPER'S FIGHTERS (S)

No. 209 (7.3.42) – No. 216 (13.6.42)

When an island's population of king penguins is threatened by rats, one of the penguins, Freddie Flipper, becomes commander of a penguin army which is formed to rid the island of the vermin.

THE MAGIC BOX (S)

No. 214 (16.5.42) – No. 230 (26.12.42)

Little Lady Mary, the young mistress of Humbert Castle, inherits a magical chest from an old woman called Mother Morag who lives in the forest. Whenever in dire need the owner of the chest can turn to it for help.
Art: Toby Baines

WILD YOUNG DIRKY (S)

No. 217 (27.6.42) – No. 225

(17.10.42) [Second Series]

More adventures, set during the 1745 rebellion, of the young Scots lad who's a whizz with daggers and dirks.
Art: James Walker

MERRY MARVO AND HIS MAGIC CIGAR (C)

No. 225 (17.10.42) – No. 329 (12.10.46)

Art: Allan Morley

HOPEFUL JIMMY STEELE (S)

No. 226 (31.10.42) – No. 244 (10.7.43)

Young Jimmy Steele is brought up by the evil Noah Craik, thinking all the while that Craik is his Uncle. When he finds this is not so Jimmy runs away to find his real parents, with his only clue to their whereabouts being his memories of a beautiful garden and a particular iron gate.
Art: James Walker

DIVER DICK (C)

No. 227 (14.11.42) – No. 268 (17.6.44)

Art: Robert MacGillivray

DICK WHITTINGTON AND HIS CAT (CA)

No. 227 (14.11.42) – No. 246 (7.8.43)

Dick's adventures before he became Lord Mayor of London.

1943

Price: 2d.

Page count: 12; published fortnightly on Friday.

LOST IN THE MAGIC FOREST (S)

No. 231 (9.1.43) – No. 240 (15.5.43)

The story of Nora and Cookie Hardy, two children lost in a vast magical forest.

WEE TUSKY (S)

[Second Series]
No. 241 (29.5.43) – No. 252 (30.10.43)

More adventures with the young Indian elephant.

TRICKY DICKY DOYLE (S)
No. 245 (24.7.43) – No. 252 (30.10.43)
High jinks in the school dormitories when schoolboy Dicky Doyle becomes the owner of a joke factory.
Art: James Walker

KING OF THE JUNGLE (A)
No. 247 (21.8.43) – No. 256 (25.12.43)
The adventures of Bill King, the famous white hunter, as he captures animals for his private zoo.
Art: James Clark

THE MAGIC KNOCKER (S)
No. 250 (2.10.43) – No. 257 (8.1.44)
If the knocker on the door of a 'haunted house' is knocked three times by someone in need and asked to help, it will do so.
Art: Toby Baines

THE WONDERFUL WIZARD (S)
No. 253 (13.11.43) – No. 264 (15.4.44)
When his Uncle dies Nick is thrown out of his public school and is forced to wander the streets, that is until he meets Zogg the Wonderful Wizard.
Art: James Walker

1944
Price: 2d.
Page count: 12; published fortnightly on Friday.

HANSEL AND GRETEL (A)
No. 257 (8.1.44) – No. 271 (30.7.44)
Extended version of the Grimm brothers' fairy tale.
Art: James Clark

THE SPITFIRE TWINS (S)
No. 258 (22.1.44) – No. 265 (29.4.44)
Not as might be supposed a war story. Instead it tells the story of two young lads, the Erral twins, in the Wild West and the adventures they have

riding on the back of their giant pet eagle.

INKY POO THE CUTE HINDOO (C)
No. 259 (5.2.44) – No. 281 (9.12.44)
Art: John R. Mason

CAPTAIN CUTLASS (C)
No. 259 (5.2.44) – No. 302 (29.9.45)
Art: Charlie 'Chic' Gordon

OLD KING COLE (S)
No. 265 (29.4.44) – No. 271 (22.7.44) [Third Series]
More adventures with the Royal Court of Koronia who are shipwrecked on an island inhabited by cannibals.
Art: Fred Sturrock

THE WANDERING WILSONS (S)
No. 266 (13.5.44) – No. 271 (22.7.44)
One day on the wireless, Jack and Kan Wilson hear that their father is marooned, without food, on the island where he is lighthouse keeper. The children, on hearing the news, load up their 'Jeep' (which is actually a soap box cart) with food and set off to help their father.
Art: Jack Prout

CLUMSY CLAUDIE (C)
No. 269 (1.7.44) – No. 278 (28.10.44)
Art: Leslie Marchant

THE AMAZING MR. X (A)
No. 272 (12.8.44) – No. 284 (20.1.45)
The adventures of Len Manners, the private enquiry agent, who dons the black costume and mask of the amazing 'Mr. X' in order to fight crime. 'The Amazing Mr. X' was the first super-hero comic strip to appear in any British comic.
Art: Jack Glass

FIVE SPUNKY DUNCANS (S)
No. 272 (5.8.44) – No. 279 (11.11.44)

The story of five children protecting the family farm from their evil Step-Uncle until their real Uncle arrives from Australia.
Art: Jack Prout

THE SLAPDASH CIRCUS (S)
No. 272 (5.8.44) – No. 289 (31.3.45)
When circus owner Duke Barnard goes away on a holiday he leaves Don, the young rough-rider and tightrope walker, in charge until he returns.
Art: Toby Baines

CHARLIE CHUTNEY THE COMICAL COOK (C)
No. 278 (28.10.44) – No. 340 (29.3.47)
Art: Allan Morley

NELLIE ELEPHANT (C)
No. 279 (11.11.44) – No. 283 (6.1.45)
Art: Leslie Marchant

BLACK BOB (S)
No. 280 (25.11.44) – No. 287 (3.3.45)
Here they are for the first time. Black Bob the champion border collie, Andrew Glenn, Bob's master, and Farmer Grant of Ettrick Farm.
Art: Jack Prout
Black Bob Books: 1950, 1951, 1953, 1955, 1957, 1959, 1961, 1965
[Black Bob appeared as a picture story in the Thomson newspaper-cum-magazine *The Weekly News* from 5 October 1946 to 2 September 1967. All picture story Black Bob adventures in *The Dandy* were reprints from *The Weekly News*.]

OLD MA MURPHY THE STRONG ARM SCHOOL MA'M (C)
No. 282 (23.12.44) – No. 404 (20.8.49)
Art: Allan Morley

1945
Price: 2d.
Page count: 12; published

fortnightly on Friday.

LAZY LARRY (C)
No. 284 (20.1.45) – No. 331 (9.11.46)
Art: Dudley Watkins

DANNY LONGLEGS (CA)
No. 285 (3.2.45) – No. 349 (2.8.47) [First Series]
The adventures of Danny Long, a ten foot schoolboy in medieval England. [For further series see 1948, 1949 and 1950.]
Art: Dudley Watkins

MARY'S MAGIC MEDICINES (S)
No. 288 (17.3.45) – No. 297 (21.7.45)
Retired Professor William Lamb goes to stay with his family at the seaside town of Freshport. It is here that he keeps a laboratory full of chemicals at the bottom of the garden and that his niece, Mary, discovers the old man to be a dab-hand at inventing strange medicines.
Art: Jack Prout

HAPPY GO LUCKY (S)
No. 290 (14.4.45) – No. 302 (29.9.45)
Jim Blake, a British boy who had lost his parents and been sent to live in the USA, discovers he is a natural ventriloquist. Unfortunately Jim is boarded with a German-American family who make his life such a misery that he runs away and tries to return home to Britain.
Art: James Walker

ABSENT-MINDED ALFIE (C)
No. 291 (28.4.45) – No. 340 (29.3.47)
Art: Fred Sturrock

BLACK BOB (S)
No. 298 (4.8.45) – No. 305 (10.11.45) [Second Prose Series]
Whilst at a sheep sale in York, Andrew Glenn is stricken with amnesia after being hit by a car.
Art: Jack Prout

THE CHEERY CHINKS (C)
No. 303 (13.10.45) – No. 331 (9.11.46)
Reprints from the boys' paper The Rover.
Art: Charlie 'Chic' Gordon

JIMMY JOHNSON'S GROCKLE (S)
No. 303 (13.10.45) – No. 310 (19.1.46)
More adventures with Jimmy Johnson and his strange pet, this time in prose form.
Art: James Crichton

WILD YOUNG DIRKY (S)
No. 306 (24.11.45) – No. 313 (2.3.46) [Third Series]
Another set of stories of the young lad who battles the Redcoats during the '45 Rebellion.
Art: Jack Glass

1946
Price: 2d.
Page count: 12; published fortnightly on Friday.

THE ABC KIDS (S)
No. 311 (2.2.46) – No. 318 (11.5.46)
The story of the six Frame children, Andy, Barbara, Clarence, Doris, Elsie and Frankie (hence ABC) who are left in charge of their house when their mother leaves them to go and tend their sick father who has been hurt in an accident in the North of England.
Art: James Crichton

BLACK BOB (S)
No. 314 (16.3.46) – No. 323 (20.7.46) [Third Prose Series]
Bob and Andrew Glenn go to Shropshire to pick up six valuable sheep to take back to Selkirk. When Glenn is taken ill with appendicitis and taken to hospital Bob takes it upon himself to take the sheep back to Selkirk alone.
Art: Jack Prout

THE CRUSOE KYDDS (S)
No. 319 (25.5.46) – No. 326 (31.8.46)
The adventures of a family castaway on a desert island.
Art: James Crichton

DAD'S GOT A BROKEN LEG! (S)
No. 324 (3.8.46) – No. 331 (9.11.46)
Benny and Eva Telford face many dangers when they set out on a 200 mile trek across the frozen wastes of Northern Canada to get help for their injured father.
Art: Fred Sturrock

BLACK BOB (S)
No. 327 (14.9.46) – No. 338 (15.2.47) [Fourth Prose Series]
Bob has to clear his name by tracking down the lookalike culprit when a local farmer, Jim Taishie, accuses him of being a sheep killer.
Art: Jack Prout

JULIUS SNEEZER, THE SNEEZING CAESAR (C)
No. 330 (26.10.46) – No. 404 (20.8.49)
Art: Allan Morley

DANGEROUS DUFF (THE MOUSE WHO'S ROUGH AND MIGHTY TOUGH) (C)
No. 332 (23.11.46) – No. 348 (19.7.47)
Art: James Crichton

WHISKERY DICK (C)
No. 332 (23.11.46) – No. 370 (22.5.48)

POOR OLD NOSEY (S)
No. 332 (23.11.46) – No. 340 (29.3.47)
Old Nosey, the High Chamberlain at the court of King Lod, has a spell put on his nose by a wizard for being too nosey. This causes his nose to grow so long that he has to carry it around in a wheelbarrow. Another wizard says he can break the spell but only if old Nosey gathers the ingredients

for the magical antidote himself.
Art: Fred Sturrock

1947
Price: 2d.
Page count: 12 until No. 340 (29.3.47), 10 pages from then on; published fortnightly on Friday.

DICKEY BIRD (THE BOY WHO KNOWS THE SECRET WHISTLE) (S)
No. 339 (1.3.47) – No. 343 (10.5.47)
The story of a boy who knows the secret of how to make friends with wild animals.
Art: James Walker

HIS MAJESTY'S WIZARD, MR G. WHIZZ (S)
No. 341 (12.4.47) – No. 350 (16.8.47) [First Series]
When King Rufus is looking for someone to fill the post of Court Wizard, the job is given by accident to Mr George Whizz, the local plumber, a guy who knows nothing at all about magic!
Art: Fred Sturrock

BLACK BOB AND BLIND BILLY (S)
No. 344 (24.5.47) – No. 352 (13.9.47) [Fifth Prose Series]
Andrew Glenn and Bob go to the Broomielaw in Glasgow to pick up Andrew's blind nephew Billy. While there Andrew saves another boy from drowning but is hurt and taken to hospital leaving Bob and Billy alone on the dockside. Not knowing what has happened to his master, Bob decides to take Billy back to Selkirk.
Art: Jack Prout

SMUDGE (C)
No. 349 (2.8.47) – No. 421 (17.12.49)
Art: Eric Roberts
['Smudge' was reprinted as 'Hy Jinks' in 1955]

OUR TEACHER'S A WALRUS (CA)
No. 350 (16.8.47) – No. 358 (6.12.47)
Picture strip version of the 1939 prose story.
Art: Dudley Watkins

CINDER EDDIE (S)
No. 351 (30.8.47) – No. 358 (6.12.47)
The adventures of Prince Eddie of Moldavia and the trouble he has with his three wicked step brothers while his father is away fighting a war.
Art: Fred Sturrock

CURLY'S TWO-TON KITTEN (S)
No. 353 (27.9.47) – No. 362 (31.1.48)
When Snook the kitten eats a fish with a wizard's spell on it, he grows to gigantic size, which 'spells' trouble for his young master, Curly.

DANNY LONGLEGS (CA)
No. 359 (20.12.47)
A one-off Christmas adventure with the ten-foot schoolboy.
Art: Dudley Watkins

BLACK BOB (S)
No. 359 (20.12.47) – No. 368 (24.4.48) [Sixth Prose Series]
When Andrew Glenn is taken ill, Bob has to come to terms with the new shepherd and his dog who come to take his master's place.
Art: Jack Prout

1948
Price: 2d.
Page count: 10 until issue No. 377 (28.8.48), then 12 onwards; published fortnightly on Friday.

BOUNCING BILLY BALLOON (C)
No. 360 (3.1.48) – No. 381 (23.10.48)
Art: Charlie 'Chic' Gordon

BRAVE YOUNG BLACK-HOOF (A)
No. 360 (3.1.48) – No. 371 (5.6.48) [First Series]

Black-Hoof, the youngest foal in a herd of wild horses, is tracked by Hawkeye an Indian boy. Hawkeye's tribe believes an old legend that they will become the greatest tribe of all when they capture a horse with four black hooves, attributes which Black-Hoof possesses.
Art: Dudley Watkins

HIS MAJESTY'S WIZARD, MR. G. WHIZZ (S)
No. 363 (14.2.48) – No. 373 (3.7.48) [Second Series]
More adventures with the inept Court Wizard.
Art: Fred Sturrock

BIG BONEHEAD (S)
No. 369 (8.5.48) – No. 380 (9.10.48) [First Series]
An engineer in Africa sends his eight-year-old son home to Britain to stay with his brother in Scotland, and sends along a Zulu warrior to act as his bodyguard on the journey.
Art: Jack Glass

CASTOR OIL CRADDOCK (C)
No. 371 (5.6.48) – No. 376 (14.8.48)
Art: Basil Blackaller

DANNY LONGLEGS (CA)
No. 372 (19.6.48) – No. 395 (7.5.49) [Second Series]
More adventures with the ten-foot schoolboy when Danny is kidnapped by the eastern potentate Prince Ali Khan as a recruit for his father's giant bodyguard.
Art: Dudley Watkins

BLACK BOB (S)
No. 374 (17.7.48) – No. 380 (9.10.48) [Seventh Prose Series]
Black Bob's adventures with lame Tim Garwood and Perky the pup.
Art: Jack Prout

MEDDLESOME MATTY (C)
No. 377 (28.8.48) – No. 421 (24.12.49) [Second Series]
Art: Malcolm Judge

RAGGY MUFFIN – THE DANDY DOG (C)
No. 378 (11.9.48) – No. 404 (20.8.49) [First Series]
Art: James Crichton

PLUM MACDUFF (THE HIGHLANDMAN WHO NEVER GETS ENOUGH) (C)
No. 378 (11.9.48) – No. 537 (8.3.52)
Art: Bill Holroyd

HOTCHA THE HOTTENTOT (C)
No. 378 (11.9.48) – No. 395 (7.5.49)
Art: Robert MacGillivray

HIS MAJESTY'S WIZARD, MR G. WHIZZ (S)
No. 381 (23.10.48)
One-off story with the hapless George Whizz.
Art: Fred Sturrock

THE SLAVE OF THE MAGIC LAMP (S)
No. 381 (23.10.48) – No. 390 (26.2.49)
Joey Brown, the ten millionth person to rub an old magic lamp, has to take the place of the genie while he takes a holiday.
Art: Fred Sturrock

THE CROAKER HOLDS THE CLUE (S)
No. 382 (6.11.48) – No. 392 (26.3.49)
The story of a nameless highland boy during the '45 Rebellion who with the aid of a talking raven sets out on an amazing quest.
Art: Jack Glass

1949
Price: 2d.
Page count: 12; published fortnightly/weekly on Tuesday.

BLACK BOB (S)
No. 391 (12.3.49) – No. 399 (2.7.49) [Eighth Prose Series]
The story of the black man, Alabama Johnny, who comes to the Glen and lures

Black Bob away from his master.
Art: Jack Prout

HIS MAJESTY'S WIZARD, MR G. WHIZZ (S)
No. 393 (9.4.49) – No. 402 (6.8.49) [Third Series]
Art: Fred Sturrock

BRAVE YOUNG BLACK-HOOF (A)
No. 396 (21.5.49) – No. 402 (6.8.49) [Second Series]
Art: Dudley Watkins

WUZZY WIZ, MAGIC IS HIS BIZ (C)
No. 396 (21.5.49) – No. 721 (17.10.55)
Art: Bill Holroyd

MARY'S MIGHTY UNCLE (S)
No. 400 (16.7.49) – No. 414 (29.10.49)
When Mary Cassidy moves to Texas to live with her Uncle, Mighty Chip Cassidy, she believes he's a real tough guy. Mary's in for a big surprise!
Art: Fred Sturrock
[Reappeared as a picture story in 1953]

LION BOY (A)
No. 403 (13.8.49) – No. 439 (22.4.50) [First Picture Series]
Picture strip version of the prose story 'Straight from the Jungle to the Magic Land' (1939).
Art: Jack Glass

BLACK BOB (S)
No. 403 (13.8.49) – No. 410 (1.10.49) [Ninth Prose Series]
Black Bob does battle with a gang of crooks led by the evil Scarface.
Art: Jack Prout

DANNY LONGLEGS (CA)
No. 405 (27.8.49) – No. 407 (10.9.49)) [Third Series]
Danny does battle with a mechanical dragon.
Art: Dudley Watkins

SIR SOLOMON SNOOZER (CA)
No. 408 (17.9.49) – No. 437 (8.4.50)
The adventures of Sir Solomon Snoozer, a medieval knight, Ribshanks his horse and Roger his page, when they are awoken from a centuries-long sleep in a cave by some engineers building a tunnel.
Art: Paddy Brennan

BIG BONEHEAD (S)
No. 411 (8.10.49) – No. 422 (24.12.49) [Second Series]
Art: Jack Glass

BLACK BOB (S)
No. 415 (5.11.49) – No. 426 (21.1.50) [Tenth Prose Series]
After a train crash a Siberian Wolf on its way to Edinburgh Zoo escapes into the Selkirk hills; Black Bob helps to track it down.
Art: Jack Prout

RAGGY MUFFIN THE DANDY DOG (C)
No. 422 (24.12.49) – No. 444 (27.5.50) [Second Series]
Art: James Crichton

COCKY SUE THE COCKATOO (SHE'S THE BRAINS OF THE PIRATE CREW) (C)
No. 422 (24.12.49) – No. 483 (24.2.51)

HIS MAJESTY'S WIZARD, MR G. WHIZZ (S)
No. 423 (31.12.49) [one-off story]
Art: Fred Sturrock

1950 ....
Price: 2d.
Page count: 12; published every Tuesday.

JAMMY JIMMY JOHNSON (THE BOY WITH LUCKY HANDS) (S)
No. 424 (7.1.50) – No. 429 (11.2.50)
The adventures of a lad who sticks his right hand into a magic bottle and finds

afterwards that everything he touches with it turns to grub.
Art: Fred Sturrock

QUICK NICK – THE LIGHTNING LOCK-PICKER OF LONDON (S)
No. 427 (28.1.50) – No. 438 (15.4.50)
In 18th-century London, Nick Morrow, apprentice to the cruel blind locksmith Tappity John, joins a group of other trade apprentices in a secret society whose mission is to punish those masters who treat their apprentices harshly.
Art: Jack Glass

BLACK MAGIC BONGO (THE SCHOOLBOY FROM THE CONGO) (S)
No. 430 (18.2.50) – No. 444 (27.5.50) [First Series]
Bongo, a practitioner of Black Magic, comes from the jungles of Africa to work his amazing spells on the teachers and pupils of Corkham College.
Art: Fred Sturrock

DANNY LONGLEGS (CA)
No. 438 (15.4.50) – No. 444 (27.5.50) [Fourth Series]
Fun when Danny's reflection in a magic mirror comes to life.
Art: Bill Holroyd

BLACK BOB AND THE MAD BULL (S)
No. 439 (22.4.50) [one-off adventure]
Art: Jack Prout

BARNEY'S BEAR (CA)
No. 440 (29.4.50) – No. 499 (16.6.51) [First Series]
The comical adventures of Smarty, a young bear cub, when he's adopted by Barney Brennan and Digger Merry, two gold prospectors, in the wilds of Northern Canada.
Art: George Ramsbottom

GRANDPA GALLANT RIDES AGAIN! (S)
No. 440 (29.4.50) – No. 451 (15.7.50)
When Jim Gallant and his family enter Lost Valley (a red Indian sacred place) in search of radium deposits, Jim's grandfather, an old Indian fighter, insists he comes along to protect them.
Art: Fred Sturrock

TOMMY BROWN'S SLAVE (CA)
No. 445 (3.6.50) – No. 457 (26.8.50)
Tommy Brown finds he has a bottle with a genie in it when he's given a box of odds and ends by a junk shop man.
Art: Dudley Watkins

RUSTY (C)
No. 445 (3.6.50) – No. 675 (30.10.54)
Art: Paddy Brennan

BLACK BOB (S)
No. 445 (3.6.50) – No. 456 (19.8.50) [Eleventh Prose Series]
Bob and Andrew Glenn become involved with Tex Mason and his team of horses when they are shipwrecked off the coast of Ireland.
Art: Jack Prout

PEGGY AND HER POP'S PEG-LEG (S)
No. 452 (22.7.50) – No. 465 (21.10.50)
Peggy Parker of Saddle Creek seeks the autographs of all the famous tough guys she can get, and then brings them to justice with the unlikely help of her pop's old peg-leg!
Art: James Walker

LONG TOM'S TREASURE (S)
No. 457 (26.8.50) – No. 466 (28.10.50)
Aboard the merchant steamer S.S. *Monaveen*, Captain Long Tom Stark and his son Rod search for the treasure of Skull Island before a group of Nazis find it.
Art: Jack Glass

LION BOY (A)
No. 458 (2.9.50)
One-off adventure with Raboo and Rajah.
Art: Jack Glass

SIR SOLOMON SNOOZER (CA)
No. 459 (9.9.50)
A single adventure with the rejuvenated Knight.
Art: Paddy Brennan

FERGUS OF THE FORTY FACES (A)
No. 460 (16.9.50) – No. 477 (13.1.51)
Fergus, a wandering Highland entertainer and a master of disguise, becomes a powerful adversary of the English during the '45 rebellion.
Art: James Walker

BLACK BOB (S)
No. 466 (28.10.50) – No. 480 (3.2.51) [Twelfth Prose Series]
Black Bob in conflict with Jung the monstrous killer ape and his evil master, the circus owner, Luke Fragg.
Art: Jack Prout

THE BOY KEEPER OF THE KING'S BEASTS (S)
No. 467 (4.11.50) – No. 489 (7.4.51)
After saving Richard I from two ferocious lions due to his uncanny control over wild animals, young Wild Wulf is made keeper of the King's Beasts, which are kept in a walled garden behind the Tower of London.
Art: Jack Glass

1951 ....
Price: 2d.
Page count: 12; published every Tuesday.

FIGHTING FORKBEARD – THE SEA WOLF FROM LONG AGO (A)
No. 478 (20.1.51) – No. 492 (28.4.51)
Thrills when a Viking longship sails out of the past to attack the English seaside

town of Graysham.
Art: Paddy Brennan

BLACK MAGIC BONGO – THE SCHOOLBOY FROM THE CONGO (S)
No. 481 (10.2.51) – No. 494 (12.5.51) [Second Series]
Art: Fred Sturrock

NOAH LOTT (HE KNOWS A LOT OF ROT) (C)
No. 484 (3.3.51) – No. 645 (3.4.54)
Art: Richard Cox

BLACK BOB (S)
No. 490 (14.4.51) – No. 501 (30.6.51) [Thirteenth Prose Series]
Bob's adventures with Spitfire, the wildcat kitten.
Art: Jack Prout

BONANZA BILL (THE TRICKY TRADER OF HILLY BILLY CITY) (CA)
No. 493 (5.5.51) – No. 523 (1.12.51)
Bonanza Bill's proud boast is that his store in Hilly Billy City can supply anything under the sun and if he doesn't have it he'll make it.
Art: Bill Holroyd

SHOCKER JOCK – THE BOY FROM THE WONDER WORLD (S)
No. 495 (19.5.51) – No. 564 (13.9.52)
Fun when a boy from three hundred years in the future visits the Scots town of Blackdean in 1951.
Art: George Ramsbottom

SOOTY AND HIS SHOOTER (C)
No. 500 (23.6.51) – No. 530 (19.1.52)
The story of Sooty, a small African boy, who is marooned by his tribe in England. Sooty has a blow-pipe or 'shooter' which when blown in an object's direction makes it grow to giant size.
Art: Charlie Grigg

LION BOY (S)
No. 502 (7.7.51) – No. 518 (27.10.51)
Return of Raboo and Rajah, this time as a prose story.
Art: Jack Glass

BLACK BOB (S)
No. 519 (3.11.51) – No. 532 (2.11.52) [Fourteenth Prose Series]
Black Bob on the trail of a mysterious prowler in the glen.
Art: Jack Prout

LITTLE WHITE CHIEF OF THE CHEROKEES (S)
No. 524 (8.12.51) – No. 558 (2.8.52)
Part reprint of the 1939–40 picture strip.
Art: George Ramsbottom

1952
Price: 2d.
Page count: 12; published every Tuesday.

WILLIE WILLIKIN'S POBBLE (CA)
No. 531 (26.1.52) – No. 553 (28.6.52)
Fun when a creature, which eats school books and drinks petrol, comes to Earth from another world and teams up with young Willie Willikin.
Art: Paddy Brennan

HURRAY FOR THE RIP-ROARING ROBINSONS (S)
No. 533 (9.2.52) – No. 542 (12.4.52)
The story of the Robinson family from Manchester who go to run a 'ranch' in the Highlands of Scotland with the help of Red Eagle, a red Indian brave.
Art: George Drysdale

BLACK BOB (S)
No. 543 (19.4.52) – No. 553 (28.6.52) [Fifteenth Prose Series]
A mysterious stranger named Mr Nobody hypnotises Andrew Glenn into forgetting Black Bob is his dog.
Art: Jack Prout

WILY SMILEY THE JUNGLE JOKER (C)
No.554 (5.7.52) – No. 860 (17.5.58)
Art: George Martin

BARNEY'S BEAR (CA)
No. 554 (5.7.52) – No. 583 (24.1.53) [Second Series]
Art: George Ramsbottom

THE TROUBLES OF OLD SHERIFF SAGGY BAGS (S)
No. 554 (5.7.52) – No. 569 (18.10.52)
Polly Perkins runs a small pie shop in the western cow-town of Saddlehorn. When she buys some 'magic' herbs from an old Indian medicine man she thinks she's wasting her money, that is until she uses them in a pie for the town's old sheriff and he becomes invisible!
Art: Fred Sturrock

THE GALLOPING GLORY BOYS (A)
No. 559 (9.8.52) – No. 576 (6.12.52)
Adventures of a boy during the Napoleonic Wars whose father carries the Colours of the Fighting 41st.
Art: Paddy Brennan

BLACK BOB (S)
No. 565 (20.9.52) – No. 574 (22.11.52) [Sixteenth Prose Series]
Black Bob and his new pal Cripple Dick Duncan in a thrilling story of 'range' wars in the glens.
Art: Jack Prout

MICKEY FROM THE MOON (S)
No. 570 (25.10.52) – No. 591 (21.3.53)
A boy from the Moon, who can freeze anything at a touch, comes to Earth to take 'likenesses' (photographs) of as many Earth creatures as he can find.
Art: Paddy Brennan

WEE WILLIE KING AND HIS MAGIC STING (S)
No. 575 (29.11.52) – No. 585 (7.2.53)
Young Willie King finds a scorpion (Blitzkin) in a bottle in an old ruined tower, whose sting has the magical property of changing a person's natural personality completely.
Art: George Ramsbottom

LION BOY (A)
No. 577 (13.12.52) – No. 587 (21.2.53) [Second Picture Series]
Art: Jack Glass

1953
Price: 2d.
Page count: 12; published every Tuesday.

WILLIE THE WICKED (CA)
No. 584 (31.1.53) – No. 605 (27.6.53)
Willie Wilson is such a troublemaker at school that his father, who is away working in Afghanistan, sends an Afghan warrior (Mustapha Kamel) to Britain to sort the boy out.
Art: Eric Roberts

BLACK BOB (S)
No. 586 (14.2.53) – No. 597 (2.5.53) [Seventeenth Prose Series]
Bob has to cope when his master, Andrew Glenn, is blinded while they are on a trip to France.
Art: Jack Prout

THE TICKLER TWINS ON THE REDSKIN TRAIL (A)
No. 588 (28.2.53) – No. 602 (6.6.53)
The adventures of Tim and Tessie Tickler when they accompany Steve Lundigan, a pony express rider, on a journey to Fort Apache to join their parents.
Art: George Ramsbottom

TIN LIZZIE (S)
No. 592 (28.3.53) – No. 622 (24.10.53) [First Series]
The comic adventures of

Professor James Puffin and his robot maid Tin Lizzie when they embark on an expedition to South America.
Art: Jack Prout

CATS-EYE KELLY (S)
No. 598 (9.5.53) – No. 607 (11.7.53)
The adventures in 17th-century London of a link-boy who can see in total darkness and whose job it is to guide travellers through the city at night.
Art: Toby Baines

WESTWARD HO WITH PRINCE CHARLIE'S GOLD (A)
No. 603 (13.6.53) – No. 614 (29.8.53)
From sympathisers all over Europe the Red MacGregor and his brother Rab have collected gold to be used in the cause of Bonnie Prince Charlie. However, when they return to Scotland they find the cause lost and the Prince gone. When they hear that the Prince has fled to France the Red MacGregor and Rab decide they are duty bound to follow the Prince and hand over the gold.
Art: Paddy Brennan

MARY'S MIGHTY UNCLE (CA)
No. 606 (4.7.53) – No. 628 (5.12.53)
Picture strip continuation of the 1949 prose story.
Art: Charlie Grigg

BANDY SHAND AND GREAT BIG BESS (S)
No. 608 (18.7.53) – No. 619 (3.10.53)
The thrilling trail over mountain, marsh and desert of the biggest old gun in the world.
Art: George Ramsbottom

LITTLE MASTER OF THE SWOOPING MONSTER (A)
No. 615 (5.9.53) – No. 631 (26.12.53)

Johnny Jackson is sent a strange ancient trumpet from Afghanistan by his father. The trumpet is destined for the school museum until Johnny finds he can control a huge eagle called Kaloo by playing on it. This upsets the plans of Marat Singh, the 'Master of the Swooping Eagles of the Mazrakish Mountains' who has brought the great bird to Britain for a special and sinister purpose.
Art: Jack Glass

PIE FACE PETE'S SECRET PAL (S)
No. 620 (10.10.53) – No. 652 (22.5.54)
When Jek the Martian wants to test the effect of some Martian products on the people of Earth he contacts schoolboy Peter Potter by radio and asks him to test various products on his family and friends and report back with the results.
Art: George Ramsbottom

BLACK BOB (S)
No. 623 (31.10.53) – No. 640 (27.2.54) [Eighteenth Prose Series]
Mysterious happenings at the adjoining estate of Thirlwood when Bob helps in the hunt for a 'phantom' robber.
Art: Jack Prout

GREAT BIG BONZO (CA)
No. 629 (12.12.53) – No. 648 (24.4.54)
The small pup owned by Toby Tuckett, the woodcutter's son, grows to giant size after eating a mash prepared by wicked wizard Gumbo. When the wizard discovers what has happened he tries to steal the pup from Toby, who has since discovered that his dog only returns to normal size when his ears get wet.
Art: Charlie Grigg

1954
Price: 2d.
Page count: 12; published every Tuesday.

THE STREAK-O-LIGHT EXPRESS (CA)
No. 632 (2.1.54) – No. 643 (20.3.54)
The story of Smiler Smart, the pony express rider who has an ostrich for a mount.
Art: Bill Holroyd

FLEETFOOT JACK (S)
No. 641 (6.3.54) – No. 650 (8.5.54)
A young Indian chief's adventures at an English school.
Art: James Walker

YOUNG DRAKE (A)
No. 644 (27.3.54) – No. 661 (24.7.54)
The adventures of Sir Francis Drake as a boy.
Art: Paddy Brennan (first episode by Dudley Watkins.)

GOBBLE, GOBBLE GERTIE (CA)
No. 649 (1.5.54) – No. 672 (9.10.54)
Fun with the Eskimo maid who'll eat anything.
Art: Charlie Grigg

TIN LIZZIE (S)
No. 651 (15.5.54) – No. 674 (23.10.54) [Second Series]
Art: Jack Prout

CHINKEE, CHINKEE JUNKEE MAN (C)
No. 653 (29.5.54) – No. 689 (5.2.55)

BLACK BOB (S)
No. 653 (29.5.54) – No. 664 (14.8.54) [Nineteenth Prose Series]
After a plane crash Bob and his master, Andrew Glenn, become castaway on a mysterious island.
Art: Jack Prout

SHOCKER JOCK (THE BOY FROM THE WONDER WORLD) (CA)
No. 662 (31.7.54) – No. 693 (5.3.55)
Picture story continuation of the 1951 prose story.
Art: George Drysdale

MY GANG BY WHACKER WILSON (CA)
No. 665 (21.8.54) – No. 728 (5.11.55)
The adventures of Whacker Wilson and his street gang told in Whacker's inimitable prose.
Art: Ron Smith (the 'Judge Dredd' artist)

BARNEY'S BEAR (CA)
No. 665 (21.8.54) – No. 778 (20.10.56) [Third Series]
Art: George Ramsbottom

SHAGGY DOGGY (C)
No. 668 (11.9.54) – No. 860 (17.5.58)
Art: Allan Morley (some later ones by George Drysdale)

THE WEE BLACK SCALLYWAG (CA)
No. 673 (16.10.54) – No. 683 (25.12.54)
The story of a rascally black lad from Tennessee who goes to Professor Willie Winkle's travelling school.
Art: Eric Roberts

WINKER AND BLINKER (S)
No. 675 (30.10.54) – No. 683 (25.12.54)
Fun and thrills with the Wild West Sheriff who has an elephant for a steed.
Art: Fred Sturrock

LITTLE ANGEL FACE (C)
No. 676 (6.11.54) – No. 731 (26.11.55)
Art: Ken Reid

1955
Price: 2d.
Page count: 12; published every Tuesday.

CLANKY THE CAST IRON PUP (CA)
No. 684 (1.1.55) – No. 703 (14.5.55)
The adventures of Johnny Drew and his mechanical dog, built for him by his clever engineer Dad.
Art: Charlie Grigg

BLACK BOB (S)
No. 684 (1.1.55) – No. 694 (12.3.55) [Twentieth Prose Series]
Trouble for Bob when he's hypnotised by the mysterious 'Skyman' into doing his evil bidding.
Art: Jack Prout

THE WEE BLACK SCALLYWAG (CA)
No. 694 (12.3.55) – No. 695 (19.3.55) [Second Series]
Two-part adventure with Professor Winkle's travelling school.
Art: Eric Roberts

GINGER'S SUPER JEEP (S)
No. 695 (19.3.55) – No. 708 (18.6.55) [First Series]
The comical story of a lad whose soapbox cart has wheels that come all the way from Venus, and the adventures he has with the Venusian, Nik.
Art: James Walker

BIG BAD WOLFF (CA)
No. 696 (26.3.55) – No. 706 (4.6.55)
When Sheriff Logan and his four sons come from the USA to England for a holiday, they are followed by the desperado 'Big Bad Wolff' who wants to get even with the Sheriff.
Art: George Drysdale

3 JONAHS IN A WHALE (A)
No. 704 (21.5.55) – No. 715 (6.8.55)
The story of a 'whale' that's fitted with engines, has a crew of three castaways, and a cargo of loot worth a King's ransom.
Art: Jack Glass

MICKEY'S TICK TOCK MEN (CA)
No. 707 (11.6.55) – No. 720 (10.9.55)
Mickey Fender and his Grandpa, a skilled toymaker and inventor, go to Africa to try and sell their wares, protected on their travels by the life-size robotmen

designed by Grandpa.
Art: Paddy Brennan

BLACK BOB (S)
No. 709 (26.6.55) – No. 720 (10.9.55) [Twenty-First Prose Series]
Danger for Bob and his master Andrew Glenn, when Andrew's cousin Tom comes from South America to stay in the glen and is followed by his enemy, the evil lion tamer Salvador.
Art: Jack Prout

CRACKAWAY JACK (A)
No. 716 (13.8.55) – No. 735 (24.12.55) [First Series]
Adventures of an axe-wielding frontier scout on the wagon train trail as he does battle with bloodthirsty Apache Indians helped by the mysterious young 'Red Mask'.
Art: Paddy Brennan

TIN LIZZIE (CA)
No. 721 (17.9.55) – No. 751 (14.4.56) [Third Series]
Art: Jack Prout/Charlie Grigg

MILLIONAIRE MIKE (CA)
No. 721 (17.9.55) – No. 730 (19.11.55)
The story of a tinker's son who inherits a fortune from a rich uncle in America and the bizarre ways he finds of spending the money.
Art: Charlie Grigg

BIG BEARDIE (C)
No. 722 (24.9.55) – No. 757 (26.5.56)
Art: Shamus O'Doherty

THE TRICKS OF SCREWY DRIVER (C)
No. 729 (12.11.55) – No. 925 (1.8.59)
Art: Bill Holroyd

THE LION HEART LOGANS (CA)
No. 731 (26.11.55) – No. 736 (31.12.55)
Return of the four Logan boys from the 'Big Bad

Wolff' strip earlier in the year.
Art: George Drysdale

HY JINKS (C)
No. 732 (3.12.55) – No. 803 (13.4.57)
Reprint of 'Smudge' strip from 1947–9.
Art: Eric Roberts

WILD WULF (A)
No. 736 (31.12.55) – No. 749 (31.3.56)
Picture-strip version of the 1950 prose story 'The Boy Keeper of the King's Beasts'.
Art: Jack Glass

1956
Price: 2d.
Page count: 12; published every Tuesday.

MY PAL BAGGY PANTS (CA)
No. 737 (7.1.56) – No. 753 (28.4.56)
The story of a young lad who can summon a genie from the pages of a magic book by saying the word 'Bagee'.
Art: Ken Hunter

CRACKAWAY JACK (A)
No. 750 (7.4.56) – No. 760 (16.6.56) [Second Series]
Further adventures with Jack and his mysterious boy helper, Red Mask.
Art: Paddy Brennan

WILLIE'S WHIZZER BROOM (CA)
No. 752 (21.4.56) – No. 772 (8.9.56)
The comic adventures of Willie Meldrum, who finds an old broom in his grandfather's shop which, when you sit astride it and press a hidden switch, whisks you to the year 2500!
Art: Eric Roberts

BLACK BOB (A)
No. 754 (5.5.56) – No. 762 (30.6.56) [First Picture Series]
Picture-strip version of the first 'Black Bob' prose adventure from 1944.
Art: Jack Prout

JUST JIMMY (C)
No. 758 (2.6.56) – No. 860 (17.5.58)
Art: Hugh Morren

BING BANG BENNY (C)
No. 760 (16.6.56) – No. 986 (15.10.60)
Art: Ken Reid

ROLY-POLY JOE (C)
No. 760 (16.6.56) – No. 881 (11.10.58)
Art: Frank MacDiarmid

TURTLE BOY (A)
No. 761 (23.6.56) – No. 773 (15.9.56)
The story of a boy shipwrecked on a desert island who befriends a giant turtle and who does battle with pirates that come to the island looking for buried treasure.
Art: Paddy Brennan

BLACK BOB (A)
No. 763 (7.7.56) – No. 778 (20.10.56) [Second Picture Series]
Retelling of the second prose series (1945) in picture form.
Art: Jack Prout

KIPPER THE COPPER (CA)
No. 773 (15.9.56) – No. 790 (12.1.57)
When Constable Kipper drinks some pink liquid from a strange teapot he is able to behold a strange invisible being from Mars. The invisible being turns out to be the Lord High Sheriff of Mars, who has crash-landed his spaceship on Earth, and is very helpful when P.C. Kipper catches crooks.
Art: Charlie Grigg

CORPORAL KIM – THE BOY MOUNTIE (A)
No. 774 (22.9.56) – No. 783 (24.11.56)
The adventures of Kim Craddock, the son of a Sergeant in the Royal Canadian Mounted Police.
Art: Jack Glass

BUSTER'S BATTLING BEETLE (CA)
No. 779 (27.10.56) – No. 812 (15.6.57)
The comical story of Buster Hay and his pet beetle the size of a donkey, who has a predilection for mint balls!
Art: Ken Hunter

BLACK BOB (A)
No. 781 (10.11.56) – No. 789 (5.1.57) [Third Picture Series]
Bob's adventures with a Rocky Mountain Bighorn goat which escapes into the Selkirk hills from a showground.
Art: Jack Prout

RIP SNORTER – THE UGLIEST PIG IN THE WORLD (CA)
No. 784 (1.12.56) – No. 826 (21.9.57)
Rip, the terror of the Indian jungle, and his battles with the local natives.
Art: Eric Roberts

JET CARSON'S SCHOOL FOR RACERS (CA)
No. 785 (8.12.56) – No. 815 (6.7.57)
Jet Carson, the famous racing driver, gives up motor racing and sets up a school to train young boys to become champion drivers.
Art: George Drysdale

1957
Price: 2d.
Page count: 12; published every Tuesday.

BLACK BOB (A)
No. 790 (12.1.57) – No. 800 (23.3.57) [Fourth Picture Series]
Picture-strip version of the fourth prose series (1946).
Art: Jack Prout

CHARLIE THE CHIMP (CA)
No. 791 (19.1.57) – No. 985 (8.10.60)
After being hurt on a safari, Jack Marsden's big-game hunter father is confined to a wheelchair. To make ends meet they return to

Britain and open a boarding house with the family's pet chimpanzee, Charlie, acting as the house porter.
Art: George Ramsbottom/ Charlie Grigg

BLACK BOB (A)
No. 801 (30.3.57) – No. 814 (29.6.57) [Fifth Picture Series]
Picture-strip version of prose series number five, taken from 1947, with some plot emendations.
Art: Jack Prout

THE SMASHER (C)
No. 804 (20.4.57) – to 2004
Art: Hugh Morren, David Gudgeon, Brian Walker

YOUNG DANDY (A)
No. 813 (22.6.57) – No. 842 (11.1.58) [First Series]
The true-to-life story of a brave red deer fawn.
Art: James Clark

BLACK BOB (A)
No. 815 (6.7.57) – No. 819 (3.8.57) [Sixth Picture Series]
Picture-strip version of the seventh prose series (1948).
Art: Jack Prout

TIN LIZZIE (CA)
No. 816 (13.7.57) – No. 835 (23.11.57) [Fourth Series]
Art: Jack Prout

BLACK BOB (A)
No. 820 (10.8.57) – No. 821 (17.8.57) [Seventh Picture Series]
Bob helps to capture an escaped circus elephant.
Art: Jack Prout

BLACK BOB (A)
No. 822 (24.8.57) – No. 842 (11.1.58) [Eighth Picture Series]
Bob is kidnapped by dog dealer Alf Bates and taken South into England where Bates's nephew Teddy helps Bob to escape.
Art: Jack Prout

MYSTERY DICK (A)
No. 827 (28.9.57) – No. 843 (18.1.58)
The story of a boy who runs

away from his mean uncle's house to try and find his parents, and is tracked by a sinister stranger.
Art: George Ramsbottom

MY PAL, BAGGY PANTS (CA)
No. 836 (30.11.57) – No. 874 (23.8.58) [Second Series]
Art: Ken Hunter

1958
Price: 2d.
Page count: 12; published every Tuesday.

QUICK NICK – THE LIGHTNING LOCK-PICKER OF LONDON (A)
No. 843 (18.1.58) – No. 862 (31.5.58) [First Series]
Re-telling in pictures of the 1950 prose story.
Art: Jack Glass

BLACK BOB (A)
No. 844 (25.1.58) – No. 867 (5.7.58)) [Ninth Picture Series]
Bob and Andrew Glenn's adventures when they help Tom Laird set up home on the island of Birsay off the western coast of Scotland.
Art: Jack Prout

ROBIN HOOD (A)
No. 861 (24.5.58) – No. 880 (4.10.58)
Robin and his Merry Men in the 'Mystery of Sherwood Forest'.
Art: Paddy Brennan

YOUNG DANDY (A)
No. 863 (7.6.58) – No. 872 (9.8.58) [Second Series]
Art: James Clark

BRAVE BEN BOLD (A)
No. 865 (21.6.58) – No. 877 (13.9.58)
The adventures in 17th-century England of a young lad who befriends a shipwrecked elephant.
Art: Vitor Peon

BLACK BOB (A)
No. 868 (12.7.58) – No. 883 (25.10.58) [Tenth Picture Series]

Bob and Andrew Glenn's exploits when they agree to look after a mischievous young lad called Nipper.
Art: Jack Prout

QUICK NICK (A)
No. 873 (16.8.58) – No. 882 (18.10.58) [Second Series]
Art: Jack Glass

ROBINSON AND HIS DOG CRUSOE (C)
No. 875 (30.8.58) – No. 985 (8.10.60)
Art: George Martin

TIN LIZZIE (CA)
No. 878 (20.9.58) – No. 913 (23.5.59) [Fifth Series]
Art: Jack Prout

GINGER'S SUPER JEEP (CA)
No. 881 (11.10.58) – No. 892 (27.12.58) [Second Series]
Picture-strip continuation of the 1955 prose story with some plot emendations.
Art: Eric Roberts

THE CASTAWAY KIDDS (A)
No. 883 (25.10.58) – No. 908 (18.4.59)
The story of two children, Jack and Jenny Kidd, who are stranded on a small island 40 miles off the coast of Scotland.
Art: James Clark

BLACK BOB (A)
No. 884 (1.11.58) – No. 904 (21.3.59) [Eleventh Picture Series]
After being swept away by a flood, Bob is kidnapped and sold to Whitey Hilton, a thief wanted by the police.
Art: Jack Prout

1959
Price: 2d.
Page count: 12; published every Tuesday.

MR MUTT (C)
No. 893 (3.1.59) – No. 986 (15.10.60)
Art: George Martin

CIRCUS BOY (A)
No. 893 (3.1.59) – No. 908 (18.4.59)
The story of Dave Derrick, a young tightrope walker, and Growler the bear who are trapped in France in 1940 after the Nazi invasion.
Art: Jack Glass

BLACK BOB (A)
No. 905 (28.3.59) – No. 918 (27.6.59) [Twelfth Picture Series]
Picture strip version of prose series No. 6 (1947)
Art: Jack Prout

ROUND THE WORLD IN 80 DAYS (A)
No. 909 (25.4.59) – No. 925 (15.8.59)
Picture strip version of Jules Verne's classic story.
Art: Paddy Brennan

MY PAL, BAGGY PANTS (CA)
No. 911 (9.5.59) – No. 929 (12.9.59) [Third Series]
Art: Ken Hunter

DRAKE'S DRUMMER BOY (A)
No. 914 (30.5.59) – No. 931 (26.9.59)
Picture strip version of the 1939 prose story with the young hero's name changed to Dick Varney.
Art: Vitor Peon

BLACK BOB (A)
No. 919 (4.7.59) – No. 929 (12.9.59) [Thirteenth Picture Series]
Don Valdos, an evil South American gaucho, comes to the glen with his three savage dogs to work on a neighbouring farm.
Art: Jack Prout

CATS-EYE KELLY (A)
No. 926 (22.8.59) – No. 937 (7.11.59)
Picture version of the 1953 prose story.
Art: Jack Glass

BLACK BOB (A)
No. 930 (19.9.59) – No. 931 (26.9.59)
Complete Bob adventures featuring a billy-goat and a balloon seller.
Art: Jack Prout

YOUNG DANDY (A)
No. 931 (26.9.59) – No. 976 (6.8.60) [Third Series]
Art: James Clark

THE BOY WITH IRON HANDS (A)
No. 932 (3.10.59) – No. 1035 (23.9.61)
The adventures of Paul Strong, who can bend iron bars with his bare hands, on the island of Jersey during the Nazi occupation of the Second World War.
Art: Bill Holroyd
[Not to be confused with the earlier (1939) or later (1971) strips with the similar titles but different content]

BLACK BOB (A)
No. 933 (10.10.59) – No. 953 (27.2.60) [Fourteenth Picture Series]
More adventures on the island of Birsay with Tom Laird when Bob and Andrew Glenn go to the island to pick up four prize sheep.
Art: Jack Prout

GINGER'S SUPER JEEP (CA)
No. 938 (14.11.59) – No. 953 (27.2.60) [Third Series]
Art: Eric Roberts

1960
Price: 2d till No. 985 (8.10.60), then 3d onwards.
Page count: 12 till No. 985 (8.10.60), then 16 onwards; published every Tuesday.
Free gifts: No. 990 (12.11.60) – Dandy Whirlybird; No. 991 (19.11.60) – Dandy Thunderbang.

BUFFALO BILL'S SCHOOLDAYS (A)
No. 954 (5.3.60) – No. 966 (28.5.60)
Art: Michael Darling

BLACK BOB AGAINST THE SALMON POACHERS (A)
No. 954 (5.3.60) – No. 962 (30.4.60) [Fifteenth Picture Series]
Bob tries to foil Salmon poachers on the local River Torry.
Art: Jack Prout

BLACK BOB (A)
No. 963 (7.5.60) – No. 988 (29.10.60) [Sixteenth Picture Series]
Bob follows young Tommy Watt to London when the lad runs away from his uncle's house in Selkirk to search for his mother.
Art: Jack Prout

RUSTY (C)
No. 967 (4.6.60) – No. 1076 (7.7.62)
Reprints from the 1950–54 series.
Art: Paddy Brennan

RODGER AND HIS LODGERS (C)
No. 968 (11.6.60) – No. 1075 (30.6.62)
Art: Shamus O'Doherty

DOCKLAND DAVIE (A)
No. 977 (13.8.60) – No. 985 (8.10.60)
The story of young Davie Frain who hides in the docks from the police, believing he's wanted for a crime he didn't commit.
Art: James Clark

THE CRACKAWAY TWINS (CRACKAWAY JACK) (A)
No. 986 (15.10.60) – No. 1005 (25.2.61) [Third Series]
The Turpin twins set off on the long trail west to be reunion with their parents, being protected on their journey Crackaway Jack, the frontier scout.
Art: Paddy Brennan

ROBBIE THE BOBBIE (A)
No. 986 (15.10.60) – No. 1009 (25.3.61)
The adventures of a big-hearted policeman on his beat.
Art: Jack Prout

JAMMY MR SAMMY (C)
No. 986 (15.10.60) – No. 1080 (4.8.62)
Art: George Martin

DIRTY DICK (C)
No. 986 (15.10.60) – No. 1892 (25.2.78)
Many 1970s strips were reprints.
Art: Eric Roberts (some later 1960s strips by Jimmy Hughes)

ALI HA-HA AND THE FORTY THIEVES (C)
No. 986 (15.10.60) – No. 1117 (20.1.63)
Art: Ken Reid

BLACK BOB (A)
No. 989 (5.11.60)
One-off story of Bob saving a small boy from a fire on Halloween.
Art: Jack Prout

CORPORAL CLOTT (C)
No. 990 (12.11.60) – No. 1770 (25.10.75)
Art: David Law (1960–1970); Jimmy Hughes (1970–1975)

BLACK BOB AND THE BLACK PROWLERS (A)
No. 990 (12.11.60) – No. 1000 (21.1.61) [Seventeenth Picture Series]
Bob's fight against an eerie pack of dogs who roam the fells at night.
Art: Jack Prout

1961
Price: 3d.
Page count: 16; published every Tuesday.

BLACK BOB (A)
No. 1001 (28.1.61) – No. 1019 (3.6.61) [Eighteenth Picture Series]
Bob's adventures when Farmer Grant's prize ram Buffer is kidnapped.
Art: Jack Prout

THE PURPLE CLOUD (A)
No. 1006 (4.3.61) – No. 1048 (23.12.61)
The story of Dandy Jim Brewster's fight against

Purple Mask, the master of a mysterious purple cloud which sweeps across the cattle lands of the USA, spreading chaos and destruction in its wake.
Art: Charlie Grigg

WINKER WATSON (CA)
No. 1010 (1.4.61) – No. 1081 (11.8.62) [First Series]
Although 'Winker' had appeared in a 'preview' strip in the 1961 **Dandy Book**, this was the first true Winker story, with Winker arriving at Greytowers School for his first term and meeting his best friend Tim Trott and arch adversary Mr Creep for the first time.
Art: Eric Roberts

BLACK BOB IN THE LAND OF THE GRIZZLIES (A)
No. 1020 (10.6.61) – No. 1046 (9.12.61) [Nineteenth Picture Series]
Bob's adventures in the USA when he's sent there by Andrew Glenn to visit Peggy Pearson, a young girl who doted on him when she lived in the glens and who is now very sick and asking to see him.
Art: Jack Prout

BINGO – THE BLACK STREAK (CA)
No. 1036 (30.9.61) – No. 1076 (7.7.62)
Steve Halliday, while collecting animals for zoos in Africa, comes across Bingo, an African youth, who is a running and jumping sensation. Steve decides to take Bingo back to civilisation and that's when the fun and thrills really begin.
Art: Jack Glass

BLACK BOB (A)
No. 1047 (16.12.61) – No. 1063 (7.4.62) [Twentieth Picture Series]
Black Bob's exploits with Cheeky Face the pup.
Art: Jack Prout

THE HOVERCAR SNATCHERS (A)
No. 1049 (30.12.61) – No. 1069 (19.5.62)
Young Jinky Baker's adventures when he has a run in with the gang of kidnappers who ride in the fantastic Hovercar.
Art: Bill Holroyd

1962
Price: 3d.
Page count: 16; published every Tuesday.

BLACK BOB (A)
No. 1064 (14.4.62) – No. 1082 (18.8.62) [Twenty-First Picture Series]
Bob helps an archaeologist named Braddock search for some ancient Roman ruins.
Art: Jack Prout

WILLIE FIXIT (CA)
No. 1070 (26.5.62) – No. 1127 (29.6.63)
The adventures of a boy who can fix anything, from a busted football to a broken-down battleship!
Art: Bill Holroyd

CLANKY THE CAST IRON PUP (CA)
No. 1077 (14.7.62) – No. 1086 (15.9.62)
Reprints from the 1955 picture series.
Art: Charlie Grigg

SUNNY BOY – HE'S A BRIGHT SPARK (C)
No. 1081 (11.8.62) – No. 1214 (27.2.65)
Art: George Martin

DANNY LONGLEGS (CA)
No. 1082 (18.8.62) – No. 1108 (16.2.63)
The story of young Danny Kettle who at ten feet tall is the tallest hill-billy in the whole of Catskill Mountains.
Art: Jack Glass
[Not to be confused with the famous 1940s strip.

BLACK BOB AND THE FOUR-FINGERED CROOK (A)
No. 1083 (25.8.62) – No. 1098 (8.12.62) [Twenty-Second Picture Series]
Thrills when Andrew Glenn's cousin's daughter Betty comes from Canada to stay in the glen and is followed by the evil crook 'Four-fingered Gotch'.
Art: Jack Prout

BLITZ BOY (A)
No. 1087 (22.9.62) – No. 1103 (12.1.63)
The story of a mystery boy and his adventures during the London blitz of 1940.
Art: Paddy Brennan
ANN: 1963, 1964

MY HOME TOWN (FEATURE)
No. 1089 (6.10.62) – No. 1495 (18.7.70)
Art: Frank McDiarmid (cartoon); Ian MacKay (incidental); Morris Chapman (character)

BLACK BOB (A)
No. 1099 (15.12.62) – No. 1112 (16.3.63) [Twenty-Third Picture Series]
Bob battles with a cowboy rustler in the glen.
Art: Jack Prout

1963
Price: 3d.
Page count: 16; published every Tuesday.

WINKER WATSON (CA)
No. 1104 (19.1.63) – No. 1165 (21.3.64) [Second Series]
Fun when Winker's younger brother, Wally, arrives at Greytowers for the first time.
Art: Eric Roberts

DREAMY DAVE (CA)
No. 1110 (2.3.63)
One-off story of Davie Bell, the boy who always forgets to remember.
Art: Jack Prout

BOBCAT BOY (A)
No. 1111 (9.3.63) – No. 1121 (18.5.63)
The story of Bud Bolton, a young boy with a fierce bobcat for a pet, and his adventures guarding a herd of cattle en route to the Kansas City stockyards.
Art: Jack Glass

BLACK BOB (A)
No. 1113 (23.3.63) – No. 1124 (8.6.63) [Twenty-Fourth Picture Series]
Bob and Andrew Glenn encounter a band of smugglers on a visit to Cornwall to look over a flock of sheep for Farmer Grant.
Art: Jack Prout

BIG HEAD AND THICK HEAD (C)
No. 1118 (27.4.63) – No. 1332 (3.6.67)
Art: Ken Reid (April 1963–August 1964); Frank MacDiarmid (August 1964–June 1967)

ROCKET JOCK (A)
No. 1122 (25.5.63) – No. 1142 (12.10.63)
The adventures of Jock Clyde, when his scientist father designs for him a pair of jet-propelled shoes.
Art: Charlie Grigg

BLACK BOB (A)
No. 1125 (15.6.63) – No. 1132 (3.8.63) [Twenty-Fifth Picture Series]
Bob and Andrew Glenn travel to Southern Spain in search of a young Scotsman, Dan Gray, who's thought to have been shipwrecked off the Spanish coast.
Art: Jack Prout

JOE WHITE AND THE SEVEN DWARFS (CA)
No. 1129 (13.7.63) – No. 1201 (28.11.64)
When his Uncle Bertrand is hurt in a fall during his high-wire act, Joe White is entrusted with taking a letter from his uncle to his lawyers in far-off London. If the letter does not reach them,

Bertrand's evil half-brother Silas will gain control of the family circus. Silas hires two crooks to waylay Joe but he takes the seven dwarfs from the circus to act as his bodyguards.
Art: Bill Holroyd

BLACK BOB'S PELL-MELL PAL (A)
No. 1133 (10.8.63) – No. 1158 (1.2.64) [Twenty-Sixth Picture Series]
Black Bob's adventures with Billy the young boxerdog.
Art: Jack Prout

THE CRIMSON BALL (A)
No. 1144 (26.10.63) – No. 1174 (23.5.64)
It's a tank without caterpillar tracks! An armoured car without wheels! A plane without wings! It's the strangest weapon of all time and young Peter Jones sets out to defeat the mysterious device and its master.
Art: Jack Glass

1964
Price: 2d.
Page count: 16; published every Tuesday.

BLACK BOB (A)
No. 1159 (8.2.64) – No. 1172 (9.5.64) [Twenty-Seventh Picture Series]
Trouble when Andrew Glenn is sacked and told to leave his cottage on the Ettrick Farm by Farmer Grant's stand-in farm manager, the evil Jeff Nixon.
Art: Jack Prout

BARNEY'S BEAR (CA)
No. 1166 (28.3.64) – No. 1191 (19.9.64)
Reprints from the first picture series in 1950.
Art: George Ramsbottom

BLACK BOB (A)
No. 1175 (30.5.64) – No. 1189 (5.9.64) [Twenty-Eighth Picture Series]
Bob and Andrew Glenn are travelling to Vancouver in Canada to the home of Andrew's cousin, Dick

Ross, when Andrew is taken ill. While Andrew enters hospital until he recovers, Bob is sent on by plane alone. Unfortunately the plane crashes, leaving Bob stranded in the vast Canadian backwoods.
Art: Jack Prout

THE RED WRECKER (A)

No. 1190 (12.9.64) – No. 1205 (26.12.64)
The fantastic story of a giant weed that spreads terror and destruction in its path.
Art: Charlie Grigg

BLACK BOB (A)

No. 1192 (26.9.64) – No. 1207 (9.1.65) [Twenty-Ninth Picture Series]
Reprint of the second picture series (1956).
Art: Jack Prout

KIT FROM THE WILD KARROO (A)

No. 1192 (26.9.64) – No. 1209 (23.1.65)
The story of Kit Cooper, an English boy brought up on the African Karroo, who comes to England to attend school and smuggles his pet leopard into the country with him.
Art: Jack Glass

BRASSNECK (CA)

No. 1202 (5.12.64) – No. 1370 (24.2.68) [First Series]
When Charlie Brand visits his inventor Uncle Sam's house for a holiday he gets into so much mischief, because he's bored, that his uncle builds him a mechanical pal to play with.
Art: Bill Holroyd

1965

Price: 3d.
Page count: 16; published every Tuesday.

MOE AND JOE AND DADDY-O! (CA)

No. 1206 (2.1.65) – No. 1223 (1.5.65)
The adventures of Chip Malone and his three performing monkeys when they are forced to bail out of

an aeroplane into the jungle.
Art: Eric Roberts

BLACK BOB (A)

No. 1208 (16.1.65)
One-off story about a thief in the glen who steals fish and footballs.
Art: Jack Prout

BLACK BOB (A)

No. 1209 (23.1.65)
One-off story of how Bob baffles three burglars with a flock of sheep.
Art: Jack Prout

BARNEY'S BEAR (CA)

No. 1210 (30.1.65) – No. 1224 (8.5.65)
Reprints from the second picture-strip series (1952).
Art: George Ramsbottom

GREEDY PIGG (C)

No. 1215 (6.3.65) – No. 1528 (6.3.71) [First Series]
Art: George Martin

THE STINGING SWARM (A)

No. 1224 (8.5.65) – No. 1254 (4.12.65)
When a gang of crooks use a swarm of bees with paralysing stings to help them commit robberies, young Ted Drake finds he is the only person immune to the stings and therefore the only one capable of foiling the crooks' plans.
Art: Jack Glass

WINKER WATSON (CA)

No. 1225 (15.5.65) – No. 1256 (18.12.65) [Third Series]
A new term at Greytowers School and Winker comes up against the mysterious phantom grub stealer.
Art: Eric Roberts

BLACK BOB (A)

No. 1228 (5.6.65) – No. 1255 (11.12.65) [Thirtieth Picture Series]
Jack Grant, the nephew of Farmer Grant of Ettrick Farm, wants to be a farmer like his uncle when he grows up, so Farmer Grant sends

him to Andrew Glenn to learn the ropes.
Art: Jack Prout

THE UMBRELLA MEN (A)

No. 1255 (11.12.65) – No. 1290 (13.8.66)
The story of Toby Judd and his battle against a gang of jet-propelled, bowler-hatted bandits.
Art: Charlie Grigg

BLACK BOB (A)

No. 1257 (25.12.65) – No. 1283 (25.6.66) [Thirty-First Picture Series]
Bob is kidnapped and taken to Argentina where he befriends a young boy called Pedro.
Art: Jack Prout

1966

Price: 3d.
Page count: 16; published every Tuesday.

WINKER WATSON (CA)

No. 1258 (1.1.66) – No. 1295 (17.9.66) [Fourth Series]
Fun when Winker's Uncle Arnold becomes the P.T. instructor at Greytowers School.
Art: Eric Roberts

BLACK BOB (A)

No. 1284 (2.7.66) – No. 1306 (3.12.66) [Thirty-Second Picture Series]
Bob and Andrew Glenn's adventures with Professor Mills, one of Britain's top scientists, and Scotty, his West Highland terrier.
Art: Jack Prout

HANK AND HIS MINI-TANK (A)

No. 1291 (20.8.66) – No. 1309 (24.12.66)
Hank Marvel is a young mechanical wizard and when his father leaves the family garage in Algiers to join up during the Second World War, Hank does his bit by building himself a small tank to use against the Nazis in the North African desert.
Art: Jack Glass

WINKER WATSON (CA)

No. 1296 (24.9.66) – No. 1343 (19.8.67) [Fifth Series]
The fun starts when Creepy's brother John, the black sheep of the Creep family, arrives at Greytowers School.
Art: Eric Roberts

BLACK BOB (A)

No. 1307 (10.12.66)
One-off story of Bob and the escaped elephant.
Art: George Ramsbottom

BLACK BOB (A)

No. 1308 (17.12.66)
One-off story of Bob and the missing key.
Art: George Ramsbottom

BLACK BOB (A)

No. 1309 (24.12.66)
One-off story of Bob and the black cat.
Art: George Ramsbottom

CRACKAWAY JACK (A)

No. 1310 (31.12.66) – No. 1319 (4.3.67)
Reprints from the first picture series (1955).
Art: Paddy Brennan

1967

Price: 3d.
Page count: 16; published every Tuesday.

SOUTH WITH THE HOVERCAR (A)

No. 1320 (11.3.67) – No. 1341 (5.8.67)
The story of the Starkey family and their journey from England to the heart of Africa in the most terrific craft ever built, the tremendous Hovercar!
Art: Jack Glass

BLACK BOB (A)

No. 1324 (8.4.67) – No. 1342 (12.8.67) [Thirty-Third Picture Series]
Bob's adventures with young Ben Neil, a gipsy boy, and a briefcase full of secret plans.
Art: Jack Prout

BULLY BEEF AND CHIPS (C)

No. 1333 (10.6.67) – 1997

Art: Jimmy Hughes, Richard Nixon, Sid Burgon

CAPTAIN WHOOSH (A)

No. 1342 (12.8.67) – No. 1359 (9.12.67)
The adventures of young Terry Bail when he does battle with two fantastic crooks, Captain Whoosh the thief with the jet-pack on his back, and his side-kick the bowler-hatted Smart Alec Bone.
Art: Charlie Grigg

BLACK BOB (A)

No. 1344 (26.8.67) – No. 1378 (20.4.68) [Thirty-Fourth Picture Series]
Thrills when Bob and Andrew cross swords with a vicious great dane and its mysterious owner.
Art: Jack Prout

BUTCH AND HIS POOCH (C)

No. 1344 (26.8.67) – No. 1402 (5.10.68)
Art: Shamus O'Doherty

SPUNKY AND HIS SPIDER (CA)

No. 1360 (16.12.67) – No. 1488 (30.5.70)
Spunky Bruce goes to play on the moors near his home one day and meets a huge spider which climbs out of a hole on a disused drilling site. Spunky calls the spider Scamper and it becomes his pet.
Art: Bill Holroyd

1968

Price: 3d until issue No. 1373 (16.3.68), then 4d.
Page count: 16; published every Tuesday.

WINKER WATSON (CA)

No. 1365 (20.1.68) – No. 1450 (6.9.69) [Sixth Series]
Creepy's sister Agnes, the principal of Heathcliffe Girls' School, brings herself and her girls to stay at Greytowers when her own school burns down.
Art: Eric Roberts

BODGER THE BOOKWORM (C)
No. 1371 (2.3.68) – No. 1528 (6.3.71)
Art: Shamus O'Doherty

GUNSMOKE JACK (A)
No. 1376 (6.4.68) – No. 1386 (15.6.68)
When young Jack Nelson finds a strange gun on a piece of wasteland, where it's been hidden by a gang of crooks, he finds himself tracked by the gang as they try to retrieve the weapon.
Art: Jack Glass

BLACK BOB (A)
No. 1379 (27.4.68) – No. 1402 (5.10.68) [Thirty-Fifth Picture Series]
Adventures with Bob and Andrew Glenn when they travel to Holland to find Andrew's young nephew Jimmy.
Art: Jack Prout

SUPER SAM (CA)
No. 1387 (22.6.68) – No. 1401 (28.9.68)
The story of a little guy who comes from another world to find out all about life on Earth, and who brings a mighty big slave to help him!
Art: Jack Prout

THE PURPLE CLOUD (A)
No. 1403 (12.10.68) – No. 1445 (2.8.69)
Reprint of the 1961 picture story.
Art: Charlie Grigg

1969
Price: 4d.
Page count: 16; published every Tuesday.

BLACK BOB (A)
No. 1446 (9.8.69) – No. 1451 (13.9.69) [Thirty-Sixth Picture Series]
Adventures with Bob and Andrew Glenn when a mysterious fire raiser enters the glen.
Art: Jack Prout

THE ISLAND OF MONSTERS (A)
No. 1451 (13.9.69) – No.

1493 (4.7.70)
Thrills with Davie Dunbar and Krambo his native friend when, for some inexplicable reason, the creatures on the South Seas island where they live start growing to giant size.
Art: Paddy Brennan

THE BABES 'N' THE BULLIES (C)
No. 1452 (20.9.69) – No. 1460 (15.11.69)
Art: Trevor Metcalfe

THE WOODEN SUBMARINE (A)
No. 1459 (8.11.69) – No. 1471 (31.1.70)
When the Second World War begins, a Borneo barrel-maker called Seesaw builds a 'wooden submarine' to help Mike, Ella and Dad Trubb escape from the all-conquering Japanese army.
Art: Vitor Peon

1970
Price: 4d.
Page count: 16; published every Tuesday.

WINKER WATSON (CA)
No. 1472 (7.2.70) – No. 1523 (30.1.71) [Seventh Series]
When Winker's brother Wally gets unfairly expelled from Greytowers, Winker hides him in the grounds and tries to get him reinstated.
Art: Eric Roberts

BRASSNECK (CA)
No. 1489 (7.6.70) – No. 1648 (23.6.73) [Second Series]
The return of Charlie Brand and his mechanical pal.
Art: Bill Holroyd

BLACK BOB (A)
No. 1494 (11.7.70) – No. 1507 (10.10.70) [Thirty-Seventh Picture Series]
Bob's adventures when two mischievous twins, Bill and Ben McLean, come to stay with their grandfather in the glen.
Art: Jack Prout

MY TOP STORY (FEATURE)
No. 1496 (25.7.70) – No. 2122 (24.7.82)

DINAH MITE (C)
No. 1508 (17.10.70) – No. 1539 (22.5.71)
Art: Ron Spencer

DOCKLAND DAVIE (A)
No. 1508 (17.10.70) – No. 1516 (12.12.70)
Reprint of the 1960 picture story.
Art: James Clark

BLACK BOB (A)
No. 1517 (19.12.70) – No. 1528 (6.3.71) [Thirty-Eighth Picture Series]
Bob's adventures with Butch the alsatian and his young master Billy Cooper.
Art: Jack Prout

1971
Price: 4d until No. 1525 (13.2.71), then 2p onwards.
Page count: 16 until No. 1528 (6.3.71), then 20 onwards; published every Tuesday.
Free gifts: No. 1529 (13.3.71) – Dandy Thunderbang; No. 1530 (20.3.71) – Red Racketty.

CLAUDE HOPPER (C)
No. 1529 (13.3.71) – No. 1661 (22.9.73)
Art: George Martin

WHACKO! (C)
No. 1529 (13.3.71) – No. 1657 (25.8.73)
Art: Ron Spencer

P.C. BIG EARS (C)
No. 1529 (13.3.71) – No. 1658 (1.9.73)
Art: John K. Geering

SCREWY DRIVER (C)
No. 1529 (13.3.71) – No. 1770 (25.10.75)
Reprints from the 1955 series.
Art: Bill Holroyd

IRON HANDS (A)
No. 1529 (13.3.71) – No. 1544 (26.6.71)
The story of young Nick Hardy, the boy with the grip of steel, on the run from the

police after being accused of theft by his villainous uncle.
Art: Paddy Brennan

WINKER WATSON (CA)
No. 1529 (13.3.71) – No. 1646 (9.6.73) [Eighth Series]
Fun when Robin Boodle, the boy millionaire, becomes a pupil at Greytowers.
Art: Eric Roberts

SUNNY BOY (C)
No. 1532 (3.4.71) – No. 1661 (22.9.73)
Reprints from the original series (1962).
Art: George Martin

MY WOOZY DOG, SNOOZY (C)
No. 1532 (3.4.71) – No. 1533 (10.4.71)
Art: John Edward Oliver

BLACK BOB (A)
No. 1545 (3.7.71) – No. 1558 (2.10.71) [Thirty-Ninth Picture Series]
Bob's adventures with Tom and Ted Tucker, the small twin sons of a millionaire who comes to spend a holiday in the glen.
Art: Jack Prout

BLACK BOB (A)
No. 1559 (9.10.71) – No. 1569 (18.12.71) [Fortieth Picture Series]
Bob's adventures with Lulu the poodle.
Art: Jack Prout

BLACK BOB (A)
No. 1570 (25.12.71) – No. 1579 (26.2.72) [Forty-First Picture Series]
Adventures for Bob when his master, Andrew Glenn, 'kidnaps' a small boy named Tommy Jackson.
Art: Jack Prout

1972
Price: 2p.
Page count: 20; published every Tuesday.

BLACK BOB (A)
No. 1580 (4.3.72) – No. 1589 (6.5.72) [Forty-Second Picture Series]
Bob falls foul of Constable

Clark, the new P.C. in the glen.
Art: Jack Prout

RODGER AND HIS LODGERS (C)
No. 1581 (11.3.72) – No. 1660 (15.9.73)
Reprints from the original series (1960)
Art: Shamus O'Doherty

THE BOY FROM LILLIPUT (A)
No. 1590 (13.5.72) – No. 1617 (18.11.72)
Adventures in present day Britain with young Ben Loyal and his ten tiny pals from the time-locked land of Lilliput where everything is as it was 250 years ago.
Art: Paddy Brennan

BLACK BOB (A)
No. 1618 (25.11.72) – No. 1624 (6.1.73) [Forty-Third Picture Series]
Bob does battle with a wildcat which makes the glen its home. Not to be confused with the 'Spitfire' prose series in 1951.
Art: Jack Prout

1973
Price: 2p.
Page count: 20; published every Tuesday:
Free gifts: No. 1662 (29.9.73) – Korky's Squeaky Squawker; No. 1663 (6.10.73) – Whirly Twirly.

BLACK BOB (A)
No. 1625 (13.1.73) – No. 1634 (17.3.73) [Forty-Fourth Picture Series]
Bob and Andrew Glenn are in trouble when two crooks try to retrieve some diamonds they've hidden in Bob's collar.
Art: Jack Prout

BLACK BOB (A)
No. 1635 (24.3.73) – No. 1643 (19.5.73) [Forty-Fifth Picture Series]
Bob and Andrew become involved with Harry Gibb, a detective, when he comes to the glen to investigate a smuggling ring.
Art: Jack Prout

BLACK BOB (A)

No. 1644 (26.5.73) – No. 1649 (30.6.73) [Forty-Sixth Picture Series]

Thrills when a mystery man, who is the spitting image of Andrew Glenn, is washed ashore unconscious near Ettrick Farm.

Art: Jack Prout

QUICK NICK – THE LIGHTNING LOCK-PICKER OF LONDON (A)

No. 1647 (16.6.73) – No. 1678 (19.1.74)

Reprints from the first and second picture series (1958).

Art: Jack Glass

JACK SILVER (CA)

No. 1649 (30.6.73) – No. 1770 (25.10.75) [First Series]

Fun when young Curly Perkins befriends Jack Silver, a visitor from the planet Marsuvia, and is taken by Jack back to his home planet.

Art: Bill Holroyd

BLACK BOB (A)

No. 1650 (7.7.73) – No. 1657 (23.8.73) [Forty-Seventh Picture Series]

Bob and Andrew's adventures on holiday in North-West Canada when they take care of a farm while the owner is in hospital.

Art: Jack Prout

BLACK BOB (A)

No. 1658 (1.9.73) – No. 1661 (22.9.73) [Forty-Eighth Picture Series]

Thrills when a young first-division footballer comes and hides incognito in the glen as a farmhand on Ettrick Farm.

Art: Jack Prout

WINKER WATSON (CA)

No. 1658 (1.9.73) – No. 1765 (20.9.75) [Ninth Series]

Fun when a police training college opens in the grounds next to Greytowers School.

Art: Eric Roberts

MONKEY BIZNESS (C)

No. 1662 (29.9.73) – No. 1770 (25.10.75)

Art: John K. Geering

ROBIN HOOD'S SCHOOLDAYS (C)

No. 1662 (29.9.73) – No. 1770 (25.10.75)

Art: Ron Spencer

THE TALKING BALL (A)

No. 1662 (29.9.73) – No. 1679 (26.1.74)

Chippy Chaplin, a young gipsy lad, is on the run from his wicked Uncle Ezra after finding a strange talking ball in his caravan. The ball, which can also move of its own accord, follows Chippy and promises to help him find his long lost father.

Art: Paddy Brennan

DESPERATE DAWG (C)

No. 1662 (29.9.73) – No. 1974 (22.9.79) [First Series]

Art: George Martin

SIR COWARD DE CUSTARD (C)

No. 1662 (29.9.73) – No. 1770 (25.10.75)

Art: Ken Harrison

1974

Price: 2p till No. 1701 (29.6.74), then 3p onwards.

Page count: 20; published every Tuesday.

YOUNG DANDY (A)

No. 1679 (26.1.74) – No. 1702 (6.7.74)

Reprint of the first 'Young Dandy' series (1957)

Art: James Clark

BLACK BOB (A)

No. 1680 (2.2.74) – No. 1696 (25.5.74) [Forty-Ninth Picture Series]

After being struck blind in a thunderstorm Bob is taken by Andrew Glenn to see a veterinary eye specialist in Manchester. The specialist tells Andrew he will have to leave Bob in his care for the time being, but when

Andrew does so Bob escapes and tries to find his way back home, still blind, to Ettrick Farm.

Art: Jack Prout

BLACK BOB (A)

No. 1697 (1.6.74) – No. 1706 (3.8.74) [Fiftieth Picture Series]

After delivering a flock of sheep to a farm in Canada, Bob and Andrew Glenn meet an old prospector called Ned Benson who is on his way to Fort McLeod to register a gold claim. Two half-breed brothers, Jacques and Jules Burget, steal old Ned's claim form and set out for Fort McLeod to file the claim in their own names; in consequence, Andrew and Ned send Bob on with a new claim form hoping that he will beat the Burgets to the claim office.

Art: Jack Prout

MYSTERY DICK (A)

No. 1703 (13.7.74) – No. 1719 (2.11.74)

Reprint of the 1957 picture story.

Art: George Ramsbottom

BLACK BOB (A)

No. 1707 (10.8.74) – No. 1717 (19.10.74) [Fifty-First Picture Series]

Reprint of picture series No. 18 (1961).

Art: Jack Prout

BLACK BOB (A)

No. 1708 (26.10.74) – No. 1724 (7.12.74) [Fifty-Second Picture Series]

Bob and Andrew's adventures with young Danny Gray and his father who they find taking refuge in the derelict Torwood Tower.

Art: Jack Prout

THE CASTAWAY KYDDS (A)

No. 1720 (9.11.74) – No. 1745 (3.5.75)

Reprint of the 1958 picture story.

Art: James Clark

BLACK BOB (A)

No. 1725 (14.12.74) – No. 1730 (18.1.75) [Fifty-Third Picture Series]

Reprint of picture series No. 24 (1963).

Art: Jack Prout

1975

Price: 3p to No. 1751 (14.6.75), then 4p onwards.

Page count: 20; published every Tuesday.

Free gifts: No. 1771 (1.11.75) – Korky Glow Mask; No. 1772 (8.11.75) – Funny Face Maker.

BLACK BOB (A)

No. 1731 (25.1.75) – No. 1743 (19.4.75) [Fifty-Fourth Picture Series]

Reprint of picture series No. 16 (1960).

Art: Jack Prout

BLACK BOB (A)

No. 1744 (26.4.75) – No. 1757 (26.7.75) [Fifty-Fifth Picture Series]

Reprint of picture series No. 19 (1961).

Art: Jack Prout

YOUNG DANDY (A)

No. 1746 (10.5.75) – No. 1770 (25.10.75)

Reprint of the second picture series (1958).

Art: James Clark

BLACK BOB (A)

No. 1758 (2.8.75) – No. 1769 (18.10.75) [Fifty-Sixth Picture Series]

Reprint of picture series No. 21 (1962).

Art: Jack Prout

WILLIE FIXIT (CA)

No. 1766 (27.9.75) – No. 1770 (25.10.75)

Reprints from the 1962–3 picture series.

Art: Bill Holroyd

PETER'S POCKET GRANDPA (C)

No. 1771 (1.11.75) – No. 2148 (22.1.83)

Art: Ron Spencer

TOM TIN AND BUSTER BRASS (CA)

No. 1771 (1.11.75) – No.

1785 (7.2.76)

When Freddie Fratton's inventor dad makes him a mechanical cat called Tom Tin for a pet, Horace Harper, the bully from next door, gets his dad, also a bit of a whizz with mechanics, to make him a mechanical dog called Buster Brass. Then the fun begins.

Art: Jack Prout

RAH-RAH RANDALL (C)

No. 1771 (1.11.75) – No. 1975 (29.9.79)

Art: Ken Harrison

JACK SILVER (CA)

No. 1771 (1.11.75) – No. 1893 (4.11.78) [Second Series]

When Curly Perkins comes home from the planet Marsuvia with his alien pal Jack Silver, they are followed to Earth by the Marsuvian space crook, Captain Zapp.

Art: Bill Holroyd

IZZY SKINT (YOU BET HE IS!) (C)

No. 1771 (1.11.75) – No. 1973 (15.9.79) [First Series]

Art: George Martin

THE JOCKS AND THE GEORDIES (C)

No. 1771 (1.11.75) – 1997

Art: Jimmy Hughes

WINKER WATSON (CA)

No. 1771 (1.11.75) – No. 1786 (14.2.76) [Tenth Series]

Creepy brings tough ex-Borstal boy Slasher Scragg to Greytowers in the hope that he will get the better of Winker and his pals.

Art: Eric Roberts

SCREWY DRIVER (C)

No. 1772 (8.11.75) – No. 2239 (20.10.84)

A mixture of new and reprint strips from the 1955–9 series.

Art: Bill Holroyd

1976......................

Price: 4p.

Page count: 20; published every Tuesday.

BLACK BOB (A)
No. 1786 (14.2.76) – No. 1801 (29.5.76) [Fifty-Seventh Picture Series]
Reprint of picture series No. 30 (1965).
Art: Jack Prout

WILLIE FIXIT (CA)
No. 1787 (21.2.76) – No. 1838 (12.2.77)
Reprints from the original picture series (1962).
Art: Bill Holroyd

WAGGY, THE SHAGGY DOGGY (C)
No. 1789 (6.3.76) – No. 2118 (26.6.82)
Reprints from the 'Shaggy Doggy' series (1954–8).
Art: Allan Morley

BLACK BOB (A)
No. 1802 (5.6.76) – No. 1808 (17.7.76) [Fifty-Eighth Picture Series]
When Bob and Andrew Glenn attend a demonstration of sheep handling in Australia, an aborigine hunter named Burra uses a mixture of strange calls and whistles to gain control of Bob.
Art: Jack Prout

WINKER WATSON (CA)
No. 1809 (24.7.76) – No. 1893 (4.3.78) [Eleventh Series]
More adventures with Winker and Creepy's tough schoolboy spy, Slasher Scragg.
Art: Eric Roberts

1977......................

Price: 4p until issue No. 1851 (14.5.77), then 5p onwards.

Page count: 20; published every Tuesday.

BLACK BOB (A)
No. 1839 (19.2.77) – No. 1849 (30.4.77) [Fifty-Ninth Picture Series]
Reprint of the eleventh

picture series (1958).
Art: Jack Prout

BLACK BOB (A)
No. 1850 (7.5.77) – No. 1857 (25.6.77) [Sixtieth Picture Series]
Reprint of the fifth picture series (1957).
Art: Jack Prout

BLACK BOB (A)
No. 1858 (2.7.77) – No. 1869 (17.9.77) [Sixty-First Picture Series]
Reprint of the ninth picture series (1958).
Art: Jack Prout

BLACK BOB (A)
No. 1870 (24.9.77) – No. 1875 (29.10.77) [Sixty-Second Picture Series]
Reprint of the fourth picture series (1957).
Art: Jack Prout

BLACK BOB (A)
No. 1876 (5.11.77) – No. 1882 (17.12.77) [Sixty-Third Picture Series]
Reprint of the twelfth picture series (1959).
Art: Jack Prout

BLACK BOB (A)
No. 1883 (24.12.77) – No. 1893 (4.3.78) [Sixty-Fourth Picture Series]
Reprint of the tenth picture series (1958).
Art: Jack Prout

1978......................

Price: 5p until issue No. 1925 (14.10.78), then 6p onwards.

Page count: 20; published every Tuesday.

Free gifts: No. 1894 (11.3.78) – Dan's Nutty Nougat; No. 1895 (18.3.78) – Zooming Boomer.

THE FIZZFIST (JACK SILVER) (CA)
No. 1894 (11.3.78) – No. 1916 (12.8.78) [Third Series]
Jack Silver gains a new ally in his battles with Captain Zapp, 'The Fizzfist', a mechanical hand with the strength of an army, which has been specially sent to Earth by the Outer Space Patrol to

capture the cosmic crook.
Art: Bill Holroyd

TOM TUM (C)
No. 1894 (11.3.78) – No. 2303 (11.1.86)
Art: Keith Reynolds

BERTIE BUNCLE AND HIS CHEMICAL UNCLE (C)
No. 1894 (11.3.78) – No. 2104 (20.3.82)
Art: David Mostyn

GREEDY PIGG (C)
No. 1894 (11.3.78) – No. 2148 (22.1.83) [Second Series]
Return of Greedy Pigg in adventures with a new rival, Jasper the Janitor.
Art: George Martin

THE RED WRECKER (A)
No. 1894 (11.3.78) – No. 1909 (24.6.78)
Reprint of the 1964 adventure strip.
Art: Charlie Grigg

BLACK BOB (A)
No. 1894 (11.3.78) – No. 1899 (15.4.78) [Sixty-Fifth Picture Series]
Reprint of the third picture series (1956).
Art: Jack Prout

BLACK BOB (A)
No. 1900 (22.4.78) – No. 1910 (1.7.78) [Sixty-Sixth Picture Series]
Reprint of the eighth picture series (1957).
Art: Jack Prout

WINKER WATSON (CA)
No. 1911 (8.7.78)
One-off story featuring Slasher Scragg.
Art: Eric Roberts

BLACK BOB (A)
No. 1912 (15.7.78) – No. 1922 (23.9.78) [Sixty-Seventh Picture Series]
Reprint of the twenty-sixth picture series (1963).
Art: Jack Prout

WINKER WATSON (CA)
No. 1917 (19.8.78) – No. 1975 (29.9.79) [Twelfth Series]
Winker does battle with the mysterious 'Hooded Terrors'.
Art: Eric Roberts

BLACK BOB (A)
No. 1923 (30.9.78) – No. 1929 (11.11.78) [Sixty-Eighth Picture Series]
Reprint of the twenty-second picture series (1962).
Art: Jack Prout

BLACK BOB (A)
No. 1930 (18.11.78) – No. 1943 (17.2.79) [Sixty-Ninth Picture Series]
Reprint of the twenty-eighth picture series (1964).
Art: Jack Prout

1979......................

Price: 6p to No. 1975 (29.9.79), then 7p onwards.

Page count: 20; published every Tuesday.

Free gifts: No. 1976 (6.10.79) – Packet of Pop Rocks (sweets); No. 1977 (13.10.79) – Howly Yowlie Balloon.

BLACK BOB (A)
No. 1944 (24.2.79) – No. 1956 (19.5.79) [Seventieth Picture Series]
Reprint of the fourteenth picture series (1959).
Art: Jack Prout

BLACK BOB (A)
No. 1957 (26.5.79) – No. 1961 (23.6.79) [Seventy-First Picture Series]
Reprint of the fifteenth picture series (1960).
Art: Jack Prout

BLACK BOB (A)
No. 1962 (30.6.79) – No. 1967 (4.8.79) [Seventy-Second Picture Series]
Reprint of the thirteenth picture series (1959).
Art: Jack Prout

BLACK BOB (A)
No. 1968 (11.8.79) – No. 1974 (22.9.79) [Seventy-Third Picture Series]

Reprint of the twenty-seventh picture series (1964).
Art: Jack Prout

THE SPLUDGES (CA)
No. 1975 (29.9.79)
A one-off strip with script supplied by ten year-old Dandy reader Carl R. Thompson of Hastings.
Art: Bob McGrath

JACK SILVER (CA)
No. 1976 (6.10.79) – No. 2065 (20.6.81) [Fourth Series]
Fun and thrills when Jack and his earth pal Curly Perkins help defend Marsuvia from invaders from the planet Zorg.
Art: Bill Holroyd

HARRY AND HIS HIPPO (C)
No. 1976 (6.10.79) – 1986; 2011 to date
Art: Ken Harrison/ Torregrosa; Andy Fanton from 2011

DAVE THE BRAVE (C)
No. 1976 (6.10.79) – No. 2031 (25.10.80)
Art: Paddy Brennan

DUMB BELLE (C)
No. 1976 (6.10.79) – No. 1992 (26.1.80) [First Series]
Art: Jan Sitek

THE HAIRY GANG OF ROBBERS (A)
No. 1976 (6.10.79) – No. 2016 (12.7.80)
Young Rusty Rider, the assistant keeper at Dinsdale Zoo, helps to combat the threat of a crook who can make all apes do his evil bidding.
Art: Bill Holroyd

1980......................

Price: 7p until No. 2016 (12.7.80), then 8p onwards.

Page count: 20; published every Tuesday.

DESPERATE DAWG (C)
No. 1993 (2.2.80) – No. 2104 (20.3.82) [Second Series]
Art: George Martin

WINKER WATSON (CA)

No. 2017 (19.7.80) – No. 2048 (21.2.81) [Thirteenth Series]
Reprint of the third series (1965).
Art: Eric Roberts

1981

Price: 8p until No. 2049 (28.2.81), then 9p onwards.
Page count: 20; published every Tuesday.

WINKER WATSON (CA)

No. 2049 (28.2.81) – No. 2085 (7.11.81) [Fourteenth Series]
Reprint of the fourth series (1966).
Art: Eric Roberts

BLACK BOB (A)

No. 2066 (27.6.81) – No. 2083 (24.10.81) [Seventy-Fourth Picture Series]
Reprint of the thirty-fourth picture series (1967).
Art: Jack Prout

BLACK BOB (A)

No. 2084 (31.10.81) – No. 2096 (23.1.82) [Seventy-Fifth Picture Series]
Reprint of the thirty-fifth picture series (1968).
Art: Jack Prout

WINKER WATSON (CA)

No. 2086 (14.11.81) – No. 2132 (2.10.82) [Fifteenth Series]
Reprint of the fifth series (1966).
Art: Eric Roberts

1982

Price: 9p until No. 2104 (20.3.82), then 10p onwards.
Page count: 20; published every Tuesday.
Free gifts: No. 2105 (27.3.82) – Korky's Kazoo; No. 2106 (3.4.82) – The Dandy Thunderbang.

BLACK BOB (A)

No. 2097 (30.1.82) – No. 2110 (1.5.82) [Seventy-Sixth Picture Series]
Reprint of the thirty-first

picture series (1965).
Art: Jack Prout

BRASSNECK (CA)

No. 2105 (27.3.82) – No. 2225 (14.7.84) [Third Series]
More adventures with Charlie Brand and his metal chum.
Art: Bill Holroyd

DUMB BELLE (C)

No. 2105 (27.3.82) – No. 2127 (28.8.82) [Second Series]
Art: Jan Sitek

BLACK BOB (A)

No. 2111 (8.5.82) – No. 2122 (24.7.82) [Seventy-Seventh Picture Series]
Reprint of the thirty-second picture series (1966).
Art: Jack Prout

BIG CHIEF ITCHY SNITCH (C)

No. 2123 (31.7.82) – No. 2148 (22.1.83)
Art: Bill Holroyd

IZZY SKINT (C)

No. 2123 (31.7.82) – No. 2207 (10.3.84) [Second Series]
Art: George Martin

MICKY THE MOUTH (C)

No. 2129 (11.9.82) – No. 2234 (15.9.84)
Art: David Mostyn

WINKER WATSON (CA)

No. 2133 (9.10.82) – No. 2179 (27.8.83) [Sixteenth Series]
Reprint of the seventh series (1970).
Art: Eric Roberts

1983

Price: 10p until No. 2175 (30.7.83), then 12p onwards.
Page count: 20; published every Tuesday.

THE BURRD (C)

No. 2149 (29.1.83) – 1986
Art: Ron Spencer

DINAH MO (C)

No. 2149 (29.1.83) – 1996
Art: Ron Spencer, Pete Moonie

DESPERATE DAWG (C)

No. 2149 (29.1.83) – No. 2242 (10.11.84) [Third Series]
Art: George Martin

WHACKO! (C)

No. 2180 (3.9.83) – No. 2214 (28.4.84)
Reprints from the 1971–3 series.
Art: Ron Spencer

1984

Price: 12p until No. 2234 (15.9.84), then 14p onwards.
Page count: 20; published every Tuesday.
Free gifts: No. 2240 (27.10.84) – The Korky Glow Mask; No. 2241 (3.11.84) – The Space Spinner; No. 2242 (10.11.84) – Leaf Cola Flavour Bubble Gum.

JOLLY ROGER (C)

No. 2209 (24.3.84) – No. 2302 (4.1.86)
Art: George Martin

WINKER WATSON (CA)

No. 2215 (5.5.84) – No. 2242 (10.11.84) [Seventeenth Series]
Fun when a circus makes camp next to Greytowers School.
Art: Paul White

HAM AND EGGHEAD (C)

First appeared: No. 2215 (5.5.84)
Art: Steve Bright

GREEDY PIGG (C)

No. 2226 (21.7.84) – No. 2239 (20.10.84) [Third Series]
Art: George Martin

MITCH AND HIS MUMMY (C)

No. 2240 (27.10.84) – No. 2303 (11.1.86)
Art: Ken Harrison/Jerry Swaffield

DIMPLES (C)

No. 2240 (27.10.84) – 1986 and then became
CUDDLES AND

DIMPLES 1986 – to date
Art: Barrie Appleby, Gordon Bell, Nigel Parkinson

THE DOMES (C)

No. 2243 (17.11.84) – No. 2286 (14.9.85)
Art: John K. Geering

1985

Price: 14p until No. 2286 (14.9.85), then 16p onwards.
Page count: 20; published every Tuesday.

PETER PEST (C)

First appeared: No. 2287 (21.9.85) (from *Nutty*).
Art: Tom Williams

BANANAMAN (C)

No. 2287 (21.9.85) – to date (from *Nutty*).
Art: John K. Geering, Barrie Appleby, Steve Bright, Wayne Thompson

THE SNOBBS AND THE SLOBBS (C)

First appeared: No. 2287 (21.9.85) (from *Nutty*).
Art: John K. Geering

From 1986 onwards this index continues with just a year-by-year listing of new characters and the date on which they first appeared in *The Dandy*.

1986

ALI HA-HA AND THE FORTY THIEVES

Second series started: 18.1.86

DESPERATE DAWG

Fourth series started: 18.1.86

STRANGE HILL SCHOOL

First appeared: 18.1.86

POLAR BLAIR

First appeared: 1.11.86

SPOTTED DICK

First appeared 1.11.86

COMIC CUTS

First appeared: 8.11.86

1987

TED-TIME TALES

First appeared: 4.4.87

MUTT AND MOGGY

First appeared: 4.4.87

1988

ANGIE – THE LITTLE ACTRESS

First appeared: 20.2.88

GRANNY

First appeared: 20.2.88

L'IL IMP

First appeared: 20.2.88

RICHARD'S SNITCH

First appeared: 30.4.88

WOOFER AND TWEETER

First appeared: 30.4.88

SAMMY SUPERSNAIL

First appeared: 28.5.88

POSTMAN PATEL

First appeared: 6.8.88

GEORGE AND THE DRAGON

First appeared: 17.9.88

JAMES – THE WORLD'S WORST SCHOOL BOY

First appeared: 17.9.88

NORBERT'S NIGHTMARES

First appeared: 17.9.88

LOUDEN THE MOUTH

First appeared: 29.10.88

WATCH THE BIRDIE

First appeared: 3.12.88

SNEAKER

First appeared: 10.12.88

YOUNG TRAINEE SANTAS

First appeared: 17.12.88

1989

GOLDEN OL' DAYS

First appeared: 24.6.89

TRISTAN – THE VICAR'S SON

First appeared: 21.10.89

1990

KYLIE PHIZZOG
First appeared: 21.4.90

MARVO THE WONDER-CHICKEN
First appeared: 31.3.90

BILLY GREEN AND HIS SISTER JEAN
First appeared: 16.6.90

THE LAUGHING PLANET
First appeared: 14.7.90

MARTY'S HOUSE
First appeared: 1.9.90

IT'S MAGIC
First appeared: 1.12.90

TUMBA AND RUMBA – THE MIMICKING ELEPHANTS
First appeared: 15.7.89

1991

GROWING PAYNES
First appeared: 25.5.91

MOLLY
First appeared: 25.5.91

SMITTEN
First appeared: 15.6.91

BARNEY
First appeared: 27.7.91

JOE MINCE
First appeared: 5.10.91

SHERMAN TORTOISE
First appeared: 26.10.91

KING DOM
First appeared: 2.11.91

1992

WENDY'S WICKED STEPLADDER
First appeared: 2.5.92

MISS EVE L. POWERS
First appeared: 27.6.92

HYDE AND SHRIEK
First appeared: 17.10.92

REG HOG
First appeared: 21.11.92

1993

DER DAFT DACHSHUNDS
First appeared: 13.3.93

PETER PIPER
First appeared: 26.6.93

FIDDLE O'DIDDLE
First appeared: 26.6.93

OLIVER TWISTER
First appeared: 26.6.93

FIBBA
First appeared: 31.7.93

POTSWORTH AND COMPANY
First appeared: 21.8.93

BERYL THE PERIL
First appeared in *The Dandy*: 28.8.93. First appeared in *The Topper* 7.2.53 and moved to *The Dandy* when the combined *Beezer* and *Topper* ceased publication in 1993.

CARROT
First appeared: 18.9.93

JONAH
First appeared: 18.9.93

RASPER
First appeared: 25.9.93

CLAUDE CUKOOLAND
First appeared: 30.10.93

PUSS 'N' BOOTS
First appeared: 11.12.93

FIRST CLASS
First appeared: 18.12.93

1994

BLINKY
First appeared: 29.1.94

LITTLE WIN
First appeared: 19.2.94

THE VERMINATOR
First appeared: 19.3.94

EURO SCHOOL
First appeared: 13.8.94

TIK AND TAK
First appeared: 17.9.94

THE FLYING BOY
First appeared: 8.10.94

HERB'S HISTORY
First appeared: 8.10.94

BRAIN DUANE
First appeared: 17.12.94

1995

MAD MARCH HARE
First appeared: 11.3.95

BEASTIE BOY
First appeared: 22.4.95

FRAWG
First appeared: 22.4.95

BROTHER GRIMM
First appeared: 6.5.95

SPELLING MISTAKE
First appeared: 6.5.95

LITTLE BOOTS CASSIDY
First appeared: 13.5.95

1996

HECTOR SPECTRE
First appeared: 6.4.96

FOXY
First appeared: 4.5.96

COWRIN' WOLF
First appeared: 13.7.96

1997

CLASSIC CUTS
First appeared: 4.1.97

THE DANDY TREASURE ISLAND
First appeared: 11.1.97

NEIGHBOURHOOD WOOD
First appeared: 18.1.97

JAK
First appeared: 6.12.97

STICK MANIACS
First appeared: 27.12.97

BREWSTER ROOSTER
First appeared: late '97

1998

VAIN WAYNE
First appeared: 28.2.98

OWEN GOAL
First appeared: 11.4.98

P5
First appeared: 19.9.98

BEDTIME TALES WITH BRADLEY BEDSOCK
First appeared: 19.9.98

NOW SHOWING
First appeared: 24.10.98

BUSTER CRAB
First appeared: 26.12.98

1999

TWEEDLE DUMB AND TWEEDLE DUMBER
First appeared: 30.1.99

ANTCHESTER
First appeared: 20.03.99

POLLY
First appeared: 22.5.99

THE PLUCK OF PERCY
First appeared: 26.6.99

CALMSVILLE
First appeared: 10.7.99

RED HOT CHILLI DOGS
First appeared: 24.7.99

BODKINS MOOR
First appeared: 31.7.99

2000

WALTER GNOME. MILLENNIUM GNOME
First appeared: 1.1.00

BART BRIMSTON
First appeared: 8.4.00

RIDGE RESCUE
First appeared: 10.6.00

THE COMET
First appeared: 1.7.00

PHONE BONE AND DIGIT AL
First appeared: 1.8.00

AUNTIE CLOCKWISE
First appeared: 7.10.00

2001

ISLAND OF TERROR
First appeared: 10.2.01

JOCK THE RAPPER
First appeared: 21.7.01

2002

OLLIE FLIPTRIK
First appeared: 12.1.02

DALLAS DITCHWATER
First appeared: 13.7.02

CHESTER THE ALIEN CHASER
First appeared: 20.7.02

ANIMAL ASYLUM
First appeared: 10.08.02

SILLY MOO
First appeared: 19.10.02

NEVILLE'S ISLAND
First appeared: 2.11.02

THE VULTURE CLUB
First appeared: 23.11.02

THE DOYLE FAMILY
First appeared: 14.12.02

2003

THE HEAVY METAL YETI
First appeared: 11.1.03

CRACKPOT CIRCUS
First appeared: 1.3.03

BABY HERO
First appeared: 3.5.03

BAD MAX
First appeared: 14.6.03

OZZY OUTBACK
First appeared: 21.6.03

WIZZO THE WIZARD
First appeared: 12.7.03

MAKE ME A MONSTER
First appeared: 6.9.03

AGENT DOG 2 ZERO
First appeared: 20.9.03

DANDY DAYS IN BEANOTOWN
First appeared: 20.9.03

CATS
First appeared: 22.11.03

2004

NUTTERS
First appeared: 24.1.04

THE BANANA BUNCH
First appeared: 31.1.04

PIGGLES
First appeared: 21.2.04

PANTS
First appeared: 10.4.04

BAD NEIGHBOURS

ARTISTS AND THEIR WORK

This Index of Artists is taken form Ray Moore's *Dandy Monster Index* and covers all the artists known to have provided artwork up to the end of 1985, together with a list of their work for the comic. A list of recent artisits is given at the end. Abbreviations are as follows:

(**A**) = artist drew this character only for an annual(s);
(**SS**) = artist drew this character only for a summer special(s);
Where two characters of the same name are mentioned, but have different storylines, then they are differentiated either by (**C**) or (**CA**).

APPLEBY, BARRIE
Dimples.

BAINES, TOBY
Those Blinking Vaccies Again!; Cats-Eye Kelly; Cripple Charlie; There's a Curse on the King; Dickey Bird (**A**); Hassan and his Magic Carpet (**A**); Little Susie's Song Hit (**A**); The Magic Box; The Magic Knocker; The Man who owns an Ali Baba Cave; Mary's Mighty Uncle (**A**); Mary takes the (cream) cake

(**A**); Old King Cole (**A**); Rip, the Rattling Roller Boy (**A**); The Skim Along Twins (**A**); The Slapdash Circus; The Three Bears (**A**); The Twins Dare the Redskin Trail; The Two Tough Lambs; The Ugliest Pig in the World.

BALL, MURRAY
Boss of the Backyards (**A**).

BANGER, HARRY
Googly the Eskimo (**A**); Three Little Nigger Boys (**A**).

BAXENDALE, LEO
The Bash Street Kids (**SS**); Dinah Mite (**A**); Little Plum (**SS**); Minnie the Minx (**SS**); Thundering Dustbins! (**A**).

BAXENDALE, MARTIN
Corporal Clott (**A**); Tom Tum (**SS**).

BLACKALLER, BASIL
Castor Oil Craddock.

BRIGHT, STEVE
Ham and Egghead; Harry and his Hippo (**A**).

BRENNAN, PADDY
The Bearding of the Wierdies (**SS**); Blitz Boy; Bonzer the Bear Cub (**A**); The Boy from Lilliput; Chuck's Wagon (**A**); Crackaway Jack; The Crackaway Twins; Cripple Singh (**A**); Dave the Brave; Diamond Dick (**A**); Eastward Ho with Prince Charlie's Gold (**A**); Fighting Forkbeard; The Galloping Glory Boys; General Jumbo (**SS**); Guardian of the Red Raider (**A**); Iron Hands; The Island of Monsters; Jimbo and Bimbo (**SS**); Little Lucky (**SS**); Mickey from the Moon; Mickey's Tick Tock Men; My Pal Midnight (**A**); Oggie and the Ostrich (**SS**); Pete's Pranky Pup (**SS**); Rikki the Rickshaw Boy (**A**); Robin Hood; Rollo (**A**); Round the World in 80 Days; Rusty; The Secret Londoners (**A**); Sir

Solomon Snoozer; Skeet the Scrounger (**SS**); Spadger's Badger (**A**); Swordsman Sam (**SS**); The Talking Ball; Tufty's Lucky Terrier (**A**); Turtle Boy; Westward Ho with Prince Charlie's Gold; Willie Willikin's Pobble; Young Drake.

CALDER, SANDY
Blinkey's Big Blunder (**SS**); Blundering Ben (**A**); Jack's Crackshot Axe (**SS**); Lucky Doc (**SS**); The Revenge of the Sea Eagle (**SS**); Ricky's Racer (**A**); Roller Skeets (**SS**); cruffy the Bad-Luck Doggy (**A**); Tottle-Ootle Tim (**SS**); Tricky Dicky Dee (**A**); SYou Dirty Dog (**SS**).

CHAPMAN, MORRIS
My Home Town (Character).

CLARK, JAMES
Brave Little Comrade of the Cowardly Lion; The Castaway Kidds/Kydds; Centipede Pete; Conky Joe (**A**); The Cowardly Lion (**A**); Daggery Dick (**A**); Dick Turpin's Getaway; Dockland Davie; Get Rid of those Pets! (**A**); Golden King's Comeback (**A**); Hansel and Gretel; Jimmy and his Grockle (**CA**); Jimmy the Double Dunce (**A**); The Jokes of Jester Johnny (**A**); King of the Jungle; The Magic Knocker (**A**); Meg and the Mongoose (**A**); Old King Popeye's Puzzle House (**A**); Oliver wakes the Sleeping 'Beauties' (**A**); The Only Boy in Millbury (**A**); 'Ride, Effie Ride!' (**A**); The Slapdash Circus (**A**); The Three Bears; Tub, the Terrifying Trumpeter (**A**); Tufty comes to stay (**A**); The Twins Out-Brave the Braves (**A**); Wee Tusky (**A**); Whistling Jim (**A**); Young Dandy.

COX, RICHARD
Noah Lott.

CRICHTON, JAMES
The ABC Kids; The Crusoe

Kydds; Dandy Monster Comic (Cover) 1944; Dangerous Duff; How Kaspar put his foot in it! (**A**); Jimmy Johnson's Grockle; Korky the Cat; Mickey's Magic Book; Raggy Muffin; Sandy's Bad-Luck Ball (**A**).

DARLING, MICHAEL
Buffalo Bill's Schooldays.

DAVIES, HARRY
Kath and Mouse (**SS**).

DEWAR, BOB
The Micro-Chipps (**SS**).

DRYSDALE, GEORGE
Barney's Bear (**A**); Big Bad Wolff; Billy Butter (**A**); Black Magic Bongo (**A**); Hungry Horace; Hurray for the Rip Roaring Robinsons; Jet Carson's School for Racers; The Lion Heart Logans; Mary's Mighty Uncle (**A**); Shaggy Doggy; Shocker Jock; Simple Simon (**A**).

FAIR, SAM
Addie and Hermy; Dopey Dinah; Magic Mike and his Magic Shop; Meddlesome Matty; Teddy Bear; Wig and Wam the Skookum Twins; Wild Man of the Woods.

GEERING, JOHN K.
Bananaman; The Domes; Monkey Bizness; P.C. Big Ears; The Snobbs and the Slobbs.

GLASS, JACK
The Amazing Mr. X; Bash him! He's the Ugliest Pig in the World; Big Bonehead; Big Starr; Bingo – the Black Streak; Bobcat Boy; Boomerang Burke; The Boy Keeper of the King's Beasts; Buffalo Boy; Cat-Eye Kelly; Chums on the Shell-Torn Road (**A**); Circus Boy; Corporal Kim – The Boy Mountie; The Crimson Ball; The Croaker holds the Clue; The Croaker holds the Key (**A**); Danny Longlegs (cas/1962); The Daring

Deeds of Buck Wilson; Don's Green Light Stops 'Em (**A**); Drakes Drummer Boy; Gunsmoke Jack; Hank and his Mini-Tank; Jumping Sausages! (**SS**); Kit from the Wild Karroo; Lion Boy; Little Master of the Swooping Monster; Long Tom's Treasure; Never, Never Nelson; Quick Nick – the Lightning Lock-Picker of London; Randall's Vandals (**A**); Sahara Sam (**A**); The Sign of the Red Raven; The Slickest Thief in Yorkshire (**A**); South with the Hovercar; The Stinging Swarm; Straight from the Jungle to Magic Land; Three Jonahs in a Whale; The Ugliest Pig in the World; Who Killed Doc Robin? (**A**); Wildfire, the War Horse; Wild Wulf; Wild Young Dirky; Young King Cole (**A**).

GORDON, CHARLIE 'CHIC'
Bamboo Town; Bouncing Billy Balloon; Captain Cutlass; The Cheery Chinks; Mugg Muggins.

GRIGG, CHARLIE
Barefoot Bill (**A**); Big Bill's Wonder Ball (**A**); Big Brother's Boxer (**A**); Blundering Ben (**A**); Bobby Buttons (**SS**); Boomerang Bill (**SS**); Buzzy's Bottled Elephant (**A**); Captain Whoosh; Catapult Pat (**A**); Charlie the Chimp; The Circus Starrs (**SS**); Clanky the Cast Iron Pup; Dan and Korky (**SS**); The Dapple-Grey Apple Eater (**A**); Daring Doyle and the Royal Gumboil; Desperate Dan; The Flight of the Stolen Jet (**A**); The 4th Arrow (**A**); Gobble Gobble Gertie; Great Big Bonzo; The House that Joe Built (**A**); Johnny Jonah (**A**); Kat and Kanary (**SS**); King of the Sawdust Ring (**A**); Kipper the Copper; Korky the Cat; Mary's Mighty Uncle; Millionaire Mike; The Million-Pound Boys (**A**); Peter Potter's Otters (**A**); Pongo's Penny

(**SS**); The Purple Cloud; The Red Wrecker; Rip and his Roaraway Racer (**A**); Rocket Jock; The Secret of the Silver Trumpet (**SS**); Sinbad the Sea Dog (**A**); Sooty and his Shooter; The Three-Legged Champs (**SS**); Tin Lizzie; Two Goats in a Boat (**SS**); Ugly Mug! (**A**); The Umbrella Men; The Walkie-Talkie Raiders (**SS**); Whizz Bang Billy (**SS**); Willie the Conk (**SS**); The World Cuppers (**SS**).

GUDGEON, DAVID
Korky the Cat; The Smasher (**C**).

HARRISON, KEN
Desperate Dan; Harry and his Hippo; Mitch and his Mummy; Rah-Rah Randall; Sir Coward De Custard.

HOLROYD, BILL
Big Chief Itchy Snitchy; Bobby Buttons (**A**); Bonanza Bill; The Boy with the Iron Hands; Brassneck; The Brave Lad from Bradford (**SS**); Danny Longlegs; Desperate Dan; Down, Down in the Drowned Town (**A**); The Flying Boy of Woomera (**A**); The Hairy Gang of Robbers; The Hovercar Snatchers; Hurrah for Hairpin Harry (**A**); Jack Silver; Joe White and the Seven Dwarfs; Plum MacDuff; Spunky and his Spider; The Streak-O-Light Express; The Tricks of Screwy Driver; Willie Fixit; Wuzzy Wiz.

HUGHES, JIMMY
Big Head and Thick Head (**SS**); Bully Beef and Chips; Corporal Clott; Dirty Dick; The Jocks and the Geordies; Smarty Grandpa (**A**); The Smasher (**A**); Wun Tun and Too Tun the Chinese Spies (**A**).

HUNTER, KEN
Buster's Battling Beetle; Johnny and the Half-Pint Wizard (**A**); My Pal, Baggy Pants.

JACKSON, ARTHUR
Harry and Barry (**A**).

JAMESON, CALDER
The War Cruise of Willie's Raft (**A**).

JUDGE, MALCOLM
Meddlesome Matty.

LAW, DAVID
Corporal Clott; Dennis the Menace (**SS**).

MCCAIL, WILLIAM
Never-Never Nelson (**A**).

MACDIARMID, FRANK
Big Head and Thick Head; My Home Town (Cartoon); Rip the Roper (**SS**); Roly-Poly Joe.

MACGILLIVRAY, ROBERT
Diver Dick; Hotcha the Hottentot; Jock MacSwiper.

MCGRATH, BOB
The Spludges.

MACKAY, IAN
My Home Town (Incidental).

MCNEIL, HUGH
Simple Simon.

MARCHANT, LESLIE
Clumsy Claudie; Nellie Elephant.

MARTIN, GEORGE
Ali Barber and the 40 Hee-Hees! (**SS**); The Byrd Brains (**A**); Claude Hopper; Desperate Dawg; Frogville Tennessee (**A**); Greedy Pigg; Hogg's Angels (**A**); Izzy Skint; Jammy Mr. Sammy; Jolly Roger; Mr. Mutt; Robinson and his Dog Crusoe; Sunny Boy – he's a Bright Spark; Wily Smiley the Jungle Joker.

MASON, JOHN R.
Barney Boko; Grandma Jolly and her Brolly; Inky Poo the Cute Hindoo; Willy Woodpecker.

THE ART
AND HISTORY OF

THE DANDY

THE END